This fine, expertly edited volume of essays offers a roundly critical, profoundly thoughtful take on contemporary African politics – and on the political science that studies it. Careful to tack between the maniacal Afro-optimism and the dire Afro-pessimism that persists in reducing African Studies to caricature, it takes as its touchstone the Foucauldian concept of governmentality, whose productivity and limits are fruitfully interrogated and put to work anew. Anyone seriously interested in African government and politics would do well to read *Critical Perspectives on African Politics*.

John Comaroff, *Hugh K. Foster Professor of African and African American Studies, Harvard University, USA*

This edited collection is an important and exciting contribution to critical scholarship on African politics. Inspired extensively, but not exclusively, by Foucault's notion of governmentality, the book provides rich and empirically grounded illustrations of the often contradictory effects of liberal interventions to build states and create civil societies. In doing so, it demonstrates the coexistence and interaction of coercive and productive power, and underscores the urgent need to analyse African politics as part of broader transformations in global governance.

Rita Abrahamsen, *Professor, Graduate School of Public and International Affairs, University of Ottawa, Ottawa, Canada*

Critical Perspectives on African Politics is a significant and innovative volume that interrogates the international practices of state- and civil society-building programmes in Africa. It is vital to understanding not only the politics of international development, security and democracy promotion in African context but also the complexities and nuances of African states, political elites, economic classes, citizens and popular movements from the lens of postcolonial and governmentality studies. Clive Gabay and Carl Death have assembled a provocative and politically original collection that skilfully draws upon critical thought to question common liberal views of the broad project of reform that Western states and agencies engage in to 'engineer' civil society in African states. As such, this impressive collection provides new perspectives for understanding and explaining relations of power, inequality, injustice, conflict, coercion and violence that are embedded within international, liberal interventions on the African continent. The contributors' astute theoretical, case-study and empirical analyses make this an invaluable resource to students and scholars interested in 'African politics', development and governmentality studies, international relations and international political economy.

Suzan Ilcan, *University of Waterloo and Balsillie School of International Affairs, Canada*

Critical Perspectives on African Politics

Strong states and strong civil societies are now increasingly hailed as the twin drivers of a 'rising Africa'. Current attempts to support growth and democracy are part of a longer history of promoting projects of disciplinary, regulatory and liberal rule and values beyond 'the West'. Yet this is not simply Western domination of a passive continent. Such an interpretation misses out on the complexities and nuances of the politics of state-building and civil society promotion, and the central role of African agency.

Drawing upon critical theory, including postcolonial and governmentality approaches, this book interrogates international practices of state-building and civil society support in Africa. It seeks to develop a theoretically informed critical approach to discourses and interventions such as those associated with broadly 'Western' initiatives in Africa. In doing so, the book highlights the power relations, inequalities, coercion and violence that are deeply implicated within contemporary international interventions on the African continent. Providing a range of empirical cases and theoretical approaches, the chapters are united by their critical treatment of political dynamics in Africa.

This book will be of interest to students and scholars of African politics, development studies, postcolonial theory, International Relations, international political economy and peacekeeping/making.

Clive Gabay is Senior Lecturer in International Politics at Queen Mary University of London, UK.

Carl Death is Senior Lecturer in International Political Economy at the University of Manchester, UK.

Routledge studies in African politics and international relations

Edited by Daniel C. Bach, Emile Durkheim Centre for Comparative Politics and Sociology, Sciences Po Bordeaux.

1   **Neopatrimonialism in Africa and Beyond**
    Edited by Daniel Bach and Mamoudou Gazibo

2   **African Agency in International Politics**
    Edited by William Brown and Sophie Harman

3   **The Politics of Elite Corruption in Africa**
    Roger Tangri and Andrew M. Mwenda

4   **Reconstructing the Authoritarian State in Africa**
    George Klay Kieh, Jr. and Pita Ogaba Agbese

5   **Critical Perspectives on African Politics**
    Liberal interventions, state-building and civil society
    Edited by Clive Gabay and Carl Death

Critical Perspectives on African Politics

Liberal interventions, state-building and civil society

Edited by Clive Gabay and Carl Death

Routledge
Taylor & Francis Group
LONDON AND NEW YORK

First published 2014
by Routledge
2 Park Square, Milton Park, Abingdon, Oxfordshire OX14 4RN

and by Routledge
711 Third Avenue, New York, NY 10017

First issued in paperback 2016

Routledge is an imprint of the Taylor & Francis Group, an informa business

© 2014 selection and editorial matter, Clive Gabay and Carl Death;
individual chapters, the authors

The right of Clive Gabay and Carl Death to be identified as the authors of
the editorial material, and of the authors for their individual chapters, has
been asserted in accordance with sections 77 and 78 of the Copyright,
Designs and Patents Act 1988.

All rights reserved. No part of this book may be reprinted or reproduced or
utilised in any form or by any electronic, mechanical, or other means, now
known or hereafter invented, including photocopying and recording, or in
any information storage or retrieval system, without permission in writing
from the publishers.

Trademark notice: Product or corporate names may be trademarks or
registered trademarks, and are used only for identification and explanation
without intent to infringe.

British Library Cataloguing in Publication Data
A catalogue record for this book is available from the British Library

Library of Congress Cataloging in Publication Data
A catalog record for this book has been requested

ISBN 13: 978-1-138-21490-3 (pbk)
ISBN 13: 978-0-415-81824-7 (hbk)

Typeset in Times New Roman
by Wearset Ltd, Boldon, Tyne and Wear

Contents

List of contributors	ix
Acknowledgements	x

1   **Introduction: critical perspectives on liberal interventions and governmentality in Africa**   1
CARL DEATH AND CLIVE GABAY

PART I
The liberal project in Africa   19

2   **Engineering civil society in Africa**   21
DAVID WILLIAMS AND TOM YOUNG

3   **Governing rural poverty and development in postcolonial Zimbabwe: insights from Foucault's governmentality approach**   40
KUDZAI MATEREKE

4   **Legitimacy and governmentality in Tanzania: environmental mainstreaming in the developing world**   67
CARL DEATH

PART II
Building communities   89

5   **Business and the uses of 'civil society': governing Congolese mining areas**   91
JANA HÖNKE

viii *Contents*

6 **Connecting state, citizen and society? The externalised context of community groups in Zambia** 108

KAREN TREASURE

PART III
Resistance and the everyday 127

7 **Informality and the spaces of civil society in post-apartheid Johannesburg** 129

ALEX WAFER

8 **Citizenship, contested belonging and 'civil society' as vernacular architecture** 147

MORTEN BØÅS

9 **Escaping state-building: resistance and civil society in the Democratic Republic of Congo** 163

MARTA IÑIGUEZ DE HEREDIA

Index 180

Contributors

Morten Bøås is Research Professor at the Norwegian Institute of International Affairs (NUPI).

Carl Death is Senior Lecturer in International Political Economy at the University of Manchester.

Clive Gabay is Senior Lecturer in International Politics at Queen Mary University of London.

Marta Iñiguez de Heredia is Teaching Associate at the University of Cambridge.

Jana Hönke is Lecturer in International Relations at the School of Social and Political Science, University of Edinburgh.

Kudzai Matereke earned his PhD in Political Philosophy from the University of New South Wales.

Karen Treasure is Associate Lecturer in International Relations and Human Geography at Plymouth University.

Alex Wafer is in the School of Geography, Archaeology and Environmental Studies, University of the Witwatersrand, South Africa, and the Max Planck Institute for the Study of Religious and Ethnic Diversity, Germany.

David Williams is Senior Lecturer at the School of Politics and International Relations, Queen Mary University London.

Tom Young is Senior Lecturer in Politics at the Department of Politics and International Studies, SOAS.

Acknowledgements

Collaborations on this project began with two panels on 'Global Civil Society in Africa' at the British International Studies Association (BISA) Annual Conference in Leicester in December 2009, and they were followed with a workshop in Aberystwyth in January 2011 funded by BISA, the Africa and International Studies working group, Aberystwyth University and the Department of International Politics, the Africa Studies Association UK, and the Democracy of Space Network. This led to a special issue of the *Journal of Intervention and Statebuilding*, 6(1), 2012, on 'Civil society and intervention in Africa' (Gabay and Death 2012). The current volume contains some expanded and revised versions of these papers, together with four completely new chapters and a new Introduction.

1 Introduction

Critical perspectives on liberal interventions and governmentality in Africa

Carl Death and Clive Gabay

Strong states and strong civil societies are now increasingly hailed as the twin drivers of a 'rising Africa'. At the end of US President Barack Obama's first extended tour of Africa in 2013 he declared that 'with the right approach Africa and its people can unleash a new era of prosperity' (Robinson 2013). His visit was dominated by talk of new international economic partnerships, 'putting muscle behind African efforts', and supporting democratic states and 'people power' in a new age of good governance and growth on the continent. 'It's going to be good for Africa, it's going to be good for the United States and it's going to be good for the world,' he said (Robinson 2013). This book seeks to develop a theoretically informed critical approach to discourses and interventions such as those associated with the US and more broadly 'Western' initiatives in Africa, highlighting the power relations, inequalities, coercion and violences that are deeply implicated within contemporary international interventions on the African continent.

Of course, there are no shortages of critical voices on the US and other 'great powers' and their role in Africa. Sometimes, as was the case with the genocide in Rwanda, it seems as though they are inevitably either doing 'too little' (Barnett 2002; Dallaire 2004); or, alternatively, they are imposing their interests and intervening 'too much' (a small selection from the last decade: Harrison 2004; Williams 2008; Ilcan and Lacey 2011). Some have warned of a new 'great game' of geopolitical competition between the major powers in Africa, often focusing on China, and the phenomenon of land and resource 'grabs' dominates much critical commentary (Carmody 2011). Certainly, you don't have to look too far to see evidence of security agendas and military build-up in Africa, extending far beyond the one official US base at Camp Lemonnier in Djibouti. The September 2013 attack on the Westgate Mall in Nairobi, which left at least 72 people dead, has only amplified Western security concerns in the region. The spectre of terrorism sat uneasily alongside Obama's talk of trade and partnerships throughout his visit; in South Africa he spoke of the 'senseless terrorism that all too often perverts the meaning of Islam – one of the world's great religions – and takes the lives of countless innocent Africans' (Robinson 2013). In one of the last ceremonies of his trip he made a rare public appearance side-by-side with former US President George W. Bush to honour the memory of

2   C. Death and C. Gabay

those killed in the 1998 US embassy bombing in Dar es Salaam. The shadow of the past continues to shape contemporary interventions in Africa.

This book attempts to position the politics of international development, security and democracy promotion in Africa in the context of a longer history encompassing the colonial *mission civilisatrice*, the modernisation programmes of the 1960s and 1970s, the structural adjustment programmes of the 1980s, and the promotion of multiparty democracy and 'good governance' in the 1990s (Gabay and Death 2012: 1). Current attempts to support growth and democracy, and foster resilient African states and civil societies – whether against terrorism, climate change or pandemic diseases – are part of this longer history of promoting and fostering various and sometimes cross-cutting projects of disciplinary, regulatory and liberal rule and values beyond 'the West'. Importantly, however, interpretations of such interventions as merely Western domination of Africa, or great power rivalry, miss out on the complexities and nuances of the politics of state-building and civil society promotion: these are not homogenous or unified (or even often coherent) projects, and they also presume, rely upon and even foster various forms of African agency (Brown 2012; Brown and Harman 2013). A more theoretically sophisticated critical perspective on the multiple rationalities and effects of international state-building and civil society promotion is the aim of this collection of essays – and such an analysis must take into account the active and even leading role of African states, political elites, economic classes and popular movements.

As such, this book, and the conference panels and workshop from which it has emerged, had two particular concerns in mind in attempting to advance the study of these international interventions (Gabay and Death 2012: 1). First, it seeks to grasp some of the 'messy actualities' (Bachmann 2012) and contradictions of these state- and civil society-building programmes in a variety of specific contexts. Each of the chapters in this volume is based on substantial empirical research and illustrates some of the tensions and the manifestations of local resistance to what Young and Williams have referred to as the 'liberal project' (Chapter 2 in this volume and 2007). Second, contributors to the conference panels and workshop were asked to reflect explicitly on the utility of our existing theoretical frameworks and conceptual toolkits for comprehending these liberal interventions in Africa. As such this volume is positioned within a rich tradition of critical reflection about how to theorise the relationship between Africa and international relations (Comaroff and Comaroff 2012; Cornelissen *et al.* 2012; Dunn and Shaw 2001). The following chapters each combine rich empirical detail with theoretical reflection and development, and present a broad range of critical tools and theoretical lenses through which to interpret contemporary African politics. By exploring specific country and local case studies in some depth, and comparing regions and regimes, the collection is able to provide more nuanced and variegated analysis of the heterogeneity of 'African politics' than the more generalised representations of the continent that characterise many policy and journalistic accounts. Many of the chapters deploy Michel Foucault's (2007a) work on governmentality, but others interpret the critical project in rather different ways, so this introduction begins by making the case for the importance of critical perspectives on African politics.

Critical African politics

The starting point for critical perspectives on African politics, shared by all the contributors to this volume, is the assumption that the current world order does not work well for the majority of people. Africa has tended to encapsulate this condition: the continued existence of extreme poverty, violence, inequality, environmental hazards, disease and limited life opportunities are perhaps more evident in parts of this continent than anywhere else. There are many dangers in this stereotypical portrayal of an entire continent, however, and indeed much recent literature on Africa reveals a distinctly and confusingly manic-depressive set of approaches to Africa's current condition. A more 'manic' or Afro-optimist perspective can be found in the work of Dowden (2009), Brown (2012) and Rotberg (2013), whilst a more 'depressive' or Afro-pessimist approach can be found in Ferguson (2007), Englebert (2009) and Carmody (2011). Part of the aim of this volume, then, is to present a more nuanced picture of the politics of the cases examined, in which politics is an inevitable mixture of domination and freedom, oppression and liberty, violence and creativity. This is true of the rest of the world as well as in Africa, and a critical perspective should draw attention to the social, economic, political, gendered, racial and epistemological violences and power relations everywhere in the world, as well as the potential for change, wherever they exist. As such it is an appropriate starting point to note that critical perspectives are not broadly content with the status quo, and that as Milja Kurki has pointed out, '[d]espite its sceptical outlook, critical and philosophical theory is still valuable in reminding us that, while it does not seem so, we do not live in a world without any alternatives' (2011: 146).

In some senses, of course, all good research should be critical: reflexive, questioning, testing answers carefully and thoroughly, rigorous, and dealing with important issues. Few would argue they engage in *uncritical* analysis of African politics. But the critical perspectives presented in this volume are drawn together in terms of the types of questions asked and the particular theoretical traditions drawn upon.

There are many intellectual traditions within a broad understanding of 'critical theory' – examples include Marxist thought, neo-Gramscian approaches, Frankfurt School 'Critical Theory', poststructuralism, postcolonialism, Actor Network Theory, and many others. Many of the chapters in this volume explicitly draw upon the work of Michel Foucault, especially his notion of governmentality (Foucault 2007a), but others draw more eclectically on a range of critical traditions. These traditions have many points of disagreement, difference, and varying emphases, particularly on questions such as truth and representation, emancipation and liberation, and the question of human nature. They share, however, a number of concerns and ways of asking questions.

4   *C. Death and C. Gabay*

In 1843 Marx set out the project of critical theory as the '*ruthless criticism of the existing order*, ruthless in that it will shrink neither from its own discoveries, nor from conflict with the powers that be' (Marx 1843). More recently, and drawing on Antonio Gramsci, Robert W. Cox made a famous and widely quoted distinction between 'problem-solving' and 'critical' theory: if the former 'takes the world as it finds it', then the latter 'stands apart from the prevailing order of the world and asks how that order came about' (1981: 129). Thus 'critical theory can be a guide to strategic action for bringing about an alternative order, whereas problem-solving theory is a guide to tactical actions which, intended or unintended, sustain the existing order' (ibid.: 130).

Neither the Marxist nor the Coxian starting point are unproblematic characterisations of the critical project, but they do highlight certain features shared by many of the chapters that follow. In addition, it might be possible to suggest that critical approaches to African politics share, to a greater or lesser extent, an awareness of and sensitivity to four particular *types* of question. These four questions concern the role and reflexivity of the scholar, the presence of conflict or contradictions within society, a 'big-picture' perspective, and the importance of normative, moral and ethical issues.

First, the contributions to this volume are not characterised by positivist approaches to science, in which the objective observer tests theories against empirical data (Brigg and Bleiker 2010; Escobar 1995: 130). Rather, the influence of post-positivist methodologies, meta-theoretical reflection and philosophical enquiry is more evident here. As Cox suggests, critical theory is 'more reflective upon the process of theorising itself' (1981: 128). An important tenet of critical research methods is that the author is present within both the social world under study, and the text produced through that study. This, we would argue, is particularly important in critical approaches to African politics, where everything is not always as it seems to the observer. The contrast between formal and informal realms of politics, public and private transcripts, the worlds of culture and belief, and the light and the shadow mean that we must approach the process of 'data-gathering' with considerable flexibility and caution (Comaroff and Comaroff 2012: 38–41; Ferguson 2007; Jensen 2012).

Second, the critical approaches collected here tend to share a perspective on society which is attuned to the presence of conflict and contradictions. Famously, of course, for Marx and Engels '[t]he history of all hitherto existing society is the history of class struggles' (Marx and Engels 1848; see also Rose 1999: 227). Foucault is also concerned with the conflict beneath the apparently consensual surface of society: he suggested that we invert Clausewitz' maxim to see how 'politics is a continuation of war by other means' (2003: 15). Whether conflicts are interpreted in terms of class conflict, or ethnic or identity clashes, or environmental degradation, or violence and hegemony, or fractured subjectivity, such perspectives on the world draw attention to the fundamental role of power relations. Whilst there will be many different accounts of the possibility or desirability of emancipatory politics, all critical perspectives tend to share a concern with the inequalities, injustices and violences of the here and now. Whilst some of the chapters in this volume look at more obvious regions of conflict in Africa – the Democratic Republic of the Congo (DRC), Côte d'Ivoire, Sierra Leone and Zimbabwe – critical perspectives on African politics should draw attention to the conflicts, tension and contradictions present in other cases and places, such as in Ghana, Tanzania, South Africa and Zambia.

Third, critical theory as defined here is concerned with 'big picture' analysis: the attempt, however incomplete and partial and doomed to failure, to address significant trends, discursive tropes and silences, systemic characteristics, and features of the social world in some kind of holistic way. As Cox defined it, critical theory seeks to examine the 'social and political complex as a whole' (1981: 129). It is necessary to be quite careful and specific here, because this should not be read as meaning that critical analysis must necessarily focus on structural power relations, underlying explanations, great power politics, or the 'big events' of politics and social life. It is perfectly possible to present a critical analysis of the small-scale, the grassroots, the everyday, the private and the apparently insignificant, whilst retaining a 'big picture' perspective in the way we mean it, and many of the chapters here do just that (see also Comaroff and Comaroff 2012; Ferguson 2007a; Mbembe 2001). The alternative to such a 'big picture' or holistic approach, however, is an atomistic approach in which arbitrary conceptual divisions – between the national and international, nature and society, economy and politics, public and private, self and other, and so on – are taken as self-evident, such that it is possible to conduct relatively self-contained, laboratory-style analysis in which variables are controlled and the dimensions of a problem un-problematically restricted. This is particularly the case in Africa where we cannot assume that many of the conceptual categories derived from the Western philosophical tradition – such as the state, civil society, ethnicity, religion, warfare, the economy, and even the continent itself as an analytically coherent unit of analysis – are automatically applicable or work in exactly the same way (Dunn and Shaw 2001). As such, the contributions to this volume share a concern with the broader social world – its history, culture, values, economic relationships – that is a characteristic of critical theory in contrast to problem-solving theory. As Richard Norgaard points out, '[o]ur ability to comprehend as a whole is all that matters in the end' (1994: 9).

Fourth, it must be recognised that it is impossible to completely separate morality and ethics – normative judgements – from our arguments and analysis (Cox 1981; Norgaard 1994). This, we suggest, is particularly important for critical research on Africa: researchers should be as clear as possible about why they are interested in the topic of study, and why they think it matters. Whilst the chapters vary in terms of the degree to which they set out explicit normative positions and commitments, and from where they derive these positions, a critical perspective on African politics is motivated by a personal and political assertion that these issues are important, and that they involve value judgements and ethical commitments. For this volume, our starting point is that the world as it is does not work well for the majority of its inhabitants, particularly in Africa: on the whole it is neither fair, just, equitable, secure nor sustainable. We suggest

6   C. Death and C. Gabay

that programmes of Western intervention – through state- and civil society-building initiatives – play some role in producing and perpetuating this state of affairs, although in a more nuanced and complex manner than some critics of 'Western imperialism' or 'neo-colonialism' would have us believe.

Indeed, this is the most important, and broadest, way in which this volume has a shared sense of being critical. There is a critical *ethos* which motivates it: these issues are important, too important not to be studied, however we define and approach them. It is important not to allow projects of state-building and civil society promotion – or development interventions and good governance, security restructuring or democracy support – to be treated as neutral and unproblematic 'public goods'. They are interventions into power relations which interact with peoples' lives in highly significant ways. A critical ethos is one committed to unsettling conventional ways of seeing and doing things; casting things in a new light; making quick judgements and small violences more problematic; increasing the political and conceptual resources available to those who have been marginalised, silenced or damaged; disrupting the status quo (Comaroff and Comaroff 2012: 19; Inayatullah and Blaney 2004: 4–5). For Foucault, '[c]riticism consists in uncovering that thought and trying to change it: showing that things are not as obvious as people believe, making it so that what is taken for granted is no longer taken for granted. To do criticism is to make harder those acts which are now too easy' (2000: 456). These concerns unite the chapters which follow.

African governmentalities

Many of the chapters that follow – such as those by Death, Matereke, Hönke and Iñiguez de Heredia – explicitly draw upon Michel Foucault, and concepts like biopolitics, governmentality, disciplinary and sovereign power, and critically examine their applicability and utility in African settings. Foucault's (2007a) study of governmentality – literally mentalities or rationalities of government – grew out of his broader project of seeking to locate the specific and individualising practices he identified in the analysis of madness, prisons and sexuality within a broader context of shifting rationalisations of the relationship between states and societies, government and the population. Governmentality, Foucault argued, emerged in the context of eighteenth-century Europe and later became more fully realised in neoliberal economic doctrines in twentieth-century Germany and the USA (Foucault 2007a; see also Gabay and Death 2012; Rose 1999; Rose *et al.* 2006; Vrasti 2013). The central insights developed in the course of this work were that 'government' should be understood as including the diverse range of actors and institutions implicated in 'the conduct of conduct', going far beyond merely the sovereign state or the political executive; and, second, that power relations in such societies can and do work through practices of freedom as well as straightforward domination or coercion. Foucault's work has of course been enormously influential, and the concept of governmentality has been subsequently extended far beyond the domains within which Foucault himself was concerned. In the field of African studies, for example, the use of Foucauldian governmentality by authors such as Rita Abrahamsen (2003), Jean-François Bayart (2009), John and Jean Comaroff (1999), James Ferguson (2007), Achille Mbembe (2001) and others inspired the initial formulation of the conference panels and the workshop. Criticisms of such theoretical applications to the study of African politics are not new. Foucault has been caricatured as a Euro-centric, inward-looking theorist obsessed with textuality, discourse and representation, and having little of value to say to those outside metropolitan café culture (Williams 1997). In response, more recent postcolonial theorists have drawn attention to the African influences upon Foucault and his contemporaries, particularly Tunisia and Algeria (Ahluwalia 2010), as well as noting that the concept of governmentality in particular lends itself to more empirical focused and concrete forms of analysis (Abrahamsen 2003). Indeed, Foucault himself understood his overall project as providing an analytical 'toolbox' from which 'others could dig around to find a tool that they can use however they wish in their own area' (in Walters 2011: 138; see also Rose *et al.* 2006: 18).

Nonetheless, in recent years a debate has emerged around the kinds of societies Foucault's analysis was devised for, and the uses (or abuses) of Foucauldian analyses of non-European contexts. This is part of a broader concern within fields like International Relations (IR) about the suitability or effectiveness of mainstream theoretical traditions in comprehending and explaining forms of politics outside 'the West' (Comaroff and Comaroff 2012; Cornelissen *et al.* 2012; Death 2013; Gabay and Death 2012; Inayatullah and Blaney 2004; Vrasti 2013). Mainstream IR has tended to assume the centrality of the state; to focus on problems such as inter-national war, international organisations and formal diplomacy; and to marginalise questions of gender, race, identity, poverty, development, the environment and ideology. Critical perspectives, including those drawn from Foucault's work, have sought to provide new tools for understanding and explaining global politics in ways which avoid some of these limitations.

Healthy debates have arisen regarding the strengths and weaknesses of some of these newer attempts to explain politics in parts of the world like Africa through concepts like governmentality. Theorists like Jan Selby (2007) and Jonathan Joseph (2010) have worried that governmentality-based analyses of liberal interventions in Africa sometimes appear to suggest that African countries are becoming increasingly liberal, civil, and dominated by practices of freedom rather than forms of domination and coercion. Joseph (2010: 224) argues that 'contemporary forms of governmentality can only usefully be applied to those areas that might be characterised as having an advanced form of liberalism'. Whilst Foucauldian forms of governmentality might successfully create free, rational, responsible, and civil individuals and societies in places like Europe and North America, he suggests, '[i]n other parts of the world the management of populations may have to rely on cruder disciplinary practices' (Joseph 2010: 239).

8 *C. Death and C. Gabay*

We would argue that in fact there are two reasons to continue to bring a governmentality framework to the study of African state-society relations. First of all, we argue that the success and/or failure of liberal interventions on the ground is an empirical question for researchers. We would therefore strenuously reject Selby's (2007: 336) suggestion that 'the globalization of a Foucauldian model of power ends up inspiring a quintessentially liberal, rather than realist, reading of international politics' in which all societies everywhere are becoming progressively more free and liberal as a result of liberal interventions. Rather, adopting a governmentality framework can contribute to understanding how states and civil societies are being built in Africa by Western interventions and (crucially) with what success; how African agency is exercised in these projects; and what the implications of Western interventions are for African politics at local, national and transnational levels. In short, the success and/or failure of liberal interventions on the ground is an empirical question for researchers which lends itself to Foucauldian sets of analytics (Gabay and Death 2012: 3).

A second factor for the utility of governmentality approaches to African cases emerges from arguments which have been recently made about Africa from a more optimistic perspective. High-profile Africanist scholars such as Crawford Young (2012: 222–224), and in particular Robert Rotberg in *Africa Emerges* (2013), have suggested that African polities have become increasingly politically pluralised, and democratic. Whilst we would share Young's cautious approach when he contends that for most African countries this opening up has signified a move 'away from authoritarianism rather than to full democracy', the introduction of more regular elections and freer civil societies than has previously been the case on the continent surely poses a challenge to those critics of governmentality approaches in Africa which have rejected Foucault's methodological utility precisely on the grounds that African societies are ruled by more nakedly disciplinary methods (Joseph 2010: 239). Indeed, even if such apparently liberal procedures as elections and a free press are uneven or illusory to greater or lesser extents across the continent, this surely makes a governmentality approach more, not less applicable, in understanding why populations submit themselves to them with such increasing regularity. Even in weak or collapsing states it is possible to identify such processes at work. Englebert argues that in states which should perhaps have disintegrated long ago the writ of the state stills holds through the spread of petty officialdom in rural as well as urban areas. Central governments unable to assert the state's authority have not meant the death of the state, for 'it will not be uncommon for state agencies in remote provinces of the country to continue to exert local authority' (Englebert 2009: 42; for rather different accounts see Chapters 6 and 9 in this volume). At the same time, those not directly in the employ of the state continue to assent to the state's power, even where the state's central authority has been eroded. Getting the appropriate stamps on the appropriate paperwork still holds the key for most people to access the services they require and desire, and the state is still viewed by most people as *the* site of legitimate power and distribution, even where such functions are poorly performed, if at all, leading to what Englebert calls 'the puzzle of acquiescence' (2009: 4). In this volume the central but problematic role of the state – whether as an idea, a set of practices, or institutions – emerges as a key question in most chapters; from the fractured or 'irresponsible' states of the DRC (Iñiguez de Heredia and Hönke; see also Vogel 2013), Côte d'Ivoire (Bøås) and Zimbabwe (Matereke), to the more 'liberal' but still bifurcated states of Tanzania (Death), Ghana (Williams and Young), South Africa (Wafer) or Zambia (Treasure). It seems to us that Foucauldian analytics provides one useful way to explore the micro and macro power relationships at work in such settings.

More generally, those who argue that Foucault's ideas are inapplicable beyond advanced liberal societies may be at risk of displaying a degree of idealism about the liberalism of these societies and implicitly a supposition of backwardness about African societies. For instance, whilst the lack of policy differentiation, similar career trajectories and ideological affinities between many candidates for public office in African countries led Thandika Mkandawire to label these countries as 'choiceless democracies' (1999; see also Ferguson (2007: 69–89) for the transnational class-based nature of African and Western political-economic elites), an Afrobarometer survey in 20 African countries (ranging from Zimbabwe to Botswana) revealed that an average of 57 per cent of respondents perceived there to be a fully or near-fully functioning democracy in their country (Afrobarometer 2009). This suggests a fertile ground for exploring issues of the conduct of conduct through freedom, of how supposedly free subjects render themselves *subjected*, and so on (Vrasti 2013).

Indeed, perceptions of political conditions in many parts of the African continent are not so dissimilar from the Euro-American contexts to which scholars like Joseph and Selby suggest Foucauldian analyses should be tied. Positive perceptions of democracy in Africa is not at a much lower rate than that reported in a YouGov survey of attitudes to democracy in the UK, which revealed a 67 per cent positive response (YouGov 2012: 4).[1] Similarly, as critical scholars such as Stuart Hall (2011) and David Harvey (2007) have argued, UK and US politicians of apparently different political hues have long drawn from the same conceptual and ideological toolbox of neoliberalism, thus arguably rendering these democracies 'choiceless' in similar terms to their African counterparts. What we attempt to suggest here then is not that Africa is becoming progressively and uniformly freer as a result of exogenous liberal interventions, but that neither does African politics represent an anomaly or illiberal backwater (Comaroff and Comaroff 2012). Rather, the often contradictory blend of freedom and coercion which the following chapters illuminate in Ghana, Sierra Leone, DRC, Côte d'Ivoire, Liberia, Tanzania, South Africa, Zambia and Zimbabwe – the mutual interdependence between the conduct of conduct and sovereign power, and the blurring of once-familiar binaries such as public and private, state and society, power and freedom – implies that 'African politics, so long misunderstood as backward, is starting to look very up-to-date indeed' (Ferguson 2007: 210). The chapters in this collection illuminate this claim.

Chapter summaries

The volume is divided into three broad sections or themes, although many of the concerns and conceptual tools are cross-cutting. The first section is entitled 'The Liberal Project in Africa' and is centrally concerned with the conceptual and political complexities of liberalism and liberal values in an African setting. This section also serves to raise and elucidate some key issues that recur throughout the rest of the volume.

David Williams and Tom Young's Chapter 2 looks at the politics of what they have termed here and elsewhere the 'liberal project' of social transformation in Ghana and Sierra Leone (see also Young and Williams 2007). They are particularly interested in the politics of liberal strategies to 'engineer' civil society: 'to construct and reconstruct social groups and their relations with the state'. Of particular significance in this chapter is the tension they identify within liberalism between what they term the 'liberation narrative' and the 'transformation narrative'; or 'between creating the conditions for the flourishing of social groups and engineering such groups in the first place'. These tensions are mapped out through consideration of the involvement of non-governmental organisations (NGOs) in processes like the Poverty Reduction Strategy Papers (PRSPs), and in the tensions between 'modern' governments and civil society, and the chiefs and traditional authorities, in both countries. A fundamental question they raise concerns the degree to which liberal states are able and willing to justify interference in other states to bring about the right kind of civil society, liberalism and capitalist development. As they note, this debate is by no means restricted to Africa but the stakes and politics are perhaps particularly stark here. This chapter maps up some of the conceptual issues and stakes in the politics of liberalism and civil society particularly clearly; themes which many of the subsequent chapters take up in a variety of ways.

Kudzai Matereke's Chapter 3 follows by addressing the politics of liberal interventions in one of the continent's 'hard cases': ZANU-PF's Zimbabwe. He shows how governmental interventions in rural development, even under President Mugabe, 'produced citizens with new forms of subjectivity and agency', including classic liberal tropes like the entrepreneur and the self-help community. Through a detailed and careful analysis of devolution and decentralisation policies, the creation of new local government structures, and the promotion of entrepreneurial citizens and self-help programmes, Matereke shows how the governmentality framework, and the importance of 'power through freedom', have as much purchase in the analysis of the distinctly illiberal political environment of Mugabe's Zimbabwe as in Western Europe and North America. He concludes that 'the interactions between the different forces at the level of the rural village is a reciprocal interplay of dialogical practices, thus signalling that power in rural Zimbabwe cannot be confined to the sovereign domination of either ZANU PF or Western neoliberalism'. Crucially, his analysis shows how forms of coercion and hierarchical authority (sovereign power) interact with, reinforce, and supplement other forms of power: disciplinary, biopolitical, capillary and governmental power through freedom.

Introduction 11

Carl Death's Chapter 4 on environmental mainstreaming in Tanzania, in contrast, tackles what might be regarded as a 'best case' context for the liberal project in Africa. This chapter highlights the continuities between environmental mainstreaming as a relatively recent technique of liberal governance and other more familiar instruments such as the World Bank's Poverty Reduction Strategy Paper (PRSP) process. Like the PRSP process, Death reveals how environmental mainstreaming in Tanzania has led to the creation and legitimisation of 'expert' civil society organisations, as well as domestic and external corporate actors who are taking advantage of new profit-making opportunities which have arisen as a result of environmental mainstreaming. Following James Ferguson, Death argues that environmental mainstreaming programmes are thus far from simply neutral or technical fixes to problems of governance in Tanzania. Rather, 'they are an important technique through which liberal forms of governmentality are able to reshape states and civil society in international politics, and open up access to lucrative natural resources and populations for "legitimate" state agencies, civil society organisations and private corporations'. By seeking to bring critical approaches to governmentality into closer dialogue with literatures on the concept of 'legitimacy', this chapter highlights the importance of normative issues in any critical assessment of the liberal project in Africa.

The second section of the volume is entitled 'Building communities', and seeks to explore in more detail different ways in which various kinds of liberal intervention have sought to construct communities or building civil societies in Africa. Jana Hönke's Chapter 5 explicates the historical continuities between strategies of corporate rule in Africa, specifically Katanga in DR Congo. Whilst corporate social responsibility vis-à-vis local community engagement is commonly understood as a relatively recent and progressive phenomenon in corporate governance, Hönke illustrates how contemporary forms of community engagement parallel forms of indirect rule practiced by foreign corporations in early twentieth-century Katanga. Moreover, she suggests that the more coercive means employed in that era to ensure community compliance continue in various forms today. Discourses of civil society and community participations thus 'run alongside these other forms of exercising power. The liberal claim of self-determination is thus compromised by the recourse to indirect rule and coercion in order to secure stable working conditions'.

Karen Treasure's exploration of community groups in Zambia in Chapter 6 illuminates the constraints posed by international and structural forces on developmental projects at the local level. Drawing on in-depth fieldwork examining the interventions of international and local NGOs, she argues that 'by focusing on local self-reliance and community-scale resource generation, these groups actively deter national democratic participation, embracing the reality that national level politics is an unproductive arena to pursue greater capacity'. She concludes that such community groups provide 'increased resilience to current patterns of global inequalities through stabilising neo-liberal structures and discourses in African communities'. As such she emphasises the limits to the freedoms of entrepreneurial individuals and self-help communities when faced

12   C. Death and C. Gabay

with global price fluctuations in fertilisers and crops, or changing NGO discourses around gender and good governance.

The final section of the volume is entitled 'Resistance and the everyday', and serves to emphasise the centrality of the routine messy actualities and everyday resistances to liberal interventions in Africa. Such a perspective is imperative in order to avoid the dangers of a 'programmers view' (Bachmann 2012: 42) of the liberal project: the everyday agency of a multitude of subjects reconfigures this project in all sorts of heterogeneous ways. Alex Wafer's account of the development of the Metro Mall in Johannesburg in Chapter 7 is a good example of this in a way that avoids taking a straightforward 'resistance' perspective. He takes us into a very different setting to many of the other chapters: inner-city Johannesburg, the heart of one of the continent's wealthiest, but also most insecure, urban spaces. The interventions studied here are in one sense those of the local municipality in its interactions with informal traders, but global commodity chains and discourses about appropriate forms of development, citizenship and business are never far away. Crucially, processes of civil society building are seen here that have many similarities with those examined elsewhere, as he suggests that the mall development 'represents not simply an attempt to discipline urban space, but to deliberately implicate informal traders into a relationship with the post-apartheid state – that is, into *civil* society'. He argues that, through the Metro Mall, 'the municipality has attempted to actively constitute new forms of entrepreneurial citizenship'. What comes through most strongly here though, are the ways in which informal traders respond and translate these interventions in their own ways, producing new spaces and new forms of citizenship. These do not always involve 'escape' from the liberal project: he makes the important point that 'while individuals resist the obligations and disciplining of the state, they nevertheless make claims for inclusion within that state'.

In his Chapter 8, Morten Bøås explores the historical processes which underpin 'wars on who is who' in African states undergoing often violent conflict over who is to be included in the polity in question. Taking Côte d'Ivoire, Liberia and Democratic Republic of the Congo (DRC) as case studies, Bøås draws our attention to the question of whether under conditions of inherent tension between the nation state and global capital flows, civil society becomes a 'vernacular architecture' which is 'an organisational form of collective action that reflects an environment of ontological uncertainty and nervousness, bordering on pure social angst'. This angst manifests itself through the deployment of hierarchical and patronage-based relationships between individuals and groups deemed to be autochthonous and those deemed to be 'strangers'. He asks whether, given the ways in which these communities struggle, sometimes violently, between themselves, the state, and the interventions of global capital through fluctuating commodity prices, civil society in Africa can fulfil its 'assumed historical mission as an organisational form that combines autonomy from the state with its ability to create the bonds of trust and friendship that the concept's origin in European Enlightenment assumes?'. As such the chapter forcefully restates the ongoing concern in this volume over the fate of liberal interventions in largely illiberal contexts.

Introduction   13

In the final Chapter 9, Marta Iñiguez de Heredia follows a similar trajectory to Bøås, drawing our attention to the manner in which civil society in DRC takes on multiple and contradictory roles, sometimes working against the grain of the neoliberal conception of civil society in Africa. Working within James Scott's definition of resistance, Iñiguez de Heredia presents details of her fieldwork in DRC, and the ways in which resistance to the state-building project is conducted utilising discursive, violent and survival strategies. In particular, Iñiguez de Heredia illustrates, through examples of civil society organisations working alongside violent militias, and where the state withdraws its services from areas where local communities engage in social provision, how the international policy agenda of linking in the development and functioning of a vibrant civil society sector with the state-building project overlooks the ways in which 'civil society needs to be considered in its role as a site where strategies of mitigation provide the ground, not to foster and support state-building but also to reject it'. The possibility of an 'escape' from the liberal state-building project seemed an appropriate point at which to draw the volume to a close, if not a conclusion.

The future of critical African politics

In the next chapter, Williams and Young suggest two further important areas for research: first, to explore the nuances and contradictions and tensions within and between 'liberal' development projects and institutions. This is of particular importance given the proliferation of aid agencies and actors in recent years: the rise of new powers such as Brazil, Russia, India, China and South Africa (the BRICS) and the BRICS-Bank in development is another obvious example of ways to explore the varied governmentalities of development and aid in the contemporary world. The second is to study the modification of programmes and agendas within liberal aid agencies over time, and various forms of adaptation to local 'realities'. Here they note the rise of discourses of 'going with the grain' and developmental patrimonialism, which have begun to undermine notions of good governance and free markets in certain settings. Both of these issues pose important questions for further empirical research; they also remind us that an attitude of 'constant critique' and self-reflection is an important aspect of critical approaches. In this spirit, we end our introduction by offering some thoughts on some of the major challenges for future critical research agendas, including (but not limited to) those mobilising the concept of governmentality.

First, given the critical commitment to destabilising binaries and questioning existing frameworks, it is worth noting the absence of sustained reflection on the analytical utility of the concept of 'Africa' itself, both within the broader discipline of international politics, but also in this volume and some of our own work. There are important political and institutional reasons for an African-studies focus, but given the enthusiasm with which critical perspectives have attacked the conceptual division between the domestic and the international 'levels', one is tempted to ask what are the politics of the continued strength of regional or area studies framings. As the rise of the BRICS – as well as

Indonesia, Mexico, Nigeria and Kenya – further destabilises categories like 'the West' and the rest, critical approaches have a great deal of potential to contribute to these conversations about the appropriateness of our scales, categories and units of analysis.

A second area in which critical theories, and literatures on governmentality, could contribute more effectively and directly is to debates on how to theorise agency in world politics. The return of 'African agency' to the literature has been notable in recent years (e.g. Brown 2012; Brown and Harman 2013), and the 'Rise of the South' (UNDP 2013) has focused attention back onto the political programmes of African elites and state bureaucrats. Increased interest in popular mass movements – most obviously in North Africa and Egypt, but also across the continent south of the Sahara (see Manji and Ekine 2011; Dwyer and Zeilig 2012) – has contributed to a need for thinking in more sophisticated ways about how to understand agency and subjectivity. Critical and governmentality literatures can provide alternative perspectives here, drawing attention to the discursive production of subjects in all sorts of different forms.

Finally, there is an opening for more reflective conversations about ethics, norms, values and political visions. There is certainly no need or desirability for a common or shared ethical stance or political project amongst critical commentators on African politics. However, whereas some branches of critical theory – particularly the more emancipatory branches associated with the Marxist, Gramscian or Habermasian traditions – have been quite clear with regard to their normative project, those drawing upon Foucauldian or governmentality approaches have been more reluctant to explicitly discuss ethics and values. This is perhaps surprising, given the extent to which Foucault's own work was increasingly concerned with these questions: for Foucault, 'to constitute oneself as a governing subject implies that one has constituted oneself as a subject who cares for oneself' (1997: 293).

There is space here, therefore, for critical theorists to think about the challenge James Ferguson presents in a recent article: what are the potential opportunities and spaces opened up by transformations in global politics to address the sorts of 'left arts of government' or 'progressive governmentalities' that might be both politically desirable and possible (Ferguson 2011: 64). Foucault, for example, was very clear that he was not advocating anarchism. When describing what he meant by the 'critical attitude', he asserted that

> I do not mean by that that governmentalization would be opposed by a kind of face-off by the opposite affirmation, 'we do not want to be governed and we do not want to be governed at all'. I mean that, in this great preoccupation about the way to govern and the search for the ways to govern, we identify a perpetual question which would be: 'how not to be governed *like that*, by that, in the name of those principles, with such and such an objective in mind and by means of such procedures, not like that, not for that, not by them.'
>
> (Foucault 2007b: 44)

Introduction 15

It is notable that studies of governmentality in Africa have hitherto somewhat neglected the role of both counter-conducts (movements, dissent, resistance and protest), and the question of whether there might be possibilities for advocating more progressive or politically desirable governmentalities. Whilst these would always be contingent, contextual, experimental and built on unstable ethical foundations, it does seem that the theoretical approaches discussed here and in the essays that follow might have more to contribute to these conversations than is usually imagined. Nikolas Rose declares that the 'political function' of governmentality studies must be 'to strengthen the resources available to those who, because of their constitution as subjects of government, have the right to contest the practices that govern them in the name of their freedom' (1999: 60). This is a challenge to which this book begins to respond in the African context, but it is a task which is only just beginning.

Note

1 The Afrobarometer question asked: 'In your opinion, how much of a democracy is your country today?'. Positive responses included those who indicated that full or almost full democracy exists. The YouGov question asked: 'Would you describe Britain as a democratic country or not?'. Answers were restricted to 'yes' or 'no' responses.

References

Abrahamsen, R. (2003) 'African studies and the postcolonial challenge', *African Affairs*, 102(407), 189–210.
Afrobarometer Briefing Paper no. 67, May 2009. Available at http://afrobarometer.org/publications/afrobarometer-briefing-papers/261-bp-67 (accessed 27 June 2013).
Ahluwalia, P. (2010) 'Post-structuralism's colonial roots: Michel Foucault', *Social Identities*, 16(5), 597–606.
Bachmann, J. (2012) 'Governmentality and counterterrorism: appropriating international security projects in Kenya', *Journal of Intervention and Statebuilding*, 6(1), 41–56.
Barnett, M.N. (2002) *Eyewitness to a Genocide: The United Nations and Rwanda*, New York: Cornell University Press.
Bayart, J.-F. (2009) *The State in Africa: The Politics of the Belly*, Cambridge: Polity.
Brigg, Morgan and Roland Bleiker (2010) 'Autoethnographic International Relations: exploring the self as a source of knowledge', *Review of International Studies*, 36(3), 779–798.
Brown, William (2012) 'A question of agency: Africa in international politics', *Third World Quarterly*, 33(10), 1889–1908.
Brown, W. and S. Harman (eds) (2013) *African Agency in International Politics*, Abingdon: Routledge.
Carmody, P. (2011) *The New Scramble for Africa*, Cambridge: Polity.
Comaroff, J.L. and J. Comaroff (eds) (1999) *Civil Society and the Political Imagination in Africa: Critical Perspectives*, Chicago: University of Chicago Press.
Comaroff, J.L. and J. Comaroff (eds) (2012) *Theory from the South: Or, How Euro-America is Evolving toward Africa*, Boulder, CO: Paradigm.
Cornelissen, S., F. Cheru and T.M. Shaw (eds) (2012) *Africa and International Relations in the 21st Century*, Basingstoke: Palgrave Macmillan.

Cox, Robert W. (1981) 'Social forces, states and world orders: beyond International Relations Theory', *Millennium: Journal of International Studies*, 10(2): 126–155.

Dallaire, R. (with B. Beardsley) (2004) *Shake Hands with the Devil: The Failure of Humanity in Rwanda*, London: Carroll and Graf.

Death, C. (2013) 'Governmentality at the limits of the international: African politics and Foucauldian theory', *Review of International Studies*, 39(3), 763–787.

Dunn, K.C. and T.M. Shaw (eds) (2001) *Africa's Challenge to International Relations Theory*, Basingstoke: Palgrave.

Dowden, R. (2009) *Africa: Altered States, Ordinary Miracles*, London: Portobello Books.

Dwyer, P. and L. Zeilig (2012) *African Struggles Today: Social Movements since Independence*, (Illinois: Haymarket Books.

Englebert, P. (2009) *Africa: Unity, Sovereignty and Sorrow*, Boulder: Lynne Rienner.

Escobar, Arturo (1995) *Encountering Development: The Making and Unmaking of the Third World*, Princeton: Princeton University Press.

Ferguson, J. (2007) *Global Shadows: Africa in the Neoliberal World Order*, London: Duke University Press.

Ferguson, J. (2011) 'Toward a left art of government: from "Foucauldian critique" to Foucauldian politics', *History of the Human Sciences*, 24(4), 61–68.

Foucault, M. (1997) 'On the ethics of the concern for self as a practice of freedom', in Paul Rabinow (ed.) *Ethics, Subjectivity and Truth: Essential Works of Foucault 1954–1984*, Vol. 1, New York: The New Press.

Foucault, M. (2000) 'So it is important to think?' in James D. Faubion (ed.) *Power: Essential Works of Foucault 1954–1984*, Vol. 3, New York: The New Press.

Foucault, M. (2003) '*Society Must Be Defended': Lectures at the Collège de France, 1975–1976*, New York: Picador.

Foucault, M. (2007a) *Security, Territory, Population: Lectures at the College de France 1977–1978*, Basingstoke: Palgrave Macmillan.

Foucault, M. (2007b) 'What is critique?' in Sylvère Lotringer (ed.) *The Politics of Truth*, Los Angeles: Semiotext(e).

Gabay, C. and C. Death (2012) 'Building states and civil societies in Africa: liberal interventions and global governmentality', *Journal of Intervention and Statebuilding*, 6(1), 1–6.

Hall, S. (2011) 'The neoliberal revolution', *Cultural Studies*, 25(6), 705–728.

Harrison, G. (2004) *The World Bank and Africa: the construction of governance states*, Abingdon: Routledge.

Harvey, D. (2007) *A Brief History of Neoliberalism*, Oxford: Oxford University Press.

Ilcan, S. and A. Lacey (2011) *Governing the Poor: Exercises of Poverty Reduction, Practices of Global Aid*, McGill-Queens University Press.

Inayatullah, Naeem and David L. Blaney (2004) *International Relations and the Problem of Difference*, London: Routledge.

Jensen, S. (2012) 'Shosholoza: political culture in South Africa between the secular and the occult', *Journal of Southern African Studies*, 38(1), 91–106.

Joseph, J. (2010) 'The limits of governmentality: social theory and the international', *European Journal of International Relations*, 16(2), 223–246.

Kurki, M. (2011) 'The limitations of the critical edge: reflections on critical and philosophical IR scholarship today', *Millennium*, 40(1), 129–146.

Manji, F. and S. Ekine (2011) *African Awakening: The Emerging Revolutions*, Oxford, Nairobi: Fahamu Books.

Marx, Karl (1843) 'Letter from Marx to Arnold Ruge in Dresden'. Available at www. marxists.org/archive/marx/works/1843/letters/43_09-alt.htm (accessed 1 February 2013).

Marx, Karl and Friedrich Engels (1848) *The Communist Manifesto.* Available at www. marxists.org/archive/marx/works/1848/communist-manifesto (accessed 1 February 2013).

Mbembe, A. (2001) *On the Postcolony*, Berkeley: University of California Press.

Mkandawire, Y. (1999) 'Crisis Management and the Making of "Choiceless Democracies" in Africa', in Richard Joseph (ed.) *The State, Conflict and Democracy in Africa*, Boulder, Colorado: Lynne Rienner.

Norgaard, Richard B. (1994) *Development Betrayed: The End of Progress and a Coevolutionary Revisioning of the Future*, London: Routledge.

Robinson, D. (2013) 'Africa: Obama ends Africa trip, voices confidence in future', Voice of America, Washington, D.C., 2 July 2013. Available at http://allafrica.com/stories/201307031613.html?viewall=1.

Rose, Nikolas (1999) *Powers of Freedom: Reframing Political Thought*, Cambridge: Cambridge University Press.

Rose, N., O'Malley, P. and Valverde, M. (2006) 'Governmentality', *Annual Review of Law and Social Science*, 2: 1–22.

Rotberg, R. (2013) *Africa Emerges: Consummate Challenges, Abundant Opportunities*, London: Polity Press.

Selby, J. (2007) 'Engaging Foucault: discourse, liberal governance, and the limits of Foucauldian IR', *International Relations*, 21(3), 324–345.

UNDP (United Nations Development Programme) (2013) *Human Development Report 2013. The Rise of the South: Human Progress in a Diverse World*, New York: UNDP.

Vrasti, W. (2013) 'Universal but not truly "global": governmentality, economic liberalism, and the international', *Review of International Studies*, 39(1), 49–69.

Walters, W. (2011) 'Foucault and frontiers: notes on the birth of the humanitarian border', in U. Bröckling, S. Krasmann and T. Lemke (eds) *Governmentality: Current Issues and Future Challenges*, New York: Routledge, pp. 138–164.

Williams, A. (1997) 'The postcolonial flâneur and other fellow-travellers: conceits for a narrative of redemption', *Third World Quarterly*, 18(5), 821–841.

Williams, D. (2008) ' "Development" and Global Governance: The World Bank, Financial Sector Reform and the "Will to Govern" ', *International Politics*, 45(2), 212–227.

Young, C. (2013) *The Postcolonial State in Africa: Fifty Years of Independence, 1960–2010*, Madison: University of Wisconsin Press.

Young, T. and D. Williams (2007) 'The World Bank and the liberal project', in D. Moore (ed) *The World Bank: Development, Poverty, Hegemony*, Scottsville, South Africa: University of KwaZulu-Natal Press.

Vogel, C. (2013) *Why Herbst and Mills are Wrong about Congo's 'Invisible State'.* Available at http://africanarguments.org/2013/06/27/why-herbstmills-are-wrong-about-congo%E2%80%99s-%E2%80%9Cinvisible-state%E2%80%9D-%E2%80%93-by-christoph-vogel (accessed 28 June 2013).

YouGov (2012) YouGov Survey Results. Available at http://d25d2506sfb94s.cloudfront.net/cumulus_uploads/document/w3436dvzzd/Democracy%20Results%20120124%20GB%20sample%20%282%29.pdf (accessed 27 June 2013).

Part I
The liberal project in Africa

2 Engineering civil society in Africa

David Williams and Tom Young

Introduction

'Civil society' has become an important term within the discourse and practice of contemporary development.[1] In this chapter we examine attempts by Western states and development agencies to 'support' and 'encourage' civil society in two African states: Ghana and Sierra Leone. These cases, while very different, nonetheless exemplify some of the typical forms of interventions that target 'civil society' in African states. Our discussion of these interventions is informed by an understanding of the broad project of reform that Western states and development agencies are attempting in most African states, which we have called, following Margaret Canovan, a liberal project (Canovan 1990; Young 2002; Williams 2008). This phrase seems to us to better capture the general character of liberalism, moving beyond understanding it as simply a body of theory (although it does, of course, take a theoretical form) to understanding it as a project of social transformation which informs the concrete practices of political agents. One form this project of transformation takes is a variety of strategies to 'engineer' civil society: to construct and reconstruct social groups and their relations with the state.

This account rests on a series of claims about the relationship between political concepts, categories and arguments and the activity of political agents, an account which is to be distinguished from at least two other possibilities. First, we reject the view that the activities of these agencies can be fully understood simply by reference to their 'interests' or the interests of powerful states. There are very significant difficulties with conceiving of an agency devoid of any 'ideas', even if it is only ideas about what is in one's interests, and why. If this is right the question is not 'do ideas matter?' but 'which ideas matter?'. And this is an empirical question. Second, our focus is narrower than one that explores the broad discursive structures that shape the activities of development agencies (Escobar 1995). Our understanding of liberalism as a project leads us to focus more precisely on the particular concepts, arguments, tensions and ambiguities found within it as a way of understanding the activities of contemporary development agencies.

In developing this account we first explore the place of civil society within liberal thought suggesting that its conceptual ambiguities are rooted in a

22 *D. Williams and T. Young*

fundamental tension between what might be called a 'liberation narrative' and a 'transformation narrative'; that is to say, between creating the conditions for the flourishing of social groups and engineering such groups in the first place. We highlight three of these ambiguities: a tension between private interests and the public interest; concerns about which groups constitute civil society and the composition of those groups; and the relationship between civil society groups and the state, notably the idea of accountability. We suggest these ambiguities become more explicable when liberalism is viewed as a political project. We turn then to the discourses and practices of Western agencies, reviewing the way in which the term 'civil society' emerged and its place within donor discourse, and suggesting that much of this discourse tracks the ways that liberal thought has conceptualised 'civil society'. Finally our case studies show how donor activities reflect the ambiguities of civil society as a concept as well as the broader political project of liberalism. In the conclusion we suggest some ways in which donors' concerns with civil society may be shifting.

Civil society and the liberal project

Although we cannot attend to its complexities here it is worth noting that the virtually hegemonic contemporary definitions of civil society as associational life have tended to obscure the range of meanings and practices that liberalism has understood by the term. Both the idea of 'the market' and the 'public sphere' remain essential concepts in the way liberalism thinks about how free, equal and rational beings form and maintain social orders appropriate to their nature.[2] In all its various manifestations civil society has been understood to have a number of common features (Chambers and Kymlicka 2002). First, it exemplifies liberal commitments to freedom and equality constituting an arena(s) within which individuals can pursue their own particular projects through freely associating with others. In this way civil society is a plural realm comprising a wide variety of groups pursuing a wide variety of ends. Second, as a space of free debate and criticism it provides a constraint on the power of the state. The expression of diverse views and opinions within civil society makes it possible to hold the state accountable, benefits the policy-making process and provides a bulwark against the 'tyranny of the majority'. Third, civil society is conceived of as a place for the cultivation of certain attitudes and virtues that are important for sustaining liberal social life. These include law-abidingness, cooperation, tolerance and self-reliance (Rosenblum 1989). These understandings shape the familiar liberal account of the relations between state, society, economy and individual in which individuals are free to pursue their economic and political aspirations, and enabled both to cultivate the virtues that make such a society work, as well as ensure that the state, while carrying out necessary public functions, does not become oppressive or its agents corrupt.

Within this account there is however a tension between a liberation narrative in which civil society 'emerges' (because it is in a sense 'already there') from the removal of oppressive social structures, practices and ideas; and a transformation narrative in which civil society, far from being 'there', has to be both constructed and sustained. This tension characterises all the core liberal concepts (notably 'the individual' and 'the market') and reflects the central ambiguity within liberal thought between 'nature' or 'reason', on the one hand, and 'culture' or 'society' on the other: between liberating what is already there – given in human nature or reason – or constructing liberal ends and arrangements from the ground up as it were. This tension can be seen in many ways. It is manifest, for example, in the varied theoretical devices used in liberal thought to justify liberal ends and arrangements that 'strip out' the actual lived lives of people and groups to 'discover' their real nature. At the same time, however, liberal thought is replete with discussions about how influenced people actually are by 'custom', 'trust' and 'interest' (to use Locke's terms: Locke 1993). In other words, people were very often not at all like the more abstract person used to justify liberal ends. Appeals to 'nature' or 'reason' might ground liberal arguments, but when it comes to making liberal ends and arrangements real in the world, the actual lived lives of persons and groups would have to be remade.

Against this background a number of difficulties in liberal concepts of civil society can be identified. The first issue concerns how a sphere in which particular private interests are pursued through associational life can at the same time be a sphere where the public interest is advanced and protected. The key question here is the extent to which civil society can be relied upon to sustain a liberal order, or to what extent there must be other guarantees, in for example the legal system, that lie outside of civil society and importantly limit the scope of civil society action (Charney 1998). It might be noted that exactly parallel concerns animate liberal discussions about both the economy (e.g. the reliance on hidden-hand argument to secure the public interest) and the public sphere (e.g. debates about the forms that public discussion and democracy should take).

This fundamental dilemma poses two further difficulties. The first concerns the groups that constitute civil society. Liberal theory generally understands social forces in terms of organised social interests and encounters difficulties with groups organised on different socio-cognitive bases, such as race, tribe or religion. There are two aspects to this. One concerns groups that might threaten liberal ends and practices, and the other groups whose internal values and practices might be non-liberal (Kateb 1994; Chambers and Kopstein 2001). This latter issue prompts questions as to the degree to which the liberal state may require social groups have the right kind of characteristics of internal organisation and values that will allow a liberal social order to work. The second difficulty concerns relations between the state and civil society generally labeled 'accountability', that is to say to what extent may civil society constrain and make demands of the public power and through what mechanisms (lobbying, electioneering, etc).

These tensions do not only merely reflect diversity within the liberal tradition, nor a failure of internal consistency, but rather the 'political project' at the heart of all liberal thought. The commitment to 'civil society' is genuine, in large part due to liberal anxieties about the power and scope of the state. But this

24 D. Williams and T. Young

commitment is hedged around by others, to certain kinds of market arrangements or individual rights for example, which suggest that what is really being advocated or defended is a particular kind of associational life relating in particular kinds of ways to the state. 'Civil society' is then at least in part a constructed realm as certain kinds of associational life are to be reworked or even eliminated, and other forms encouraged. Finally it implies that 'civil society' can play an important part in shaping the attitudes, mores and self-understanding of individuals who are to be encouraged to conceive of themselves and their relations with others and the state in particular kinds of ways. All of this, we suggest, is visible in the discourse and practice of Western states and development agencies in their relations with African states.

Development and 'civil society'

Despite the importance of some notion of civil society within liberal thought its political deployment has of course varied with time and political circumstance. 'Civil society' first emerged within the policies of Western development agencies in the late 1980s and early 1990s as part of the broader ideas of 'good governance' and 'democracy promotion'. Almost all major Western donors and development agencies have embraced the language of civil society (Williams 2011: chap. 7). The World Bank has argued that a strong civil society participating in public affairs is an essential component of good governance (World Bank 1994a). USAID has emphasised the importance of civil society in creating a democratic culture and particularly its role as a 'counterbalance to the exercise of excessive authority by governments and economic and political elites' (USAID 2009). The UK Department for International Development (DfID) has stressed the role of civil society in enabling poor and marginalised groups to participate in decision-making and the role of civil society in providing goods and services to the poor (DfID n.d.). The liberal logic of the donor arguments is clear. In order for the state to provide the institutional and macroeconomic environment necessary for 'development' it must be made accountable for its actions. The state's activities, then, must be made as transparent as possible through the provision of information, a free press and public debate, and 'civil society' groups must be 'empowered' so that they can play a key role in pressuring the state for better performance. 'Aware that they are being monitored by citizen groups, public officials know that they may be held accountable for budget discrepancies or failure to deliver adequate services' (World Bank 2006a: vi).

But donor discourse (and as we shall see practice) also reflects the ambiguities and tensions in the liberal understandings of 'civil society'. There is a concern about whether civil society groups actually have the skills to enable them to hold governments to account: 'the effectiveness of many initiatives is impaired by civil society's lack of technical expertise in financial management and budgetary analysis' (World Bank 2006a: vii). This animates much of the concern with 'capacity building' for civil society. There is also a concern with limiting the scope of civil society:

in some spheres ... there can be little compromise. Family and ethnic ties that strengthen communal actions have no place in central government agencies where staff must be selected on merit, and public and private monies must not be confused.

(World Bank 1989: 60)

As Pierre Landell-Mills (1992: 545) argued in a wonderfully clear articulation of the liberal project: 'the challenge is to build on the elements that are compatible with modernization and development, [and reject] those that are not.'

While these generalisations hold, political practice never simply follows some theoretical template as the term 'liberal project' reminds us. Even in liberal politics broadly defined there are strategic and tactical calculations to be made, goals and policies to be formulated and outcomes to be anticipated and assessed. The West and its agencies have not blindly pursued a 'one-size-fits-all' policy in relation to civil society questions, nor are they anything like as simple-minded, unreflective, or impervious to criticism (provided it is conducive to the basic project of course) as much of the critical commentary tends to imply. For that reason it is illuminating to compare cases, not in the spirit of some positivist fetishism, but simply to illustrate the range of strategies, policies and debates that may be in play. Ghana and Sierra Leone are two relatively small West African countries (Ghana is about the size of Britain, Sierra Leone about the size of Scotland), both once British colonies, both once regarded as very promising candidates for independence. Both have suffered political turbulence in the form of coups and repression but whereas since 1992 Ghana has been politically stable, Sierra Leone experienced vicious internal conflict between 1991 and 2002.

Engineering civil society in Ghana

Ghana has had substantial engagement with Western donors for a long period of time, and donors are heavily involved in almost all aspects of Ghana's social, economic and political life. The 'promotion' of civil society in Ghana as part of a strategy to improve governance has been a long-standing part of the overall strategy of Western donors. In 2000 the then World Bank country director in Ghana said that the two main benefits of greater civil society involvement were the generation of feedback to help the public sector improve its performance and the improved accountability of government (Harrold 2000). The 2010 Ghana growth strategy said that 'the role of civil society as key stakeholders/partners in the development process is very crucial to achieving transparency and accountability' (GoG 2010: 123). In at least some respects Ghana does have a vibrant associational life. It has been estimated that there are 1000–3000 registered NGOs with a combined development expenditure of $150–200 million (Danquahz 2011). In addition, there are lots more informal associations, such as self-help and hometown associations and church-based organisations. Despite this the Bank argued that 'participation by civil society in the management of public affairs has been constrained by the lack of access to information', and the recent

26 D. Williams and T. Young

Ghana Shared Growth and Development Agenda has argued that there is 'low participation of civil society in governance' (World Bank 2004a: 21; GoG 2010: 122).

Part of the donor strategy has been to encourage NGOs to play a more significant role. For example, the Public Financial Management Project was focused on improving the central government's budget management and revenue collection processes, but it also had as one of its objectives the strengthening of 'civil society' involvement in the area of economic management (World Bank 2000: 3–4). This involved support for organisations within the Ghana Anti-Corruption Coalition (a 'civil society' organisation), funding for a variety of initiatives to encourage the participation of civil society in the oversight of economic management, including providing training for the media so it can 'play its watchdog role vis-à-vis the fiscal and economic activities of the government' (World Bank 2000: 4). We can also see this with a recent multi-donor funding mechanism to support civil society groups. STAR-Ghana (Strengthening Transparency, Accountability and Responsiveness) funded NGOs and civil society organisations operating in a number of areas, including the oil and gas industry, education, and supporting the 2012 election, with the aim of 'improving the accountability and responsiveness of Ghana's government, traditional authorities and the private sector' (STAR-Ghana 2012).

Ambiguities over the character of accountability, however, are revealed in other projects and programmes. The Ghana Poverty Reduction Strategy document says that 'groups for consultation were selected based on their ability to build broad legitimacy for the GPRS. The groups were seen as partners whose support was felt to be necessary for the implementation of the GPRS' (GoG 2003: 5) – in other words, groups that were thought to be important for its implementation (see also Kothari 2001). This is echoed elsewhere. An ODI report on DfID funding for civil society has said that 'non-traditional civil society includes groups such as grassroots organisations, faith-based organisations, diasporas, the media and private-sector associations [are important for] ... securing genuine, domestically-rooted support for a given policy direction' (ODI 2007: 28). The 2010 growth strategy says that

> the deepening of the process of promoting participation of stakeholders ... in the design and implementation of the national development agenda is an effective mechanism for promoting and consolidating broad national ownership.... Accordingly, the broad objective of policy will be to seek to promote and strengthen national ownership and achieve national consensus to ensure policy sustainability.
>
> (GoG 2010: 128)

It is hard to avoid the conclusion, not that Western donors do not really 'want' participation of civil society groups, but that such participation is designed to elicit the consent of certain kinds of groups to a development strategy that is significantly determined by the donors.[3] In this way the 'public interest' (as understood by the donors) is guaranteed not by the participation of civil society groups, but by the broader pattern of donor influence on development policy. As Harrison has put it, 'intervention is not exercised solely through conditionality and adjustment, but to a significant degree through closer involvement in state institutions and the employment of incentive finance' (Harrison 2004: 77).

Some indication of what kinds of groups Western donors consider to be 'civil society' is given by the kinds of organisations that 'participated' in the PRSP process. This 'participatory' process had a number of elements. The process started with a national forum of stakeholders involved in poverty reduction activities including the government, NGOs, civil society and advocacy groups and donors. There then followed a more extensive consultative process involving 36 community groups, the Ghanaian media, the Trades Union Congress, student unions, professional bodies, representatives of women's groups, NGOs and religious groups involved in service delivery, the Ghana Employers Association, research institutions, political parties and members of parliament (GoG 2003: 5–10). It is clear from this document that the kinds of groups understood as being ones who can 'participate' are mostly ones organised around certain 'interests'. In this sense the participatory process clearly operates with a particular view of what constitutes 'civil society' that excludes groups organised along different lines. The STAR-Ghana programme is not just about engineering accountability, by channeling funding to specific areas considered by the donors to be priorities (such as the oil and gas sector), but also evidences an attempt to engineer civil society itself. In particular, the STAR-Ghana funding programme has gender equality and social inclusion as core criteria for funding. Only those groups who have this as a stated aim will be allocated funding (STAR-Ghana 2012).

This concern with engineering civil society is evident in a series of projects the World Bank has undertaken that in one way or another are attempting to reduce and/or rework the role of Traditional Authorities – the collection of Chiefs, Queens, Priests and other traditional authority figures whose role predates colonial rule and which still maintain considerable power and legitimacy in Ghana, particularly in rural areas (and one of the aims of STAR-Ghana is to improve the 'accountability and responsiveness' of these traditional authorities). The relationship between these authorities and the state in Ghana has often been fraught, particularly in the immediate post-colonial period (Rathbone 2000). The 1992 Constitution protects Traditional Authorities but explicitly bars them from participating in party politics. The World Bank's General Counsel expressed a series of reservation about traditional legal systems. While he accepted that these systems 'help meet a fundamental need for justice', he argued they had a number of problems. These include that fact that judgments are rarely recorded in writing and therefore can be 'inconsistent and unpredictable' and make appeal difficult; that customary laws 'can be discriminatory against women, children and vulnerable minorities'; and that the 'training of officials of traditional tribunals in elements of procedure and human rights' may be necessary to improve the fairness of customary law processes (Danino 2005). In 2003 the World Bank funded a

28   *D. Williams and T. Young*

Land Administration Project (World Bank 2003). One element of the project supported the revision of laws and regulations regarding land ownership and administration. This was seen as particularly important precisely because there are a variety of different types of land tenure systems in Ghana, some tribal-, clan-, or family-based, often overseen by Traditional Authorities, some commercial, and some held by the state (see Kasanga and Kotey 2001). One expected outcome of this project is the development of a more efficient land market, which would 'instill order and discipline to curb the incidence of land encroachment, unapproved development schemes, illegal land sales, and land racketeering' (World Bank 2003: 6).

A second Land Administration Project was developed to deal with the weakness and lack of transparency in the customary land tenure system. This project funded the establishment of customary land secretariats that will establish 'minimum norms of transparency, respect for rights and quality control in documentation and record keeping' (World Bank 2011a: 9–10). The Bank also funded a Promoting Partnerships with Traditional Authorities Project that ran from 2003 to 2006 (World Bank 2007a). In some respects it was a straightforward 'capacity building' project with various training programmes and workshops, and the provision of training to improve the financial and management 'skills' of Traditional Authorities. But the project also provided support for a review of traditional laws and the role of traditional courts and reviewed the need to codify and revise customary law (it is notable that this element of the project comes under the heading of 'preserving cultural heritage'). As the World Bank has said:

> traditional authorities will be supported to assume a constructive role in national development and the modern nation-state, in particular in local land and judicial administration as well as in extra-judicial dispute settlement in conformity to the requirements of rule-of-law and national policies.
>
> (World Bank 2007a: 31)

Such social engineering is not limited to elites and reworking existing forms of association. Quite explicitly donors are constructing new social groups. Two Community Water and Sanitation Projects emphasised the provision of water and sanitation services to communities who were willing to contribute towards the capital costs and the operations and maintenance costs of water and sanitation facilities (World Bank 1994b, 2005). Recipient communities had to demonstrate that they could effectively operate, maintain and repair water facilities, collect revenue, keep records and accounts, and evaluate and resolve problems (World Bank 1994b: 38, 81). Communities were then expected to contribute 5–10 per cent of the capital costs of the project, and levy and collect tariffs to pay for operations and maintenance (World Bank 1994b: 22–28; 2005). The idea of developing community organisations is also visible in the Community Based Rural Development Project (World Bank 2004b). In this case the project supports the development of rural infrastructure and the rehabilitation of community facilities, alongside capacity building for community-based organisations (World Bank 2004b: 4–5). These organisations were given training in management, small enterprise development, 'group dynamics', planning, budgeting, record-keeping and managing back accounts (World Bank 2004b: 36).

More recently the World Bank has developed a project that has as its central aim the development of social groups. This project, Building the Capacity of the Urban Poor for Inclusive Urban Development in Ghana, has as its aim 'to strengthen the capacity of communities to actively engage in constructive, results-oriented public community dialogue'. It targets slum dwellers in Greater Accra. But this project is not providing the conditions for these groups to articulate their views, but rather about making groups in the first place. It is designed to mobilise communities to actively participate by establishing savings groups. In order to do this, local 'leaders' will be identified, and they will be given training in order to effectively 'lead' these newly created groups. They will be trained how to undertake 'effective engagement' with local government officials and other stakeholders (World Bank 2011b).

Donor engagements with civil society in the Ghanaian case illustrate all the ambiguities and tensions we noted earlier. Civil society is important for ensuring accountability and improving the performance of the government. But there are limits to the forms of accountability exercised by civil society, there is a clear understanding about the need to encourage certain attitudes and rework certain forms of association life such that they embody and pursue liberal norms (equality, transparency, rights). Finally, it is clear that the donors are building civil society, from the ground up, by encouraging the creation of certain kinds of groups, organised around certain kinds of economic and political engagements.

Engineering civil society in Sierra Leone

For all sorts of reasons the civil society project in Sierra Leone has been more problematic than in Ghana largely due to a much greater degree of instability and violence. During the 1960s and 1970s the state was massively informalised, political activity of any kind was circumscribed, and economic decline, exacerbated by corruption and smuggling, was almost continual. This situation precipitated an uprising by the Revolutionary United Front, noted for its highly destructive tactics, which resulted in a decade-long and immensely damaging internal war. The end of that war in 2002 saw very extensive involvement by the 'international community' in the country which was also characterised by new modalities, for example, formal agreements as to expected policy and institutional changes, and long-term aid commitments, with an unusually high concentration of resources on 'governance' issues. Civil society issues have been posed on the terrain of 'peace building', a combination of terminating conflict, reestablishing order and creating the conditions that will prevent a return to conflict (Paris 2010). But the peace building agenda both signifies greater ambition on the part of outside agencies and also commits them, to deeper analytic engagement with, and to deeper intrusions into, target societies.

30　*D. Williams and T. Young*

Despite these very different circumstances, donor documents for Sierra Leone also stress the involvement of civil society in recent developments in the country, hailing for example its role in bringing about peace and stability. Support for civil society is embedded in specific programmes such as the Integrated Public Financial Management Reform Project as well as a whole series of decentralisation projects (World Bank JAS and World Bank PRSP). In these and other documents consultation with 'civil society organisations' is constantly emphasised. The desirability of making public participation a major feature of the post-war recovery process has been stressed by the Sierra Leone government itself as well as international donors, and was inscribed in the Interim Poverty Reduction Strategy Paper (I-PRSP) (GoSL 2001) and later the Poverty Reduction Strategy Paper (PRSP) of 2005–2007 (GoSL 2005), as well as other documents, notably the Sierra Leone Vision 2025 (GoSL 2003), which noted that 'another critical political challenge is putting in place sound state governance systems that allow for popular participation and social inclusion, accountability, efficiency, as well as building capacity to manage the development process' (2003: 34). Yet despite the (it must be said, rather bland and formulaic) rhetoric of these documents, projects and programmes, on closer analysis even they (and certainly many others) exhibit all the ambiguities and tensions about civil society earlier identified.

It is clear that the room for debate about the 'public interest' is substantially constrained, if not exhaustively defined, by the donors and international organisations. The drafting of Sierra Leone's PRSP in 2004 involved a fairly extensive process of consultation and the participation of civil society organisations in the process was coordinated by an international NGO, ActionAid Sierra Leone, with financial support from DfID. But the main conduit for support for Sierra Leone civil society has been the (rather bizarrely named) ENCISS (Enhancing the Interface between Civil Society and the State to Improve Poor People's Lives), an organisation largely funded by DfID whose stated purpose is 'to increase the capacity of civil societies to participate in, influence, contribute to and monitor the Poverty Reduction Strategy' (ENCISS 2009: ix). In effect civil society comprises organisations which accept the premises and content of the PRSP, a document not noticeably different from many other such documents. It is generally agreed that there has been extremely little parliamentary oversight or engagement in the PRSP process in Sierra Leone and that much of its content derives from the agendas of donors. As one Sierra Leonean Government official suggested:

> [t]he World Bank had targets in their country strategy, and we incorporated these into the PRSP strategy. At that time there was no MDBS (Multi-donor budget support), but the European Commission had a number of targets, and we incorporated those too.
>
> (EURODAD 2008: 16)

Nonetheless within these rather strict parameters the donors have not been insensitive to local circumstances, especially concerning relations between state

Engineering civil society in Africa   31

institutions and the wider society. Perhaps the major issue confronting post-conflict Sierra Leone was how far dysfunctional local institutions, notably rural chieftaincy had caused the conflict and, if so, what should be done about it. Whatever misgivings there were about the chiefs the imperatives of restoring order led DFID to fund a Paramount Chiefs Restoration Programme to re-establish basic administration and to signal to the population that it was safe to return to their villages. At the same time DFID was mindful of the dangers of abuse of powers by chiefs (there was after all a long colonial history of this) and organised consultation meetings for local people, as well as issuing a revised code of conduct for chiefs and their employees. Since then the debate has rumbled on, both in academic publications and policy circles, about the legiti-macy and utility of chieftaincy, one view asserting that the roots of the conflict lay in a broken patron-clientelist system in which chiefs increasingly used their 'traditional' power illegitimately to extort labour and other resources from young men, and interpreting the conflict as 'a long deferred revolt of the rural under-class welled up, led by intransigent youth' (Richards 2005: 588). On this ana-lysis if the conflict is not to recur, the old chieftaincy system must ultimately disappear. A rather different view has suggested that much of the oppressive picture is no longer plausible, but that the institution of chieftaincy remains rooted in daily life and still retains considerable popular approval. On this account, 'the fundamental challenge' would then be 'to make chieftaincy rel-evant in Sierra Leone in the 21st Century' (Fanthorpe 2009).

Such considerations informed the promotion of an alternative model of local governance rooted in the idea of the decentralisation of government powers to local councils (Zhou 2009). Under strong donor pressure and with support from the UNDP and the World Bank a new Local Government Act created a structure of district councils responsible for providing a wide range of services, devolved from central government, while the chiefdoms continued to perform other essen-tial local functions, notably the administration of customary land rights, revenue collection and the maintenance of local law and order. The councils were dependent for their revenues either on transfers from the centre or on taxes col-lected by the chiefdoms. The Local Government legislation was ambiguous about the relationship between the councils and the chiefs, and for reformers this presented the danger that the councils would become dependent on either the central state or the chiefs. Such institutions require of course the presence of modern civil society as conventionally understood and such groups attracted funding from the donors as part of the strategy.

It might be suggested that the international engagement with Sierra Leone, in the particular circumstances of the country and especially with the overwhelming need to restore basic state functions, has generated not one but two sets of dis-courses and policies about civil society. On the one hand there is a (more or less reluctant) acceptance of the existence of traditional groups and attendant modes of administration and forms of law enforcement. This can be seen in the toler-ance of the chieftaincy system but also in a much more analytically open stance to what actually exists on the ground. World Bank studies, for example, openly

32   D. Williams and T. Young

acknowledge the conceptual difficulties in applying notions like civil society to much of Sierra Leone, and deploy such labels as 'traditional' civil society and 'formal' civil society and are not unaware that these categories are not water tight (World Bank 2007b). In the same vein the Bank has placed considerable emphasis on investigating what modes of rule and dispute resolution people actually use (World Bank 2006b).

A second stream of debate and policy concerns civil society more conventionally understood and especially its ability to hold the state 'accountable'. Here there is considerable skepticism. Report after report suggests that:

> it is clear from interviews carried out that local CSOs [civil society organisations] tend to be weak. Many will only participate in activities for which they are sponsored or paid. Lack of an organized community oversight role could weaken transparency and accountability within Councils,

or that

> while it [ENCISS] has had some success conducting public opinion surveys, producing databases on local development activity, hosting workshops and radio discussion programs and resolving local disputes between citizen groups, it has yet to develop a broader strategy for state-society engagement,

indeed that ENCISS' own staff concede that 'there is little organised civil society that is not donor driven' (Oxford Policy Management 2007; International Crisis Group 2008: 13, 15). There is a constant lament as to the weakness of civil society and the need to reshape it to more adequately carry out its role. No-one knows better than external donors how dependent civil society is on outside funding. In Sierra Leone the CIVICUS survey found that 'it is clear in the research findings that CSOs are overwhelmingly reliant on donor support for implementing their various programmes (CIVICUS n.d.: 5). As these examples suggest, 'accountability' requires not merely a vibrant civil society and an open responsive government but the right kind of relationship between them. They have to see each other as it were and this mutual visibility does not simply emerge on the ground but has to be laboriously constructed.

Such profound engagement with the internal fabric of other societies poses the question of the degree to which liberal states may interfere in other states to bring about the right kind of civil society. This is by no means restricted to Africa (and has been an essential part of the construction of liberal capitalism everywhere) but the issues are perhaps particularly stark in contemporary Africa. At its simplest this involves continuing to sponsor 'modern' civil society groupings while also exploring what kinds of arrangements can be made with 'traditional' forms to draw them into the development process. It is clear from the participation of religious and faith-based groups in the PRSP process, for example, that Western donors are not operating with a strict secular-liberal account of 'civil society' in either Ghana or Sierra Leone. On the other hand there are limits to the extent to which Western agencies are prepared to tolerate divergence from their own understandings of what are appropriate (liberal) social institutions. Traditional Authorities are not seen as 'bad' per se; indeed they are seen as being potentially important in the delivery of social services. Rather, where the social practices of these Authorities diverge from certain liberal understandings (legal norms, land markets) they are to be reformed.

In both streams there appears to be a kind of two-pronged strategy on the one hand to inculcate good (liberal) practices and on the other to at least gradually eliminate bad (illiberal) practices. It is hardly controversial to suggest that in many African countries the conduct of many civil society organisations is characterised by authoritarianism, lack of transparency and so on. As the NGO Civicus noted in a recent workshop in Freetown:

> CIVICUS' Civil Society Index (CSI) findings show that there have been high levels of financial mismanagement within civil society organisations, as well as weak internal governance and gender equity. Action must be taken to improve public trust and the credibility of the NGO sector.[4]

Effectively the elites of civil society organisations must be trained to conduct themselves properly.

This leaves a considerable field for bad attitudes and practices. In Sierra Leone 'the levels of social tolerance, particularly towards people living with HIV/AIDS, homosexuals and people of a different race remain low' (CIVICUS n.d.: 9). Much of the policy literature, despite its often emollient tone, makes it clear that these are in many ways pathological societies which simply need to be fundamentally transformed. It is here that the notion of 'civil society' is stretched to breaking point. Part of the CIVICUS survey comprises a 'sub-dimension [which] defines the extent to which the existing socio-cultural norms and attitudes are favourable or detrimental for civil society' (50). Here civil society ceases to have any connection with a particular society and becomes rather a template against which any such society is to be measured. But even in the 'real world' there is a sense in which civil society is quite literally to be created. It is a constant refrain in the literature on Sierra Leone that women and youth must be empowered or emancipated with the constant (though usually unstated) assumption that this will be done by outside forces. It is clear also that the role of civil society is not to reflect the wider society but to inform and reshape it, though this also is rarely made explicit. 'CSOs educate the public on the environment, human rights, gender equality, good governance – accountability and transparency, corruption, decentralisation, poverty eradication or alleviation, respectively' (CIVICUS n.d.: 77).

The patent absurdity of this sort of utilisation of 'civil society' in large part explains the fairly rapid disillusionment with the concept in more academic writing about Africa, which though it struggles to anticipate, track, indeed inform the demands of liberal states and agencies, is under some obligation to

34   D. Williams and T. Young

observe social realities and to demonstrate at least a degree of attachment to coherent reasoning. There was informed scepticism from early on (Kasfir 1998) and then a growing tide of findings that suggested that African civil society not only had weak links to the populations it supposedly represented, little internal democracy and remained subordinate to Western agencies and their agendas, but in many ways was positively dysfunctional in its tendencies to create new forms of inequality, promoting clientelism and corruption amongst leaders, and even weakening the capacity for collective action (Booth 2010).[5] At the risk of simplifying a complex picture liberal social science found that what was actually there it did not like and what it would like was not there.

Conclusion: civil society and the liberal project in Africa

These rather general arguments would clearly benefit from further elaboration in a number of directions. One we have already explored a little ourselves, namely the obvious historical parallels between the contemporary and the colonial periods (Williams and Young 2009). The study of the latter has tended to be dominated by perspectives that see colonialism as almost entirely deviant from the liberal tradition and which have endlessly obscured the degree to which colonial rule was committed to projects of social change that were never reducible to oppression and exploitation. The crucial difference is of course that colonial rulers, however constrained by the limits of 'hegemony on a shoestring' (Berry 1993), did have some local means of enforcement, whereas the modern armies of progress and development are perforce constrained to promote social change 'at a distance'. That difference acknowledged, however, one aspect of colonial rule – the divisions between officials of different types and backgrounds, as well as the tensions between them and missionary endeavour and capitalist enterprise – points in another direction as yet poorly understood with a strong contemporary resonance. This would involve exploring not only the agendas of modernisation (the high politics as it were) but the gaps between organisations, between policy and outcomes, between politics and 'development', between states and NGOs as a way towards a more nuanced understanding of the 'liberal project' in the twenty-first century.

A second though linked area, worthy of further scrutiny, is the degree to which, and in response to what factors, the priorities and practices of Western donors shift over time, and the effects of such changes on civil society support programmes. In Ghana, for example, it is clear that Western donors are very animated about the potential impact of significance oil and gas revenues on Ghanaian politics (unsurprisingly given experiences elsewhere in Africa). As the STAR-Ghana programmes shows, civil society organisations are understood to play a part in ensuring transparency in this area, but it is also clear that donors are attempting to bind the Ghanaian state in other ways too. This is evident in the raft of projects targeting the budgeting and spending mechanisms of the state, and the capacity of the relevant government departments. It is also evident in attempts to commit the state to participation in international regimes, such as the

Extractive Industries Transparency Initiative and the anti-money laundering regimes. This suggests that while civil society is an important part of the liberal project in Ghana, donors are flexible and adaptive when it comes to the best mechanisms for ensuring the instantiation of liberal ends and practices.

In Sierra Leone also donors (and their academic advisers) have not been slow to consider other strategies. One follows from the idea that donors should engage in further manipulation of the institutional architectures they have largely set up, and intervene, for example, in the structure of relations between central and local government. As one of the leading advocates of this approach has it:

> the World Bank should re-focus its activities in a way to direct far more resources directly to the L[ocal] C[ouncil]s. The basic aim of this is not just to make LCs better resourced and to allow them to provide services properly, but also to empower them.
>
> (Robinson 2010)

The thinking here is that strengthening local government may provide a counter balance to central government and particularly the tendency towards the centralisation of resources. This would also connect with a development of 'modern' civil society strategy at the local level. Elsewhere the same author has suggested that beyond resources, outside agencies need to take account of political realities, of the interests of elites and individual politicians, and seek to create 'incentives' for such individuals to continue to support reform processes (Robinson 2008).

Such ideas appear more bluntly in responses from expatriate advisers and officials 'on the ground', who often argue that critical to the success of their projects is the support of 'key individuals' to drive through reforms, policies and directives.[6] Successes in the Sierra Leone Ministries of Finance and Health were attributed to having a small number of committed individuals, perhaps as few as five, in key positions. Often, but not always, the individuals concerned were returning highly qualified and experienced Sierra Leoneans from the Diaspora on augmented salaries or seconded international staff, and most often a combination of the two. More than one respondent suggested that the ultimate key individual is President Koroma himself. The situation was sometimes characterised as 'lighthouse politics': when the president shone his light on a policy, it began to work. The job of the donors was to regulate the light. Alternatively, when Sierra Leonean politics is actively focused on elections, for example, it was widely conceded, that the reform process would tread water as other factors, regional, ethnic and party political come into play.

However bluntly expressed, what might be called this 'man-on-the-spot' realism now appears to be receiving acknowledgement in more theoretically sophisticated forums. In recent years there seems to have been a greater recognition that donor strategies in Africa have been rather too driven by a commitment to instantiating liberal ends and arrangements in Africa. Some considerable doubt, if not complete loss of faith, has been cast on civil society strategies, even

36 *D. Williams and T. Young*

within the World Bank. There is much more talk about the necessity of paying attention to local contexts, of 'going with the grain' of African societies, and thinking about what kind of governance would be 'good enough' (Grindle 2007, 2011; Kelsall 2008, 2011; Bunse and Verena 2012). In the light of a more general reassessment of donor strategies, it has been argued that the 'better governance that Africa needs is not so easily identified with the usual concept of 'good governance' (Booth 2012: 2; for a more general reassessment, see Lin 2012). There is little doubt that a more rigorous and informed analysis of the actual modes of governance and forms of associational life in African states would be an important step in developing more nuanced strategies. The question this poses for the major donors, however, is whether and to what extent they are prepared to substantially modify their liberal understandings of governance and civil society in future aid policies. As long as they do not, then the kinds of ambiguities and tensions we have identified will continue to characterise Western agencies pursuit of a liberal project in Africa.

Notes

1 This chapter is an expanded and revised version of an article published as David Williams and Tom Young, 'Civil Society and the Liberal Project in Ghana and Sierra Leone', *Journal of Intervention and Statebuilding*, 6, 1 (2012), pp. 7–22.
2 See the subtle discussion in Taylor 1995: chaps 11 and 13.
3 It is wrong to think of the Ghanaian government as passive in this process, but rather than being committed to the participatory process as a way of developing a better development strategy, it has been argued that the government saw the process as a necessary one to gain debt relief under the HIPIC initiative and mobilise additional donor funds (Whitfield 2010).
4 See http://civilsocietyindex.wordpress.com/2010/10/29/cso-accountability-workshop-in-sierra-leone (accessed 27 September 2011).
5 For sceptical commentary more broadly, see Encarnación 2006.
6 This section draws on research recently embarked on by Tom Young and Dr. David Harris of Bradford University.

References

Berry, S. 1993. *No Condition is Permanent: The Social Dynamics of Agrarian Change in sub-Saharan Africa*, Madison, WI: University of Wisconsin Press.
Booth, D. 2010. *Towards a Theory of Local Governance and Public Goods' Provision in sub-Saharan Africa*, London: Overseas Development Institute.
Booth, D. 2012. *Development as Collective Action Problem: Addressing the Real Challenges of African Governance*, London: Overseas Development Institute for the Africa Power and Politics Programme.
Bunse, S. and Verena, F. 2012. 'Making public sector reforms work: political and economic contexts, incentives and strategies', *World Bank Political Research Working Paper* 6176, Washington, D.C.: World Bank.
Canovan, M. 1990. 'On being economical with the truth: some liberal reflections', *Political Studies*, 38(1), 5–19.
Chambers, S. and Kopstein, J. 2001. 'Bad civil society', *Political Theory*, 29(6), 837–865.

Chambers, S. and Kymlicka, W. eds 2002. *Alternative Conceptions of Civil Society*, Princeton: Princeton University Press.

Charney, E. 1998. 'Political liberalism, deliberative democracy, and the public sphere', *American Political Science Review*, 92(1), 97–110.

CIVICUS n.d. Civil Society Index Report for the Republic of Sierra Leone: *A Critical Time for Civil Society in Sierra Leone.*

Craig, D. and Porter, D. 2003. 'Poverty Reduction Strategy Papers: a new convergence', *World Development*, 31(1), 53–69.

Danino, R. 2005. 'Leadership Dialogue with Traditional Authorities', Speech, Kumasi, Ghana, 5 December.

Danquahz, R. 2011. 'Are civil right societies and NGOs essential to Ghana's development?' [online]. Available from: http://ita.civicus.org/about/90-civil-society-accountability-in-ghana (accessed 19 December 2012).

DfID (Department for International Development) 2011. 'Ongoing Civil Society Challenge Fund Project', [online]. Available from: www.dfid.gov.uk/Working-with-DFID/Funding-opportunities/Not-for-profit-organisations/CSCF.

DfID (Department for International Development) n.d. 'What is civil society?' [online]. Available from: www.dfid.gov.uk/Global-Issues/Emerging-policy/Civil-Society.

Encarnación, O. 2006. 'Civil society reconsidered', *Comparative Politics*, 38(3), 357–376.

ENCISS 2009. *Knowledge, Attitude and Practice Baseline Survey*, September 2009.

Escobar, A. 1995. *Encountering Development: The Making and Unmaking of the Third World*, Princeton: Princeton University Press.

EURODAD 2008. *Old Habits Die Hard: Aid and Accountability in Sierra Leone*, 2008.

Fanthorpe, R. 2005. 'On the limits of liberal peace: chiefs and democratic decentralisation in post-war Sierra Leone', *African Affairs*, 105(418), 27–49.

Fanthorpe, R. 2009. *Reform is Not against Tradition: Making Chieftaincy Relevant in 21st century Sierra Leone*, Freetown: Partners in Conflict Transformation and Campaign for Good Governance.

GoG (Government of Ghana) 2003. *Ghana Poverty Reduction Strategy 2003–2005: An Agenda for Growth and Prosperity*, Accra: Government of Ghana.

GoG (Government of Ghana) 2010. *Ghana Shared Growth and Development Agenda*, Accra: Government of Ghana.

GoSL (Government of Sierra Leone) 2001. *Sierra Leone Interim Poverty Reduction Strategy Paper*, Government of Sierra Leone: Freetown.

GoSL (Government of Sierra Leone) 2002. *National Recovery Strategy: Sierra Leone 2002–2003*, Government of Sierra Leone: Freetown.

GoSL (Government of Sierra Leone) 2003. *Sierra Leone Vision 2025: Sweet Salone*, Strategies for National Transformation, Government of Sierra Leone: Freetown.

GoSL (Government of Sierra Leone) 2005. *Sierra Leone Poverty Reduction Strategy Paper 2005–2007*, Government of Sierra Leone: Freetown.

Grindle, M. 2007. 'Good enough governance reconsidered', *Development Policy Review*, 25(5), 553–574.

Grindle, M. 2011. 'Governance reform: the analytics of next steps', *Governance*, 24(3), 415–418.

Harrison, G. 2004. *The World Bank in Africa: The Construction of Governance States*, London: Routledge.

Harrold, P. 2000. 'Setting the context of civil society engagement', in K. Mackay and S. Gariba (eds) *The Role of Civil Society in Assessing Public Sector Performance in Ghana*, Washington, D.C.: World Bank, 3–4.

38   *D. Williams and T. Young*

ICG (International Crisis Group) 2008. *Sierra Leone: A New Era of Reform?* Africa Report No. 143, Dakar/Brussels: ICG.

Kasanga, K. and Kotey, N. 2001. *Land Management in Ghana: Building on Tradition and Modernity*, London: International Institute for Environment and Development.

Kasfir, N. 1998. 'Civil society, the state and democracy in Africa', *Journal of Commonwealth and Comparative Politics*, 36(2), 123–148.

Kateb, G. 1994. 'Notes on pluralism', *Social Research*, 61(3), 511–537.

Kelsall, T. 2008. 'Going with the grain in African Development', *Development Policy Review*, 16(6), 627–655.

Kelsall, T. 2011. 'Rethinking the relationship between neo-patrimonialism and economic development in Africa', *IDS Bulletin*, 42(2), 76–87.

Kothari, U. 2001. 'Power, knowledge and social control in participatory development', in B. Cooke and U. Kothari (eds) *Participation: The New Tyranny*, London: Zed, 139–152.

Landell-Mills, P. 1992. 'Governance, civil society and empowerment', *Journal of Modern African Studies*, 30(2), 543–567.

Lin, J. 2012. *New Structural Economics: A Framework for Rethinking Development*, Washington, D.C.: World Bank.

Locke, J. 1993. 'A letter concerning toleration', in D. Wootton (ed.) *John Locke: Political Writings*, London: Penguin.

ODI (Overseas Development Institute) 2007. 'Multi-Donor Support for Civil Society and "Non-Traditional" Civil Society: A Light Touch Review of DfID's Portfolio', London.

Oxford Policy Management 2007. *Making Aid More Effective through Gender, Rights and Inclusion: Evidence from Implementing the Paris Declaration – Sierra Leone case study*, Oxford: Oxford Policy Management.

Paris, R. 2010. 'Saving Liberal Peacebuilding', *Review of International Studies*, 36(2), 337–365.

Rathbone, R. 2000. *Nkrumah and the Chiefs: The Politics of Chieftaincy in Ghana, 1951–1960*, Oxford: James Currey.

Richards, P. 2005. 'To fight or to farm? Agrarian dimensions of the Mano River conflicts (Liberia and Sierra Leone)', *African Affairs*, 104(417), 571–590.

Robinson, J. 2008. *Governance and Political Economy Constraints to World Bank CAS Priorities in Sierra Leone*, World Bank Paper, Washington, D.C.: World Bank.

Robinson, J. 2010. *The Political Economy of Decentralization in Sierra Leone*, World Bank Paper, Washington, D.C.: World Bank.

Rosenblum, N. 1989. *Liberalism and the Moral Life*, Cambridge, MA: Harvard University Press.

STAR-Ghana 2012. 'Introduction' [online]. Available from: www.startgahan.org/about-star-ghana/introduction (accessed 7 February 2014).

Stewart, F. and Wang, M. 2003. *Do PRSPs Empower Poor Countries and Disempower the World Bank, or Is It the Other Way Round?*, Queen Elizabeth House Working Paper QEHWPS108, Oxford.

Taylor, C. 1995. *Philosophical Arguments*, Cambridge, MA: Harvard University Press.

Thomson, B. 2007. *Sierra Leone: Reform or Relapse? Conflict and Governance Reform*, Chatham House Report, London: Royal Institute of International Affairs.

USAID 2009. Civil Society [Online]. Office of Democracy and Governance. Available from: www.usaid.gov/our_work/democracy_and_governance/technical_areas/dg_office/civ.html.

Whitfield, L. 2010. 'The state elites, PRSPs and policy implementation in aid dependent Ghana', *Third World Quarterly*, 31(5), 721–737.

Whitfield, L. and Jones, E. 2008. *Ghana: The Political Dimensions of Aid Dependence*, Global Economic Governance Working Paper 2007/32, Oxford.

Williams, D. 2008. *The World Bank and Social Transformation in International Politics: Liberalism, Governance and Sovereignty*, London: Routledge.

Williams, D. 2011. *International Development and Global Politics: History, Theory and Practice in the Changing Global Order*, London: Routledge.

Williams, D. and Young, T. 2009. 'The international politics of social transformation: trusteeship and intervention in historical perspective', in M. Duffield and V. Hewitt (eds) *Empire, Development and Colonialism*, Oxford: James Currey, 102–115.

World Bank 1989. *Sub-Saharan Africa: From Crisis To Sustainable Growth*, Washington, D.C.: World Bank.

World Bank 1994a. *Governance: The World Bank's Experience*, Washington, D.C.: World Bank.

World Bank 1994b. *Ghana: Community Water and Sanitation Project*, World Bank report no. 12404-GH.

World Bank 2000. *Public Financial Management Reform Project*, World Bank report no. PID9535.

World Bank 2003. *Land Administration Project*, Africa Regional Office, World Bank report no. 25913.

World Bank 2004a. *Country Assistance Strategy of the World Bank Group for the Republic of Ghana*, World Bank report no. 27838-GH.

World Bank 2004b. *Community-Based Rural Development Project*, World Bank report no. 28539.

World Bank 2005. *Implementation Completion Report: Second Community Water and Sanitation Project*, World Bank report no. 32309.

World Bank 2006a. *Demanding Good Governance: A Stocktaking of Social Accountability Initiatives by Civil Society in Anglophone Africa*, Washington, D.C.: World Bank.

World Bank 2006b. *Justice for the Poor and Understanding Processes of Change in Local Governance*, Sierra Leone, Africa Region Concept Note, Washington, D.C.; World Bank.

World Bank 2007a. *Promoting Partnerships with Traditional Authorities Project: Implementation Completion and Results Report*, World Bank report no. IDA-37430.

World Bank 2007b. *The Civil Society Landscape in Sierra Leone: Understanding Context, Motives and Challenges*, Washington, D.C.: World Bank.

World Bank 2011a. *Second Land Administration Project*, World Bank report no. 58334.

World Bank 2011b. *Phase One of the Building the Capacity of the Urban Poor for Inclusive Urban Development in Ghana Project*, World Bank report no. 69614.

Young, T. 2002. '"A project to be realised": global liberalism and a New World Order', in E. Hovden and E. Keene (eds) *The Globalisation of Liberalism*, Basingstoke: Palgrave, 173–190.

Zhou, Y. 2009. *Decentralization, Democracy and Development: Recent Experiences from Sierra Leone*, Washington, D.C.: World Bank.

3 Governing rural poverty and development in postcolonial Zimbabwe

Insights from Foucault's governmentality approach

Kudzai Matereke

Introduction

This chapter seeks to make a case for the relevance of Foucault's notion of governmentality in analysing the ways power is exercised in the government of poverty and development in Zimbabwe's rural areas. Within a context of deep political and economic crises the postcolonial state (with support from the international donor community) has made interventions to ameliorate rural poverty and meet development goals. These interventions invoke a number of questions which include: How do power relations in Zimbabwe involve more than simply domination but also extend to power that works through relatively free subjects? What other actors and institutions does the Zimbabwean state enlist in its government of the rural population? What role do non-governmental organisations (NGOs) and international agencies play in governing Zimbabwe? Suggesting that power works through forms of governmentality – rationalised practices of freedom – in somewhere like Zimbabwe is a hard case, and thus this chapter has broader significance for debates about the utility of governmentality outside the 'liberal West'.

An attempt to address these questions serves two main purposes. First, it provides a chance to interrogate what analytical purchase the notion of governmentality has in our understanding of the operations of knowledge/power at the two levels of the global and the national. This understanding will help us not only to envisage how the postcolonial nation-states relate to the international economic and political order but also how they deal with their own citizens in addressing specific issues of poverty and development that emerge within their jurisdiction. Second, the strategy allows us to envision the limits to and prospects of the interventions by both international governmental and national civil society actors in postcolonial societies. Careful analyses of both aims allow us to open new spaces of inquiry into how power is both structured and exercised in postcolonial societies.

The questions I pose above are framed against the backdrop of the debates about the efficacy (or otherwise) of the international practices of state-building and civil society support in postcolonial Africa. In these debates, some African

Governing rural poverty and development 41

studies scholars and international relations theorists have doubted whether financial and technical assistance from the international and multilateral donors have the positive effect of democratising authoritarian states (Alence 2004; Diamond 2000; Joseph 2010a; Sandbrook 1993). A closer look, however, highlights how the financial and technical assistance rendered by international agencies brings about convoluted and ambiguous results. On the one hand, the technical assistance offered by local and international donors help to open up spaces for citizens to exercise their democratic agency. In this way, the assistance is a form of governmentality whose effect is to govern through free citizens, thus making the notion of 'governmentality' relevant for postcolonial societies, despite the difficulties of extending the concept outside of Western liberal societies (Joseph 2010a). On the other hand, the assistance serves to entrench the control and authority of the state in ways that may forestall transition towards more democratic forms of politics. In this chapter, I utilise the Zimbabwean postcolonial context to flesh out how the Zimbabwe African National Union – Patriotic Front (ZANU PF) government's approach to issues of rural poverty and development can be illuminated from the Foucauldian governmentality perspective. By focusing my attention at the level of the rural village, I seek to highlight the intricate ways in which ZANU PF's mobilisation structure is strategically placed to oversee and exert discipline (even in very subtle and covert ways) within the structure of the local government and village development protocols. By attending to this intricate relationship we can decipher how some of the developmental projects and poverty reduction strategies sponsored by the state and international and multilateral donors are expended with very little or no transformative effects on the broader structural level of Zimbabwean politics, but which have the effect of promoting entrepreneurial and 'free' subjects at the micro-level. The interplay of the dominant structures of power at the micro-level of the rural village need to be clearly understood if we are to assess and critique the assumption that practices of supporting state-building and civil society through financial and technical assistance from the international and multilateral donors in postcolonial Africa have the positive effect of strengthening civil society and contributing to the overall goal of democratisation.

Zimbabwe: the quest for development and alleviating rural poverty

The alleviation of rural poverty has been at the heart of development interventions in Zimbabwe, and the broader state-led development project must be understood in this context. In this section, I will provide a brief outline of the different strategies employed by the postcolonial state in its quest to reduce rural poverty and accelerate development. Attempts to account for the source of rural poverty in Zimbabwe should take into account, among other things, the structure of the country's agricultural sector. Historically, the Zimbabwean agricultural sector operated on a dualistic pattern. The commercial farms produced mainly cash crops like sugar, tobacco, flowers and fruits, and also animals and animal

42   *K. Matereke*

products. Rural-based and small-scale farms mainly produced food crops like maize and other grain crops for local consumption. Both sectors were pivotal in the production of surplus food for export. Owing to the success of labour-intensive commercial farms, the majority of rural dwellers were employed on either short-term or long-term contracts, thus ensuring a steady household income. However, the dualistic nature of the agricultural sector inherited from the previous colonial regime presented a number of challenges. At independence, the rural-based agricultural economy which comprised of approximately 77 per cent of the total population was characterised by arid conditions, poor soil quality, and low productivity, while less than 5000 European commercial farmers held the most productive lands, where large-scale commercial farming and ranching predominated (Alwang *et al.* 2002: 3). This meant that the rural population was vulnerable to droughts and serious health risks.

Given this background, it becomes clear why the postcolonial state embarked on a social and economic reform programme informed by socialist ideology and centralised planning. This entailed the state intensifying its fiscal spending on social sector reforms in order to expand rural infrastructure: building more schools, clinics and hospitals, roads and social services. In the field of education, positive gains were recorded with the establishment of free and compulsory education, increase in enrolment, improvement in literacy and numeracy levels and also a high regard for post-school academic qualifications. For these reasons, Zimbabwe achieved what has been described as an 'educational miracle' (Mackenzie 1988). The commitment to equitable educational outcomes also translated into impressive health outcomes as there was a marked improvement in immunisation levels, nutrition and child mortality (Tumwine 1992). Full subsidisation of healthcare, building of new clinics and hospitals and also upgrading existing ones ensured that all people had access to healthcare (Chikuhwa 2008). There was also a land acquisition programme that aimed to resettle families to decongest the overpopulated rural areas on the basis of the 'willing-buyer, willing-seller' provided by the Lancaster House Constitution (Dashwood 2000: 52). The programme produced better resourced farmers who ensured constant food supply to the nation and the region.

The pursuit of social and economic reform on the basis of the ZANU PF party's commitment to Marxist-Leninist scientific socialism also explains why in the first five years of its rule there was a strong drive to legislate a one-party state. In August 1984, the party adopted a new constitution in which sweeping reforms were introduced. One of the reforms was the establishment of a Politburo, the party's highest decision-making organ that would champion the socialist ideology and also lay foundations for a one-party system. In this way, ZANU PF became a vanguard party, 'one that is dedicated to a theory of society' which its adherents 'believe to be scientifically correct' thus explaining their attempts 'to enforce *its* political truth as an official orthodoxy' (Sklar 1985: 29). Despite having fought alongside its sister nationalist party, Zimbabwe African People's Union (PF ZAPU) and having formed the first independent government together, ZANU PF envisaged a political dispensation in which its nationalist partner was

Governing rural poverty and development 43

obliterated. It created the impression that the pursuit of a one-party state agenda was essential for the unity of a young postcolonial nation committed to development and modernisation. Hence the repression and violence against political opponents in general; and the attempts to outlaw PF ZAPU and the killings perpetrated against its supporters, in particular, were easily co-opted into the discourse of postcolonial nation-building and development. However, while national unity may have been a necessary prerequisite for the developmental tasks of a third-world nation like Zimbabwe, the particular resolve to legislate a one-party state went far beyond the examples of many other post-colonial African states which were moving to multi-party systems during the same period. As others have argued, the unity necessary to sustain a developmental state could even have been achieved in a multi-party framework rather than in a one-party system (Shaw 1986: 381). The process of reform also included merging former rural councils and district councils. The former had represented white commercial farming interests while the latter exercised its jurisdiction over the indigenous Africans in the communal areas, highlighting how the colonial administration had relied on a 'bifurcated state' (Mamdani 1996) – a system of racial segregation in which rural and urban councils and also African councils or African Tribal Trust Lands had different jurisdictions. The reform saw the introduction of the new District Councils under the District Administrator who was directly under the Ministry of Local government, Rural and Urban Development (Mutizwa-Mangiza 1990).

The drive towards a one-party state rule resulted in an overbearing and repressive postcolonial state which was heavily controlled if not held hostage by the party. This situation where all the formal organs and structures of the state, including the military and security services, are closely linked to the party without being officially integrated into each other is called the 'party-state phenomenon' (Masunungure 2009: 82). In this situation, state-sponsored violence is nothing but the party's attempt to confront internal dissent or opposition. The period of reform was also characterised by contradictions and ambiguities because while ZANU PF officially claimed to follow the socialist ideology as a strategy to address the question of governance and the inequalities brought about by settler-state capitalism, the party's stalwarts were embarking on a process of 'embourgeoisement' (Mandaza 1986). They utilised their role in the party and government to form ties with the semi-proletariat and the peasantry to act as the pivot between imperialist and semi-proletariat aspirations while at the same relying on the very colonial structures of industrial capitalism to draw wealth for personal gain.

As part of its reform in 1984, ZANU PF also published the Leadership Code. This was a code of conduct inspired by a Marxist-Leninist stance against the creation of a class of bourgeoisie from the political elites. The code forced leaders to declare their assets. It also discouraged them from embarking on business enterprises thus serving as a deterrent measure against elites' abuse of political power for personal economic gain. The existence of the code was an acknowledgement of the elites' propensity for using political power and influence in order to accumulate personal wealth (Dashwood 2000: 98). Despite the code's

44   K. Matereke

clarity on how political power should not play a role in business ventures, the politicians continually flouted it with Mugabe himself subsequently describing it as a 'despicable piece of paper' (Harsch 1993: 45–46; Hope 2002: 120) because it hindered the emergence of a black entrepreneurial class. For some critics, the contradictions and inconsistencies inherent in the ways the postcolonial state formulated its policies shows that the postcolonial state is a 'schizophrenic state' (Mandaza 1986; Moore 2004). Such a state is characterised by a political leadership that deploys tools of propaganda in the articulation of ideology in its advancement of homogeneity and also in its bid to suppress popular demands (Yeros 2002: 6) or to channel them to advance its own cause.

How does the development of the one-party state in Zimbabwe help us to better understand rural poverty? While the postcolonial state initiated social and economic reforms, the life of the peasants did not transform for the better. Government expenditure on social and economic reform to ameliorate rural poverty did not yield the intended results. Rather, by the end of the first decade poverty increased and living standards plummeted; the gains in the areas of health, education and economic development were also stagnating. Moreover, state expenditure on social and economic reform in the name of scientific socialism increased against a general background of political developments that undercut the achievements of the social and economic reforms. Other similar developments during this period included the ZANU PF-dominated parliament passing constitutional amendments to create an executive presidency which wielded enormous political power, thus signalling the centralisation of power in the executive at the expense of the legislature and judiciary (Alexander 2009: 188; Kagoro 2004); increasing Cabinet and presidential appointees which resulted in a bloated bureaucracy that consumed a huge chunk of the budget; the ZANU PF government's crackdown against PF ZAPU and other opponents continued unabated; there was increased lack of transparency and accountability by the government and its agencies as highlighted by cases of corruption and nepotism such as the Willowvale Scandal of 1988; and the defence force undertook a process of military expansion programme and was also involved in the Mozambican civil war which saw it absorb about 10 per cent of GDP annually (Van Der Hoven *et al.* 1993: 24). Given that government expenditure made a sharp rise within a context of declines in returns to both human and physical assets (Alwang *et al.* 2002), it is not surprising to understand why the plight of the poor remained a difficulty for the government. Hence whilst the official record in Zimbabwe during this period attributed recurrent food shortages and poverty to natural droughts, declining quality of soil and the depletion of farming assets, the real cause of food shortages and poverty stemmed from the mismanagement of the economy and political repression (Sachikonye 1992; Wilhite and Buchanan-Smith 2005: 19–20). The sum effect of the developments of the first decade was the emergence of a more disgruntled citizenry that clamoured for a more accountable and transparent political dispensation.

The adoption of the Economic Structural Adjustment Programme (ESAP) in 1991 marks a turning point for Zimbabwe's postcolonial politics. ESAP's adoption against the preceding political and economic developments needs to be understood from two perspectives. First, the adoption was because of internal or local political and economic dynamics that Zimbabwe found itself in; dynamics which stem from ZANU PF's contradictory policies. The social and economic reforms were initiated against the background of an increasingly inefficient public sector and local industry inherited from the colonial system which was showing strong signs of fatigue. Hence there was a need for an alternative policy framework. Second, the end of the Cold War saw the emergence of a new global neoliberal order championed by international economic institutions such as the World Bank and the International Monetary Fund.

In short, the postcolonial nation found itself adopting policies championed by a larger and global governmental order. Poverty in Zimbabwe thus seems to be explicable through two forms of domination: Mugabe's domination of the rural population and political opposition, and the domination of Western neoliberalism from 1991 onwards. However, it is also possible to see rural poverty as produced and governed through particular forms of freedom in Zimbabwe. My contention is that the political domination of Mugabe's party within the country was augmented by the policy domination of Western neoliberal institutions from outside, but also that rural poverty and the quest for development are governed through specific forms of freedom. This takes me to the work of Michel Foucault. Below I undertake an analysis of how his ideas illuminate my argument.

The Foucauldian view of power and governmentality

Foucault's view of power and the notion of governmentality can help to inform how Zimbabwean postcolonial politics has restructured citizen-state relations and also how the state has intervened to ameliorate rural poverty and achieve development. One key element of Foucault's thought is to trace and examine how the notion of power and its exercise within the European state shifted from the Middle Ages through to the eighteenth century. In particular, Foucault traces how states developed the capability not only to create a more stable society that can defend its territory against both internal and external enemies, but also to create forms of knowledge and techniques by which to order its population in pursuit of 'reason of state', a Foucauldian term which refers to actions informed by political rationalities and knowledge directed at specific ends which reinforce and sustain the state itself (Foucault 1988: 150). Foucault's most important theoretical novelty is to deconstruct the dominant account that saw power as repressive and as a zero-sum game; or as a substance that can be possessed or wielded; or an entity that inhabits a single and specifiable place and flows in a single direction. For Foucault, this dominant conception of power (which he terms the juridico-discursive model of modern power) is depictive of the monarchy as articulated in the classical theories of sovereignty. It is a form of power symbolised by the sword – 'the power of life and death' – as it was the sovereign's unconditional and absolute right to defend his life and realm even if this required the death of his subjects (Foucault 1980a: 135–136).

46   *K. Matereke*

According to the classical conception of sovereignty, one of the key attributes of the sovereign is the exercise of 'the right to make live and let die', an attribute which constitutes a 'theoretical paradox' in that the subjects' right to life or death is dependent on the sovereign who has the will over the right (Foucault 2003: 240). Looking at how the ruling party in Zimbabwe sought to advance the one party-state agenda through repression of perceived opponents and domination of the political sphere, it is easy to cast President Mugabe into this conception of sovereignty. The ruling party's strategies to amend the national constitution so as to create executive presidency was aimed at creating a framework of law and legality in which the sovereign had enough space to monitor, incite, repress and optimise all the forces under its jurisdiction. In this way, it can be argued that Mugabe's ruling party exercised a form of power that renders political activity as nothing but the means to increase the might of the sovereign. This form of power is hierarchical and it puts the repressed and subordinated people in a perpetually asymmetrical relationship with those who repress and subordinate them as it allows 'an extremely limited margin of freedom' (Foucault 1997: 292).

Foucault contrasts sovereign conceptions of power with 'relations of discipline', and the notion *discipline* here refers to mechanisms and techniques that emerged in the seventeenth and eighteenth centuries which targeted individual bodies and ensured that they are controlled, rendered visible, separated, aligned, hierarchised and serialised and also put under surveillance (Foucault 1977). With the emergence of industrial capitalism in the nineteenth century, Foucault identifies another shift characterised by the emergence of 'a second seizure of power' called 'bio-power'; a form of power that is neither individualising nor directed at man-as-body, but rather massifying and directed at man-as-species (Foucault 2003: 243). The major shift was that whereas the juridico-political model of power placed the interests of the sovereign at the centre of politics and also saw the individual as its target, bio-power targeted the population or multiplicity of men, not to the extent that men are individual bodies but to the extent that they are 'a global mass that is affected by overall processes characteristic of birth, death, production, illness, and so on' (Foucault 2003: 242–243). The emergence of bio-power means the notion of population occupies a central place in the object of government or the domain of the political, and this is very significant for Foucault. It highlights how the aims of all forms of government revolve around enhancing and improving the life of the people who constitute the nation or *population* by identifying and defending against any internal and external attacks. It also entails that the activity of governing involves ensuring the stability of forces within the state through generating economic efficiency thus guaranteeing the population's material well-being. However, the emphasis on the population does not entail that the individual immediately lost significance. Rather interest about the individual (that is, knowledge about her life, death, activities, work and joys) becomes 'important to the extent that these everyday concerns became politically useful' (Dreyfus and Rabinow 1986: 139). Such a perspective alerts us to the ways in which the 'rural poor' in Zimbabwe were

Governing rural poverty and development 47

actually produced as an object of development interventions by colonial and postcolonial governmentalities.

At the core of Foucault's view of the exercise power is an attempt to address two key questions: '*who* governs (*who* exercises power)?' and '*how* is the power exercised?'. The Foucauldian conception of power as ubiquitous and also as a relation between forces shows that these two questions are inextricably interwoven. Since power is produced and applied by way of techniques, strategies and tactics that form a network of relations amongst individuals and groups, then its source is diffused and its flows are multi-directional. The process of governing entails how individuals, groups and institutions conduct their own behaviour and that of others. Thus governing implies freedom insofar as it relates to how we shape and regulate ourselves and our needs in order to make decisions and choices about our lifestyles. Governing is the 'conduct of conduct' by constituting an array of activities that 'structure the possible field of action for others' (Foucault 1982: 220). Thus the term 'governmentality' describes a form of exercising power in the conduct of conduct by using types of rationality. Lemke offers a semantic definition of this term by linking governing (*gouverner*) and modes of thought (*mentalité*) so as to show how knowledge and rationality are imputed in the process of governing, thus highlighting how it is impossible 'to study the technologies of power without an analysis of the political rationality underpinning them' (Lemke 2001: 190).

Foucault's view of power and its manifestations as sovereign, disciplinary, biopower and governmentality can help us to understand that, even in the case of Zimbabwe where power can so easily be identified as the domination of Mugabe, his party and/or Western neoliberal institutions, power can also be seen as productive insofar as it works through the freedom of citizens. If we envisage the reforms initiated by Zimbabwe's ruling party as the deployment of structures of coercion and domination, we can see how the exercise of power in the postcolonial state is a refinement of techniques of domination over individuals. This form of exercising power takes 'recourse to processes by which the individual acts upon himself', thus showing how 'the techniques of the self are integrated into structures of coercion and domination' (Foucault 1993: 203). The notion of government points to the convergence between domination and self-conduct. Foucault elaborates this by arguing that what he terms 'government' is 'the contact point, where the way individuals driven by others is tied to the way they conduct themselves' (Foucault 1993: 203). This entails that

> governing people is not a way to force people to do what the governor wants; it is always a versatile equilibrium, with complementarity and conflicts between techniques which assure coercion and processes through which the self is constructed or modified by himself.
>
> (Foucault 1993: 204)

This conception of government highlights the multiple ways in which power operates and it also points to the complex ways in which social relations between

48 K. Matereke

actors constitute fields of possibility for action and resistance. This conception of government and power is important for the ways the Zimbabwean postcolonial state responded to poverty and the quest for development after the first decade of independence.

Zimbabwe reconsidered from the governmentality approach

Zimbabwe seems to be a hard case for a governmentality approach. Given that the Zimbabwean postcolonial regime is repressive and has perpetuated its hold on power through internal domination, how can it be an archetypal example of the exercise of power through freedom? Some critics, such as Jonathan Joseph, think that Foucault's idea of governmentality is irrelevant in sub-Saharan African countries. As the argument goes, these countries are 'currently non-starters' for the governmentality approach since they 'are relatively bare spots on the [international] map'; zones in which 'networks of capital and information associated with postindustrial progress are sparse and stretched' (Joseph 2010a: 239 and 236; see Death 2013, for a discussion of this argument). In contrast, I suggest that a governmentality approach can provide illuminating insights into the operation of politics in societies outside Western liberal democracies.

It must be noted, however, that Foucault uses the notion governmentality with reference to liberalism. For him, liberal societies are guided by 'the principle of the self-limitation of governmental reason' or a governmental rationality which exercises a 'new type of calculation' in limiting 'forms and domains of governmental action' (Foucault 2008: 20–21). Understood in this way, liberalism is a general principle which establishes on the part of citizens conditions of the possibility of resistance to the manner in which they are governed. Foucault's conception of governmental reason as characterised by a search for the principle of self-limitation highlights how a liberal society provides a context for resolving the complex interaction of individual and collective interests. As many African societies – particularly Zimbabwe under Mugabe – are regarded as illiberal (or are not liberal in the way Foucault describes above), how can they be analysed from the standpoint of a theory concerned with liberalism? I attempt to address this question below.

My discussion in the previous section highlights how the Zimbabwean economic and political landscape is a site of both internal domination by Mugabe's party and external domination from the Western neoliberal order. Yet the interventions of the IMF and World Bank suggest ways in which government through freedom become relevant in Zimbabwe. The enforced liberalisation of the economy was characterised by a movement towards a *laissez faire* form of government. The adoption of a liberal economy is a response to the deep seated concern that characterises liberalism itself: that the intricacies of the economy are to be governed by laws, processes and procedures that must be kept beyond the reach of the state. Hence there is need to separate, on one hand, state (public) and, on the other, market (private) realms – a separation which, in the dominant discourses of liberalism, marks the emergence of civil associations that are beyond the reach of

Governing rural poverty and development 49

the state. This position adequately captures what Foucault identifies as the art of government in modern liberal democratic societies which is an exercise of sovereignty through the regulation of populations not by attending to the minute details of their everyday life but by avoiding 'excessive' government. The maxim, derived from the eighteenth-century English statesman Robert Walpole, 'Let sleeping dogs lie', denotes the principle of internal self-regulation of power such that the essential precept of liberalism is underpinned by commitment to planning and calculation as forms of exercising 'modern governmental reason' in order to address the problem of 'how not to govern too much' (Foucault 2008: 1 and 13).

How do the principles of internal self-regulation and not 'governing too much' play out in Zimbabwe's adoption of ESAP and accompanying policies like the Social Dimensions of Adjustment (SDA) programme which sought to mitigate the socio-economic effects of structural adjustment? One may argue that the adoption of ESAP and SDA signals 'the so-called "retreat of the state"' which is in actual fact 'a prolongation of government' insofar as it 'is not the end but a transformation of politics that restructures the power relations in society' (Lemke 2000: 11). By adopting policies that allow the market to regulate supply and demand, the state actually formed, developed and adopted new governmental practices in which, though its hold appeared to have faded away into the background, it remained central in the transformed power-dynamics. This contention forms my overall argument that the adoption of ESAP and the concomitant measures to ameliorate its effects on citizens need to be conceived not in terms of governmental practices imposed from a single source or direction (that is, from those who govern to those who are governed), but as a practice of 'internal limitation' (Foucault 2008: 12). Rather, the political and economic changes involved the reorientation, reinvention and deployment of different institutional and administrative mechanisms in the economic, socio-cultural and political spheres which governed through conducting the conduct of citizens.

By advancing the argument above, I seek to challenge the perspective that sees the exercise of political power in repressive political regimes solely from the perspective of Foucault's 'disciplinary power'. Rather, a closer look at the exercise of power in repressive regimes may reveal a proliferation and utilisation of a complex network of social and economic relations that involves both state and non-state agencies. Such an approach serves to highlight the efficacy of the governmentality perspective to the African postcolonial context. Foucault's view is that *internal limitation* 'is a practice that fixes the definition and respective positions of the governed and governors facing each other and in relation to each other', and rather than term 'limitation' as an imposition by either side, we should term it a 'transaction', thus rendering it as an 'action between' parties insofar as the relationship is marked 'by a series of conflicts, agreements, discussions, and reciprocal concessions' (Foucault 2008:12). By taking the relationship of power between the governed and those who govern as constituted by complex 'transactional realities' (Foucault 2008: 297), we can attend to how the material and rhetorical practices in the postcolonial state are structured by, and also how they conduct, political outcomes.

50 *K. Matereke*

Any attempt to establish how poverty reduction strategies and development initiatives are structured by, and also have a structuring effect on, the ways power is exercised in the postcolonial context requires us to clearly identify the key aspects of the context and configurations of the structures of rural life. This involves an analysis of the empirical realities of the rural village as space in which discourses of poverty and development engender relations that defy the usual over-generalisations about power and the ways it is exercised. At independence, Zimbabwe inherited a two-tier system of rural authorities: on one hand, district councils which administered black peasant communities under customary authority and law; and, on the other, rural councils representing largely white commercial farming communities that had belonged directly under settler administration and civil law. How do the systems of local government and traditional authority operate? I attempt to address this question below by trying to highlight how the two relate to each other and also to show the political implications of this relationship.

The postcolonial reforms that redefined the local government structure and the traditional authority structure sought to transform a colonial 'bifurcated system' in which the former operated on the basis of decentralised despotism and the latter relied on centralised despotism (Mamdani 1996). The transformation gave way to two local structures of power which operate at different and lateral levels and are also characterised by pervasive mobility and interpellation. On one hand, customary authority consists of three structures: a *sabhuku* (village head), a *sadunhu* (sub-chief) and an *ishe* (paramount chief). Since Zimbabwean society is patriarchal, one is accorded the position of *ishe* by virtue of one's lineage within a clan which lays autochthonous claims on a specific territory. The clan member (usually male) is conferred the title of *ishe* after consultations within the clan. Under the current constitution, the country's president appoints the *ishe*, thus making the traditional authority structure a central part of the government bureaucratic system. As part of his task, the *ishe* consults and supervises the sub-chiefs and the village heads and also plays a prominent role in their appointment. In some contexts, however, the relationship between *ishe* and *sadunhu* is too complex, because though the *sadunhu* may be positioned under the authority of *ishe*, the former 'could be more powerful' than the latter, hence making the customary structure of authority a 'triad-in-motion' that can unsettle 'any stable grid of power that might secure a singular, nested hierarchy of rule' (Moore 2005: 276). Despite this complexity, there is a clear hierarchy that can easily be discerned in practice. On the other hand, the local government structure consists of three structures: the village development committee (VIDCOs); the ward development committee (WADCOs); and the rural district council. The first two are representative bodies that oversee all development initiatives at the grassroots level. The rural district council coordinates the activities of the WADCOS. The hierarchical structure of traditional authority forms formal and informal channels of communication with the structures of local government and they cooperate at various levels in pursuit of developmental goals laid by the state and also initiated by the citizens.

Governing rural poverty and development 51

The amalgamation process which gave rise to the new local government structure was mainly done under the banner of 'decentralisation', and the enactment of the District Councils Act in 1980 and the decentralisation policy that started in 1984 culminated in the Rural District Councils Act of 1988. The process was understood along four main dimensions: devolution of local government; deconcentration of central government's field administration; delegation of authority to parastatal organisations; and privatisation (Mutizwa-Mangiza 1990). The processes of devolution and deconcentration involved the transfer of authority and responsibilities (or the relocation or dispersal of agents or office bearers) to a lower or more local level where they would perform their duties and responsibilities. In some cases, authority and responsibility were delegated to parastatal bodies or organisations in order to promote a competitive and dynamic system controlled by the market forces. All these, it was hoped, would bring about efficiency and effectiveness. Under the colonial system, traditional chiefs and headmen had the authority of allocating land to their subjects and also presiding over customary law under a system of community courts. The process of decentralisation saw the transfer of authority of land allocation and power over judicial matters from the traditional leaders to the district councils and the district magistrates under the Ministry of Justice respectively (Mutizwa-Mangiza 1990: 427). With some chiefs being renowned for their resistance to colonial authority, while others stood accused for collaborating with colonial authorities (Moore 1998; 1999), it is understandable why some scholars argue that the reform of the local governance structure in the post-independence era was a retributive exercise against some chiefs for their role as functionaries of the colonial system (Makumbe 1998). However, as I will argue below, this process can also be seen as the proliferation of subjects of governance, and the introduction of forms of power through freedom into the rural sphere of Zimbabwean politics.

As the basic and bottom unit of local governance, the VIDCO comprises about 100 family units and it is headed by a chairperson and six other committee members (Herbst 1990: 172). The chairperson and four members are elected while the two remaining positions are filled in by members drawn from interest groups like women and youths. The WADCO comprises of about six VIDCOs (depending on the population density of the catchment) and its membership is drawn from those members who constitute the VIDCOs. Like the VIDCOs, two positions are reserved for youth and women. The task of the VIDCO is to work out plans for local development by way of identifying the needs of the village and articulate them through the development of a local village plan (Mandondo 2000: 10). The WADCO, which is presided over by an elected councillor who is also the representative at the District level, has the responsibility to collate the developmental plans from the VIDCOs and then create a consolidated ward plan of action which is forwarded to the Rural District Development Committee. It is from these consolidated plans that districts develop annual and five-year plans (Mandondo 2000: 10). In the development of these long-term plans and objectives a whole range of NGOs become crucial in offering financial and technical assistance. Projects that may feature in the ward plans include dressmaking, small-scale irrigation, smallholder livestock production, soap making, local savings and credit associations, and caregiving for those affected by HIV and AIDS. A number of NGOs have given assistance in these projects. For example, World Vision, CARE International and Plan International have offered both financial and technical assistance to promote projects such as construction of dams and imparting to communal farmers new and effective farming methods, irrigation and animal production. They have also worked with rural women to run 'village saving and loan schemes'. Another NGO, Africare, works to teach HIV and AIDS and reproductive health and also to promote volunteer caregivers (Campbell 2011). Thus the voluntary associations so characteristic of liberal civil society play a central role in governing rural populations in Zimbabwe.

Since colonialism, the problem of governing rural areas has remained highly politicised as issues of land tenure and usage of natural resources, revenue collection, poverty reduction and also rural development raise the question of who has legitimate control over the rural population. This question explains why traditional leaders and the state are often in constant conflict which also engenders dynamic relations of manipulation, strategic cooperation and subordination. The conflict was brought out clearly in the Land Tenure Commission Report of 1994 which highlighted, among other things, concerns about the depletion of natural resources, destruction of farming and grazing land which it attributed to the erosion of the authority of the traditional leaders in the management and use of natural resources. According to the Commission, the persistent problems of depletion of land and natural resources pointed to how the post-independence reforms in local government had eroded the powers of the traditional leaders (Government of Zimbabwe 1994). Given that traditional leaders are unelected while the development committees are elected on the basis of such skills as improved farming methods, numeracy and literacy, and also ability to articulate views about development, it is understandable why the antagonism between the two structures of authority existed. Thus there had been a growing tendency by the former to view the latter as having usurped their traditional power (Maxwell 1999: 151). The Commission's findings justified its recommendation that traditional leaders should occupy a more central role in the management and distribution of the resources. In pursuance to the recommendations, the government passed the Traditional Leaders Act of 1998 whose primary objective was to restore the authority of the traditional leaders in the management of natural resources and coordination of issues of rural development; in the collection of revenue in the form of taxes and levies; and also in the coordination and dissemination of information about culture, health, education, records and also natural disasters. The emergence of the Movement for Democratic Change (MDC) party as a strong political opposition in 1999 and also the rising agitation for land reform saw the passing of the Traditional Leaders Act of 2000 which provided for salaried chiefs and village heads and their reinsertion into the local government and development protocol. The move by the government to pass the act served 'as part of the state's attempt to extend its hegemony deeper in the rural areas at a time of political discontent' (Wolmer 2007: 55).

Governing rural poverty and development 53

The re-engagement of chiefs and headmen to play a more central role in, among other things, coordinating development, allocating land, and managing natural resources entailed a restoration of a wide range of powers in the planning system (Masendeke *et al.* 2004: 41). This change triggered struggles which were fundamentally contests over the form of governmentality at work in governing rural populations. The crucial questions that need to be analysed are: What impact did the restoration of traditional power and authority to the chiefs and village heads have on the role of local government in the attempts to confront poverty and initiate rural development? What are the implications of this restoration for the ways in which the local government hierarchy exercised its power? I will attempt to address these questions by showing the intricate configurations of the local government structure, on one hand, and traditional authority on the other, and also discuss how these two structures relate to each other. This discussion will also proceed to show how the ZANU PF hierarchy relates to these two structures and what effects the relationship has on the overall exercise of power in the postcolonial society. The postcolonial reforms produced two structures of power which are organised and run on two different logics. The chiefs, headmen and village heads exercise power on the basis of traditional authority, which is centralised in an individual and/or a family. In most cases, their authority goes unquestioned. The local government structure, unlike the structure of traditional authority, can be understood as 'rational' in the Weberian sense insofar as the ways its decisions are reached and implemented aim to limit opportunities for arbitrariness and at achieving outcomes based on calculable rules.

An analysis of the re-enactment of the two acts of parliament that restored power to the traditional leaders in the postcolonial context brings into sharper focus the conflict between these two structures of power. The existence of a traditional leader at each level of the local government hierarchy points to how traditional authority is expected to have a place and role at each committee that is mandated to address issues of rural development. This entails that the traditional leader has some amount of influence to determine political outcomes at each level of the local government structure. While the formal system of communication at each hierarchy has both a 'top down' and a 'bottom up' direction of flow, at an informal level, however, the chiefs, being appointees of the President who is also the leader of the ruling party ZANU PF, are positioned to wield more control because they can exercise their coercive powers over village heads and development committees to determine political outcomes. This point can be demonstrated by looking at how the adoption of ESAP and SDA policies transformed the relations between the different players. In this vein, I will briefly discuss how the economic and political policies of ESAP and SDA transformed the social context. I will then highlight how the ruling party positioned itself in this transformed context.

The introduction of ESAP in 1991 marked a shift from the state's proclaimed socialist ideology – through which it had established a regulated and welfare-based policy since independence – to a more *laissez-faire* form of capitalism. The currency was devalued, the economy and the labour market deregulated,

54   K. Matereke

state-controlled institutions and assets were privatised, inflation-control measures were put in place, and also foreign exchange and investment regimes and protocols were liberalised. To prepare for the newly adopted regime of economic reforms, the government promulgated the SDA programme whose aim was, among other things, 'to mitigate the social costs of adjustment' by designing and implementing programs that 'protect and support vulnerable groups so that they are better equipped to face the demands of a liberal order' (Government of Zimbabwe 1991a: 2). The SDA programme sought to minimise strains on the national budget by maximising the participation and support of other players like NGOs, private enterprises and local authorities. The strategies adopted by the state were expected to liberalise the economy thus making it more competitive in attracting and retaining domestic and international investment. Implementation of the economic recovery policies involved the state assessing the extent of the vulnerability of the reform agenda on citizens. It was observed that the most vulnerable group comprised those who lived in rural areas, those who worked in large-scale commercial farms, and also a section of unemployed and unskilled workers in the urban areas (Government of Zimbabwe 1991b: 20). Since the rural areas serve as 'the residual refuge of those who have not been absorbed into the modern formal and informal sectors' (Mhone 1995: 107), the vulnerability of rural households had to be mitigated by ensuring access to income and other entitlements like farming assets (land, livestock and draft power, farming implements and inputs, etc.) and also ability to engage in other forms of wage labour.

To accomplish the SDA programme's aim to cushion the effects of increases in prices of commodities, the state initiated a broad range of measures including rolling out new forms of social welfare which covered the areas of commodity prices, education and health. The state also identified food products like maize meal (the nation's staple diet), bread, beef, sugar, cooking oil and fats as basic consumption items that needed to be controlled in terms of pricing and also to provide government subsidies to ensure their availability (Government of Zimbabwe 1991b: 13). In the area of health and education, new fee structures favourable to rural areas – mostly to be determined on the basis of parental ability to pay – were introduced. This meant a waiver in both education and health for most rural peasants. On the other hand, the government introduced a public works scheme or 'food-for-work programmes' (Sachikonye 1992: 91) in which rural villagers engaged in productive work in return for food or cash handouts. This was a two-pronged measure in that, on one hand, it ameliorated food shortages, while on the other it also achieved infrastructural development as villagers were co-opted in projects such as construction of local roads and dams and also land reclamation projects.

The deregulation of the labour market, however, triggered a spate of retrenchments as companies either downsized or closed down. This had a domino effect on the vulnerability of the rural population. On one hand, they lost remittances from their urban kin. On the other hand, a high influx of city-rural migration increased the pressure on the rural welfare system (Potts and Mutambirwa 1998:

64; Potts 2010: 89). To abate the rampant cases of malnutrition and infant mortality in the rural population, the Child Supplementary Feeding Program was intensified (Bijlmakers *et al.* 1996: 16). The programme had been initiated by NGOs in 1980 when drought affected the region of Southern Africa (Demery and Addison 1987: 40). To further complement the poverty-reduction efforts, the government (through the cooperation of a range of NGOs) encouraged the formation of small community-based groups at the grassroots level to come up with an array of 'self-help' projects aimed at promoting self-sustenance, entrepreneurial skills and income-generation. For example, savings club projects with rural women were encouraged as a way for women groups to pool resources together to buy farming inputs in bulk and take advantage of wholesale prices and transport costs (Lacoste 1998; Lacoste *et al.* 2000). Some of the projects targeted areas of nutrition, food production and preservation with specific focus on the impact of HIV/AIDS on both sufferers and orphans (Food and Agricultural Organization Report 2007).

In order to deal with the challenges of rural poverty, the state also encouraged citizens, mainly unemployed youths and women, to venture into small-scale and medium enterprises (SMEs) in the manufacturing sector which included food processing activities such as baking, oil processing and grain milling, and also other projects like pottery, garment production and brickmaking (Kapoor *et al.* 1997: 6). A special ministry to focus on SMEs and an agency, the Small Enterprise Development Corporation (SEDCO), were specifically created to cater for the needs of small and medium businesses and enterprises. These agencies would spearhead the mobilisation, administration and funding of this sector of the economy. They encouraged the emergence of a new type of citizen: self-enterprising agents who have the potential of creating employment for fellow citizens and contributing to the growth of the economy. In this vein, SMEs have become the government's way of pushing forward the objective of economic indigenisation. In a complete reversal of the precepts of Marxist-Leninist scientific socialism, the pursuit of economic indigenisation was aimed at creating a black capitalist class that would create jobs for the citizens, thus help to speed up the growth of a black middle class. Within a context of staggering unemployment and an intensified de-industrialisation as the government and major companies scaled-down and retrenched workers (Tevera 1998), the initiative to produce self-enterprising agents amongst the indigenous population was a strategic intervention to govern poverty and also to create opportunities to achieve key developmental goals through productive work, especially in agriculture and small-scale manufacturing. In its promotion of national developmental goals and calls to combat poverty, the government utilised new vocabulary of 'self-employment', 'self-sufficiency', 'self-sustenance', and 'self-help'. This new vocabulary highlights how the transformation from formal to informal employment was a form of empowerment for the citizens. In the same vein, the education policy was also expected to co-opt the new vocabulary because it had been observed that since rural life depended on agriculture, 'it would be economic folly and social deception to educate children as if they were going to end in

56 K. Matereke

industrial or office work' (Stoneman and Zvobgo 1981: 55). It is interesting also to note that because the vocabulary that gave currency to the calls for black empowerment was widely accepted as the official party policy, it re-emerged in the land take-overs of 2000 and beyond as party elites and the 'war veterans' within ZANU PF captured the economic indigenisation agenda through threats and intimidation against the opposition.

Some experts claim that small and medium enterprises are an important plank of industrial policy in developing countries given how this sector aims to create jobs, improve welfare, alleviate poverty, raise incomes, enhance technical and entrepreneurial capacities, as well as the often expedient, political considerations of fostering key constituencies of civil society (Nadvi 1995: 3). This claim is especially instructive in the case of Zimbabwe because the introduction of a ministry specifically devoted to small and medium enterprises created an impetus for collaboration between a plethora of NGO agencies that provided services such as technical training and support and local government in order to realise support intervention and collaboration. This collaboration produced citizens with new forms of subjectivity and agency. For example, the involvement of such NGOs as Self-Help Development Foundation (SHDF), Zambuko Trust, community-based savings and credit organisations in assisting women to venture into different forms of entrepreneurship, highlights a correlation between engaging in self-employment or self-help projects and the ability to exercise different forms of freedom. The development of entrepreneurial competencies and abilities amongst women in Zimbabwe's turbulent economic and culturally conservative environment has transformed the economic, political and social space. Against the backdrop of systemic patriarchal prejudice against women and discriminatory laws and policies, it can be demonstrated that the involvement of women in various forms of economic entrepreneurship enhances women's social and financial freedom (Mboko and Smith-Hunter 2009). The social and economic freedom that entrepreneurship brings about is also important for citizens' response to the configurations of political power around them. The state's interventions to ameliorate the demands of a liberalised market economy have produced an entrepreneurial individual – a kind of an 'economic man' or *homo economicus* – who can actively sustain competitive relations of the market and also advance political claims or demand that power be exercised in certain ways that secure their interests.

The development of entrepreneurial skills aimed at poverty reduction through the strategy of 'self-help projects' which citizens choose for themselves, or are at least agreeable to, highlights that the forms of government employed by the state do not always mean that the governor always has his way, but that the governed and the governor exist in a 'versatile equilibrium' in which techniques of negotiation and calculation are employed. Further, the implementation of the projects is mediated through interplay of different structures of authority, each aimed at achieving its own goals and objectives. An example suffices here. Local villagers who engage in a microfinance project may choose to diversify and take up a project in small-scale animal rearing (e.g. chicken or dairy production). The choice is based on their needs, skills and competencies and also availability of resources or prospects of external aid from the government or donor agencies. They approach their respective development committee, which then consults or petitions traditional leaders to allocate land and other resources like water and pasture. The traditional leaders ought to expedite the process by closely cooperating with the development committees because the self-help group in his area is competing with groups from other jurisdictions for the limited aid. By granting access to resources, the traditional leader is bringing to fruition initiatives for both development and poverty reduction for his area.

If the success of development initiatives and poverty-reduction strategies depends on the cooperation among self-help groups, development committees and traditional leaders, then it is also important to probe into how the involvement of the ruling party further complicates the interplay of the forces represented by each significant player in the power dynamics of the rural village. In order to put this point into perspective, it is important to remember that the reform of the local government protocols which had scaled down the powers and responsibilities of the traditional authorities in the 1980s and also the restructuring of the party's hierarchy coincided with the ZANU PF's determined attempt to institute a one-party state system (Onslow 2011). The command structure of the ZANU PF party is implicated in the ways the new local government structure and traditional authority are constituted and also function on a daily basis. The party's constitution is crafted as a voluntary organisation in which members have a choice join in or opt out. Yet the party's mobilisation strategy suggests that by virtue of one's membership to the village, one automatically becomes a member of the party. The structure is designed to fit and also permeate into the pre-existing hierarchy of both the traditional institutions and the rural development protocol.

According to the party's constitution, the 'cell', which is the basic element of the party's structure, exists at the level of the village and its role is to represent the member's interests and to mobilise members to work together for the development of their area (ZANU PF Constitution 2012). Ten cells make up a 'branch' and ten branches make up a 'district'. Each 'branch' and 'district' is headed by an executive committee elected every two years. The range of duties and obligations to the party are generated on the assumption that membership to the village translates to membership to the party, and the circumscription of the party's structure within the traditional authority structure and the local government protocol is a deliberate strategy to reproduce a hierarchy that conscripts existing structures of authority to the party's overall mechanisms of hegemonic control. This justifies the argument that the ZANU PF command structure runs 'parallel to the governing system from the parliament right down to the village level in rural areas' (Makura-Paradza 2010: 96) because its committees' representatives infiltrate into the governing structures of the VIDCOs and WADCOs both by default and by design. For example, the common practice at the elections of VIDCOs and WADCOS to fill in the positions of 'interest groups' with members from the party's youth and women's leagues gives a leverage to the party since its interests are represented in the standing committees. While the

58 *K. Matereke*

structures of governance at the village level are characterised by overlapping and not wholly concordant resource units, memberships and jurisdictions, user-defined interests and uses, and varying degrees of association and affection within and among them (Mandondo 2000: 12), owing to its mobilization strategies at the village level, the ruling party has an upper hand over not only traditional leaders and local government but also other political parties.

The involvement of the ruling party in the power dynamics at the level of the rural village and the quest to alleviate poverty and achieve development seems to lend weight to the claim that the ways the state engages the global governmental practices of Western neoliberalism have given rise to a ruling party whose structure and mobilisation strategy are designed to permeate local government structures and the rural development protocol. This claim supports the argument that political power in Zimbabwe primarily works through sovereign domination. However, political relations in rural Zimbabwe do not solely – or even primarily – rely upon the formal hierarchies and networks of power that are inherent in the dominant depictions of sovereign power. In addition there is a range of ways in which the power of civil society and the market is mobilised to intervene in rural poverty. This takes the form of the adoption of neoliberal economic reforms which saw the introduction of 'enterprise' as a mode of governance of citizens' behaviour and their relationship to each other, the state and the market. Hence what needs to be shown is how consultative processes and negotiations are conducted between the structures of local government, traditional authority and the ruling party to mediate the power of the latter, and also how such mediation processes suggest that power is exercised through freedom and not just through the sovereign's hegemonic practices through the party. This will help to demonstrate that the interactions between the different forces at the level of the rural village is a reciprocal interplay of dialogical practices, thus signalling that power in rural Zimbabwe cannot be confined to the sovereign domination of either ZANU PF or Western neoliberalism. Just as Foucault thought that 'power is not something that is acquired, seized, or shared, something that one holds on to or allows to slip away', my analysis seeks to establish how we can conceive the rural village as a social field within which 'power is exercised from innumerable points, in the interplay of nonegalitarian and mobile relations' (Foucault 1980a: 94). In this way, I think it is prudent to argue that this interplay encompasses a complex network of multiple sites and rationalities.

Earlier, I argued that traditional authority and the local government structure constitute two different logics. The relationship between the tradition of chieftaincy, on one hand, and the modern institutions of local governance, on the other, remains a key issue in the analyses of democratisation in contemporary postcolonial African states (Mamdani 1996). The existence of a ruling party that seeks to manipulate the disjuncture created by the two logics adds even more complexity. It is understandable why some scholars have argued that these two logics represent two dialogically opposed poles of politics, one representing authority, and the other representing power, or others even suggested that the future of Africa's democratisation lies in the consensual, creative and balanced

Governing rural poverty and development 59

synthesis between traditional structures and the modern state (Skalník 1996, 1999). In my view, however, such arguments or suggestions are inadequate if they do not specify how the different structures of power and authority interact and what possibilities and transformative effects the forms of interaction yield.

Through an analysis of how different power structures (and agents within them) interact, we can understand how certain actions and reactions create and also limit possibilities for further actions. Such an understanding allows us to envisage what can be termed 'the logic of power' which is an attempt to specify how power relations between or amongst different agencies are 'imbued with calculation' as there is no form of 'power that is exercised without a series of aims and objectives' (Foucault 1980a: 95). This conception of power is more poignantly articulated in Foucault's powerful metaphor of the 'capillary' which he strategically uses to deploy his view that power has the capacity and mechanism to be pervasive such that we can envisage 'the point where power reaches into the very grain of individuals, touches their bodies and inserts itself into their actions and attitudes, their discourse, learning processes and everyday lives' (Foucault 1980b: 39). Letting citizens come up with proposals for the development of their community on the basis of their identified interests, skills and abilities points to how the governmentality paradigm provides a conception of personal autonomy that is not antithetical to political power but that is key to its exercise, and also that individuals are not merely subjects of power but they play a part in its exercise (Rose and Miller 1992: 174). Foucault's capillary conception of power carries analytical weight in Zimbabwe's postcolonial politics because it dissuades us from a preoccupation with a juridical perspective of power or what Foucault terms 'sovereignty's old right' – a perspective which conceives power only in terms of the sovereign's right 'to take life or let live' (Foucault 2003: 241). A conception of power that sees power as concentrated in the sovereign who, by use of force or threat of force, guarantees or withdraws the rights and responsibilities of citizens, is limited as it omits how individual subjects and agents are enmeshed in shifting and mobile relations at the micro-level.

Foucault's concept of government draws attention to the contact between being externally driven and conducting oneself, and points to the convergence between domination and self-conduct. Hence force or coercion in and by itself is inadequate to describe agency. As Foucault would have it, a conception of government that depicts this convergence highlights the quality of 'a versatile equilibrium' in which techniques of domination contest and mediate techniques of the self between the governed and governors. The self can be involved in its own construction and modification and has an ability to attain a new ethos. Hence the Zimbabwean state's determined aim to use the notion of 'entrepreneurship' in the production of self-reliant and economically self-sufficient citizens can be used to highlight how practices of 'enterprise' were co-opted in both thought and practices of government in the construction of an autonomous self that is capable of thought and action within the domain of the market. In this way, 'governance through enterprise construes the individual as an entrepreneur of his own life,

60 *K. Matereke*

who relates to others as competitors and his own being as a form of human capital' (McNay 2009: 63). By alleviating the effects of neoliberal reforms through SDA policies and also fostering entrepreneurial skills through the cooperation of an array of NGOs projects in the rural areas, the state sought to achieve two related aims. First, to preserve a competitive environment in which the free market becomes the driver of the economy. Second, it aimed to produce disciplined yet free subjects who can actively participate in national economic processes. Hence the interventions of the state (and the Western neoliberal institution that underwrote the economic reforms) were aimed at organising individuals such that discipline and freedom became complementary. The governmental techniques that undergird the reforms produced a certain kind of power which sought to produce disciplined individuals who could optimise their capabilities for positive national economic outcomes. Thus economic reform was a 'theme program of a society' in which action was 'brought to bear on the rules of the game rather than on the players'; it was 'an environmental type of intervention instead of the internal subjugation of individuals' (Foucault 2008: 259–260).

Looking at how the governing structures at the level of the village are configured and interact, we can argue that the establishment of a neoliberal political agenda in the post-independence era has produced profound and unprecedented processes of social and political restructuring of society. The emphasis on enterprise gave way to the intervention of NGOs which worked with villagers in order to assist them to become economically viable citizens through meaningful engagement and agency in market relations. Ordinarily, the context of the rural village is characterised by overbearing traditional authority which is amenable to the control of the functionaries of the ruling party. The reforms to the composition and jurisdiction of the local government structure, the implementation of the economic reforms and the rolling out of SDA policies which also saw the co-optation of NGOs in producing enterprising citizens has transformed this picture.

Rather than understand the rural village as social space in which sovereign domination is the mode of exercising power, we can say that the political and economic reforms that happened in the 1990s have seen the production of a citizen who can exercise an internal limit to the ways sovereign power is exercised. This point signals how the configurations of rural structures of authority and governance provide citizens with the possibility to exercise emancipatory politics. The skills essential for enterprise and self-help make citizens economically viable such that they enhance their social capital within their communities, thus providing them with the capacity to engage in oppositional political agency. The preparedness of citizens to gain entrepreneurial skills and to utilise them to engage in self-help projects enables them to exercise power less in a confrontational manner than in the way they can structure the possible field of action of those they interact with including traditional leaders and ruling party functionaries. Just as Foucault uses 'state phobia' (Foucault 2008) in an attempt to show how misleading and wrong it is to treat the entity of 'the state' as a universal

Governing rural poverty and development   61

with clear and fixed essential qualities, we can also insist that description of Mugabe and the ruling party as dominant and oppressive is potentially and at least partially misleading insofar as it attributes to the postcolonial state and the party a universality and autonomy that they rarely possess. While insisting on the dangers of seeing the notion of governmentality as a tool for legitimating the Mugabe regime, it is worth commenting here that Foucault's alertness to the dangers of 'state phobia' allows us to show how violence and coercion operate alongside power through freedom. The ways the postcolonial state is involved in 'incessant transactions' with other local powers or forces (that is, the traditional authority structure, NGOs, the ruling party and local government protocol), would show it is nothing but 'the mobile effect of a regime of multiple govern-mentalities' (Foucault 2007: 77); the postcolonial state is a force whose power is inscribed in and diffuses across multiple actors or agencies (Mbembe 1992; 2001).

The traditional leaders carry out their official duties and responsibilities by assisting the state to realise its developmental goals, and they view the role assigned to them by both tradition and the modern state as co-extensive with the agency and economic viability of enterprising citizens. Hence at best the rela-tionship between enterprising citizens and the different structures of power views political power not in terms of 'the rationality of a sovereign maximising his own power' but rather in terms of 'the rationality of those who are governed as economic subjects' insofar as the strategies and art of government are mod-elled 'on the rational behavior of those who are governed' (Foucault 2008: 312). In saying this, however, I am not suggesting that we need to entirely forget the existence of sovereign domination. Rather, I am trying to highlight that the pursuit of a type of governmentality that tracks the interests and rationality of the governed overlaps with or dovetails into and integrates with the rationality of sovereign power.

Conclusion

Foucault's governmentality approach helps to illuminate how rural populations in Zimbabwe are governed not solely in terms of the domination of President Mugabe or external forces, but also through the production of certain types of free entrepreneurial subject, and a complex network of institutions and power relations. Foucault's work allows us to see how the state employs a multiplicity of non-state agencies to discipline and regulate citizens' conduct so as to mobilise, structure and construct their capacity for self-government. This is significant in that it points to how the practice of governing operates as 'a power bent on generating forces, making them grow, and ordering them, rather than one dedicated to impeding them, making them submit, or destroying them' (Foucault 1980a: 136). In this chapter, I have attempted to extend this argument to the postcolonial state by analysing how the postcolonial state's efforts to reform the economy, to improve the life, health and longevity of its population were also ways of strengthening itself. The efforts were carried through by

62 K. Matereke

employing strategies and techniques that shape citizens' conduct, to ensure they have a level of compliance that guarantees economic productivity.

By giving priority to the *how* of government, or by focusing on the mechanisms of government in their specificity, we are able to avoid making generalisations about how the state goes about its business of exercising power. The complex relations of power at the level of the rural village highlight how the governmentality paradigm is central for the analysis of how power is exercised in the postcolonial state through the deliberate and well calibrated efforts to produce free and autonomous subjects towards specific governmental goals. Such efforts reflect how African states are agents implicated in the global political and economic sphere, yet also highlight the potential for African citizens to exercise their agency at the micro-level in ways that defy the usual generalised depictions of the postcolonial state as either authoritarian or feeble and its citizens as lacking any form of agency.

References

Alence, R. (2004) 'Political Institutions and Developmental Governance in sub-Saharan Africa,' *Journal of Modern African Studies*, 42(2): 163–187.

Alexander, J. (2009) 'Zimbabwe since 1997: Land and the Legacies of War', in Abdul Raufu Mustapha and Lindsay Whitfield (eds) *Turning Points in African Democracy*, Suffolk: James Currey.

Alwang, J., Mills, B. and Taruvinga, N. (2002) *Why Has Poverty Increased in Zimbabwe?* Washington, D.C.: International Bank for Reconstruction and Development.

Bijlmakers, L. A., Sanders, D. M. and Bassett, M. T. (1996) *Health and Structural Adjustment in Rural and Urban Zimbabwe*, Uppsala: Nordiska Afrikainstitutet.

Campbell, P. (2011) *Africare: Black American Philanthropy in Africa*, New Jersey: Transaction Publishers.

Chikuhwa, J. (2008) *Zimbabwe: Beyond a School Certificate*, Bloomington, IN: Author House.

Dashwood, H. (2000) *Zimbabwe: The Political Economy of Transformation*, Toronto: University of Toronto Press.

Dean, M. (2010) *Governmentality: Power and Rule in Modern Society*, 2nd edn, London: Sage Publishers.

Death, C. (2013) 'Governmentality at the Limits of the International: African Politics and Foucauldian Theory', *Review of International Studies*, 39(03): 763–787.

Demery, L. and Addison, T. (1987) *The Alleviation of Poverty under Structural Adjustment*, Washington, D.C.: World Bank.

Diamond, L. (2000) 'Developing Democracy in Africa: African and International Imperatives,' *Cambridge Review of International Affairs*, 14(1): 191–213.

Dreyfus, H. and Rabinow, P. (eds) (1986) *Michel Foucault: Beyond Structuralism and Hermeneutics*, Hemel Hempstead: Harvester Wheatsheaf.

Fatton, R. (1989) 'The State of African Studies and Studies of the African State: The Theoretical Softness of the "Soft State"', *Journal of Asian and African Studies*, 24(3–4): 170–185.

Food and Agricultural Organization (2007) *Garden-Based Learning for Improved Livelihoods and Nutrition Security of School Children in High HIV-Prevalence Areas in Southern Africa*, Workshop Report, Harare.

Governing rural poverty and development 63

Forrest, J. B. (1988) 'The Quest for State "Hardness" in Africa', *Comparative Politics*, 20(4): 423–442.

Foucault, M. (1977) *Discipline and Punish: The Birth of the Prison*, New York: Vintage.

Foucault, M. (1979) '*Omnes et Singulatim*: Towards a Criticism of 'Political Reason', Tanner Lectures on Human Values, delivered at Stanford University, 10 and 16 October 1979.

Foucault, M. (1980a) *The History of Sexuality, Vol. 1: An Introduction*, trans. R. Hurley, London and New York: Penguin.

Foucault, M. (1980b) *Power/Knowledge: Selected Interviews and Other Writings 1972–1977*, ed. Colin Gordon, New York: Pantheon Books.

Foucault, M. (1982) 'The Subject and Power', in *Michel Foucault: Beyond Structuralism and Hermeneutics*, 2nd edn, ed. Hubert L. Dreyfus and Paul Rabinow, Chicago: University of Chicago Press.

Foucault, M. (1988) 'The Political Technology of Individuals,' in Luther H. Martin, Huck Gutman and Patrick H. Hutton (eds) *Technologies of the Self: A Seminar with Michel Foucault*, Amherst: University of Massachusetts Press, pp. 145–162.

Foucault, M. (1993) 'About the Beginning of the Hermeneutics of the Self: Two Lectures at Dartmouth', trans. and introduction Mark Blasius, *Political Theory*, 21(2): 198–227.

Foucault. M. (1997) 'The Ethics of the Concern for the Self as a Practice of Freedom', in *Ethics: Subjectivity and Truth: The Essential Works of Michel Foucault, 1954–1984*, Vol. 1, ed. Paul Rabinow, trans. Robert Hurley *et al.*, New York: The New Press.

Foucault, M. (2003) *Society Must be Defended: Lectures at the Collège de France, 1975–1976*, New York: Picador.

Foucault, M. (2007) *Security, Territory, Population: Lectures at the Collège de France, 1977–1978*, ed. M. Senellart, trans. G. Burchell, Basingstoke: Palgrave Macmillan.

Foucault, M. (2008) *The Birth of Biopolitics: Lectures at the Collège de France, 1978–1979*, ed. M. Senellart, trans. G. Burchell, Basingstoke: Palgrave Macmillan.

Government of Zimbabwe (1991a) 'Social Dimensions of Adjustment (SDA): A Programme to Mitigate the Social Costs of Adjustment', Harare: Government of Zimbabwe.

Government of Zimbabwe (1991b), *Zimbabwe: A Framework for Economic Reform 1991–1995*, Harare: Government of Zimbabwe.

Government of Zimbabwe (1994) *Report of the Commission of Inquiry into Appropriate Agricultural Land Tenure Systems*, October 1994, Harare: Government of Zimbabwe.

Harsch, E. (1993) 'Accumulators and Democrats: Challenging State Corruption in Africa', *Journal of Modern African Studies*, 31(1): 31–48.

Herbst, J. I. (1990) *State Politics in Zimbabwe*, Berkeley: University of California Press.

Hope, K. (2002) *From Crisis to Renewal: Development Policy and Management in Africa*, Leiden: Brill Academic Publishers.

Jackson, R. H. (1990) *Quasi-States: Sovereignty, International Relations and the Third World*, Cambridge, New York: Cambridge University Press.

Jackson, R. H. and Rosberg, C. G. (1982) *Personal Rule in Black Africa: Prince, Autocrat, Prophet, Tyrant*, Berkeley: University of California Press.

Joseph, J. (2010a) 'The Limits of Governmentality: Social Theory and the International', *European Journal of International Relations*, 16(2): 223–246.

Joseph, J. (2010b) 'Poverty Reduction and the New Global Governmentality', *Alternatives*, 35: 29–51.

Kagoro, B. (2004) 'Constitutional Reform as Social Movement: A Critical Narrative of the Constitution-Making Debate in Zimbabwe, 1997–2000,' in Brian Raftopoulous and

64 *K. Matereke*

Tyrone Savage (eds) *Zimbabwe: Injustice and Political Reconciliation*, Cape Town: Institute for Justice and Reconciliation.

Kapoor, K., Mugwara, D. and Chidavaenzi, I. (1997) *Empowering Small Enterprises in Zimbabwe*, Discussion Paper No. 379, Washington D.C.: The World Bank.

Lacoste, B. (1998) 'Evaluation of the Technical Training Programme', Harare: SHDF/ ADRAI.

Lacoste, J.-P., Mungoshi, V. and Wachenuka, D. (2000) 'Management of Resources Poor Households in Zimbabwe: A Case Study of Savings Club's Members', Harare: SHDF/ ADRAI.

Lemke, T. (2000) 'Foucault, Governmentality, and Critique', paper presented at the Rethinking Marxism Conference at University of Amherst, Massachusetts, September 2000.

Lemke, T. (2001) ' "The Birth of Bio-politics": Michel Foucault's Lecture at the Collège de France on Neo-liberal Governmentality', *Economy and Society*, 30(2): 190–207.

Mackenzie, C. (1988) 'Zimbabwe's Educational Miracle and the Problems it Created', *International Review of Education*, 34(3): 337–353.

Makumbe, J. (1998) *Democracy and Development in Zimbabwe: Constraints of Decentralisation*, Harare: Sapes Trust.

Makura-Paradza, G. G. (2010) *Single Women, Land and Livelihood Vulnerability in a Communal Area in Zimbabwe*, Wagenigen: Wageningen Academic Publishers.

Mamdani, M. (1996) *Citizen and Subject: Contemporary Africa and the Legacy of Late Colonialism*, Princeton, NJ: Princeton University Press.

Mandaza, I. (ed.) (1986) *Zimbabwe: The Political Economy of Transition, 1980–1986*, Dakar: Codesria Books.

Mandondo, A. (2000) *Situating Zimbabwe's Natural Resource Governance Systems in History*, Centre for International Forestry Research, Occasional Paper No. 32.

Masendeke, A., Mlalazi, A., Ndlovu, A. and Gumbo, D. (2004) *Empowering Communities through CBP in Zimbabwe: Experiences in Gwanda and Chimanimani*, International Institute for Environment and Development, PLA Notes 49.

Masunungure, E. (2009) *Defying the Winds of Change: Zimbabwe's 2008 Elections*, Harare: Weaver Press.

Maxwell, D. (1999) *Christians and Chiefs in Zimbabwe: A Social History of the Hwesa People* c.*1870s-1990s*, Edinburgh: Edinburgh University Press.

Mbembe, A. (1992) 'Provisional Notes on the Postcolony', *Africa: Journal of the International African Institute*, 62(1): 3–37.

Mbembe, A. (2001) *On the Postcolony*, Berkeley and Los Angeles: University of California Press.

Mboko, S. and Smith-Hunter, A. (2009) 'Zimbabwe Women Business Owners: Survival Strategies and Implications for Growth', *Journal of Applied Business and Economics*, 11(2): 82–104.

McNay, L. (2009) 'Self as Enterprise: Dilemmas of Control and Resistance in Foucault's *The Birth of Biopolitics*', *Theory Culture Society*, 26(6): 55–77.

Mhone, G. (1995) 'The Social Dimensions of Adjustment (SDA) Programme in Zimbabwe: A Critical Review and Assessment', *European Journal of Development Research*, 7(1): 101–123.

Moore, D. (2004) 'Marxism and Marxist Intellectuals in Schizophrenic Zimbabwe: How Many Rights for Zimbabwe's Left?' *Historical Materialism*, 12(4): 405–425.

Moore, D. S. (1998) 'Subaltern Struggles and the Politics of Place: Re-mapping Resistance in Zimbabwe's Eastern Highlands', *Cultural Anthropology*, 13(3): 344–381.

Moore, D. S. (1999) 'The Crucible of Cultural Politics: Reworking 'Development' in Zimbabwe's Eastern Highlands', *American Ethnologist*, 26(3): 654–689.

Moore, D. S. (2005) *Suffering for Territory: Race, Place, and Power in Zimbabwe*, Durham, NC: Duke University Press.

Mutizwa-Mangiza, N. D. (1990) 'Decentralization and District Development Planning in Zimbabwe', *Public Administration and Development*, 10(4): 423–434.

Nadvi, K. (1995) *Industrial Clusters and Networks: Case Studies of SME Growth and Innovation*, Vienna: UNIDO.

Onslow, S. (2011) 'Zimbabwe and Political Transition', London School of Economics and Political Science Strategic Update.

Potts, D. (2010) *Circular Migration in Zimbabwe and Contemporary Sub-Saharan Africa*, Oxford: James Currey.

Potts, D. and Mutambirwa, C. (1998) ' "Basics are now a luxury": Perceptions of Structural Adjustment's Impact on Rural and Urban Areas in Zimbabwe', *Environment and Urbanization*, 10(1): 57–75.

Rose, N. and Miller, P. (1992) 'Political Power beyond the State: Problematics of Government,' *British Journal of Sociology*, 43(2): 173–205.

Sachikonye, L. M. (1992) 'Zimbabwe: Drought, Food and Adjustment', *Review of African Political Economy*, 19(53): 88–94.

Sandbrook, R. (1993) *The Politics of Africa's Economic Recovery*, New York: Cambridge University Press.

Shaw, W. (1986) 'Towards the One-Party State in Zimbabwe: A Study in African Political Thought', *Journal of Modern African Studies*, 24(3): 373–394.

Skalník, P. (1996) 'Ideological and Symbolic Authority: Political Culture in Nanun, Northern Ghana', in Henri J. M. Claessen and Jarich G. Oosten (eds) *Ideology in the Formation of the Early States*, Vol. II, Leiden: Brill, pp. 84–98.

Skalník, P. (1999) 'Authority versus Power: A View from Social Anthropology', in A. Cheater (ed.) *The Anthropology of Power: Empowerment and Disempowerment in Changing Structures*, London: Routledge, pp. 163–174.

Sklar, R. L. (1985) 'Reds and Rights Zimbabwe's Experiment', *Issue: A Journal of Opinion*, 14: 29–33.

Stoneman, C. and Zvobgo, P. (1981) 'Education and Economic Development', Seminar on Education in Zimbabwe: Past, Present and Future, ZIMFEP, Harare, Ministry of Education and Culture/Dag Hammerskjöld Foundation.

Tevera, D. S. (1998) 'Micro and Small-scale Enterprises in Shamva District within the Context of an Adjusting National Economy', in L. Masuko (ed.) *Economic Policy Reforms and Meso-Scale Rural Market Changes in Zimbabwe: The Case of Shamva District*, Harare: Institute of Development Studies, pp. 253–292.

Tumwine, J. K. (1992) 'Zimbabwe's Success Story in Education and Health: Will it Weather Economic Structural Adjustment?' *Journal of the Royal Society of Health*, 112(6): 286–290.

Van Der Hoven, R., Marinakis, A., Baily, C. and Van Ginneken, W. (1993) *Structural Change and Adjustment in Zimbabwe*, International Development Project on Structural Adjustment, Occasional Paper No. 16, Geneva: International Labour Organisation.

Wilhite, D. A. and Buchanan-Smith, M. (2005) 'Drought as Hazard: Understanding the Natural and Social Context', in D. A. White (ed.) *Drought and Water Crises: Science, Technology, and Management Issues*, Boca Raton, FL: CRC Press.

Wolmer, W. (2007) *From Wilderness Vision to Farm Invasions: Conservation and Development in Zimbabwe's South-East Lowveld*, Harare: Weaver Press.

Yeros, P. (2002) 'Zimbabwe and the Dilemmas of the Left', *Historical Materialism*, 10(2): 3–16.

Young, C. (1994) *The African Colonial State in Comparative Perspective*, London: Yale University Press.

Zimbabwe African National Union-Patriotic Front (ZANU PF) Constitution, available at www.zanupf.org.zw/index.php?option=com_content&view=article&id=79&Itemid =107 (accessed 12 June 2012).

4 Legitimacy and governmentality in Tanzania

Environmental mainstreaming in the developing world

Carl Death

Introduction

The central concern of many critical approaches to state-building and civil society promotion interventions in Africa is with the power and politics of such programmes, which are frequently framed as neutral or technical attempts to improve the lives of others.[1] James Ferguson famously described development in Lesotho in terms of the 'anti-politics machine' (1994), and critical scholars – including those deploying concepts such as governmentality – have sought to re-politicise the development project. This means discussing interests and ideologies, values and ethics, and the winners and losers in development interventions. The concept of legitimacy can be useful in re-politicising the analysis of development programmes, although it is not frequently deployed by scholars drawing on Foucault or governmentality approaches. This chapter has two aims: showing how the concept of legitimacy might be utilised within a governmentality approach; and exploring the power and politics of forms of environmental governmentality in Tanzania (see also Death, 2013a).

For the former, the chapter distinguishes between two approaches to the concept of legitimacy. One is a form of normative theorising, which starts by deriving criteria for 'legitimate governance' from first principles or political theory, and then assesses actually existing interventions or forms of governance to see how they measure up. The second is a more empirical approach which draws upon the Weberian tradition of asking, in particular circumstances, how certain power relations and forms of authority come to be seen as legitimate, i.e. broadly accepted. Governmentality theorists can usefully draw upon this latter tradition to show how certain forms of governmentality – such as environmental mainstreaming projects – work as 'legitimating mechanisms' by attempting to secure popular acceptance for particular political projects.

As such this chapter argues that environmental mainstreaming in Tanzania can be seen as a legitimating mechanism for a form of state-building very similar to others associated with new governance mechanisms like Poverty Reduction Strategy Papers (PRSPs) and 'good governance' schemes. As with these interventions the beneficiaries of environmental mainstreaming do not just include 'responsible states', but an array of transnational and civil society actors. This

68 *C. Death*

works both ways: the inclusion and participation of local and transnational actors (such as Tanzanian community-based organisations, and international NGOs like the International Institute for Environment and Development (IIED)) help to legitimate particular governmental projects; and environmental mainstreaming initiatives help to produce these civil society actors – and some well-placed corporate actors – as responsible subjects of development policy. Environmental mainstreaming projects are therefore certainly not simply neutral or technical programmes: they are an important technique through which liberal forms of governmentality are able to reshape states and civil society in international politics, and open up access to lucrative natural resources and populations for 'legitimate' state agencies, civil society organisations and private corporations.

Governmentality and legitimacy

As set out in the Introduction to this volume, a governmentality approach draws on the work of Michel Foucault (2007, 2008) to explore the various mechanisms and rationalities by which power works through freedom: the conduct of conduct rather than power relations which are reducible to force, coercion or deception. This concern with power working through freedom provides a potential link to far more extensive and well-established literatures on legitimacy, which also tend to emphasise the importance of democratic freedoms in *legitimate* forms of power and authority (see Bernstein, 2011; Brassett and Tsingou, 2011; Clark, 2005, 2007). This is a reflection of the dominance of liberal traditions of political thought in shaping how mainstream political science approaches the question of legitimacy.

Unsurprisingly, most governmentality scholars have rejected this approach as a starting point for studying politics. Governmentality approaches tend to be closer to either Marxist political theory or realist accounts of power politics than the liberal tradition (see Dean, 2007; Death, 2013b: 780). In particular, taking liberal values and assumptions as the starting point, or foundation, for political analysis seems to approach things the wrong way around: Foucault was interested in showing, genealogically, how certain discourses and practices associated with liberalism and neoliberalism were historically produced at certain times and in certain places (Foucault, 2007, 2008). The poststructuralist critique of stable foundations leaves a normative approach to legitimacy on irredeemably shaky foundations. Elsewhere I have argued that governmentality approaches share 'much of the ambiguous ethical and normative alignment of Foucauldian theory' and as such they do 'not provide a set of well-grounded philosophical principles or values according to which the desirability of different forms of power relation can be assessed' (Death, 2013b: 765). This does not mean that an analytics of government framework is somehow objective or normatively neutral, however, but rather that its foundations are always contingent, contextual and somewhat unreliable. Indeed, much of Foucault's later work was explicitly focused on ethical relations, and there is much here that could be more explicitly introduced into the governmentality literature (Foucault 2010).

Legitimacy and governmentality in Tanzania   69

Moreover, there is a second tradition of thought interested in the question of legitimacy: the Weberian tradition of empirical studies of legitimation, as the degree of consent a regime manages to acquire. This derives quite straightforwardly from the foundational definition of legitimacy: acceptance of a form of rule or authority by those ruled over (Bernstein, 2004: 142; Clark, 2005: 18). Such an approach is therefore rather different to more explicitly normative attempts to formulate a set of principles by which a form of rule could be designated more or less legitimate (i.e. morally, politically or technically *right*). Legitimating mechanisms are practices or techniques of governance designed to try to secure acceptance from a particular political constituency or audience. Such an approach is far closer to the style of analysis governmentality scholars (as well as Gramscians) are used to: an empirical exploration of the techniques and technologies by which consent and order are maintained in society.

However, rather than over-emphasising this distinction between normative and analytical approaches to legitimacy, it is important to see them as tightly interwoven. This is because legitimating mechanisms (such as the forms of environmental governance this chapter will explore in Tanzania) of course do draw upon particular traditions of political thought and their criteria of what is morally, politically or technically *right*. The degree to which particular mechanisms or practices of legitimacy resonate with their audience or constituency (the subjects of governmentality) is an important factor in determining their success. Power relations which work through freedom can, by definition, be resisted, and the degree to which they are resisted is at least partly related to the success of an array of legitimating mechanisms. As such, the clear-cut distinction between empirical and normative approaches to legitimacy begins to break down (see Bernstein, 2004: 42; Brassett and Tsingou, 2011: 5).

The approach taken here is one which seeks to illuminate the broader power relations through which certain norms of legitimacy became widely accepted, and to draw attention to their sometimes obscured implications. The link between power relations and legitimacy/legitimation is crucial (Bernstein, 2004: 165; 2011: 20–21; Brassett and Tsingou, 2011: 2), and is the most important point of connection between governmentality approaches and the legitimacy literature. As Clark (2005: 20) points out:

> legitimacy cannot be divorced from power. Legitimacy constrains power, whilst also being an important element of it. Power also impacts upon the practice of legitimacy, and contributes to the substance of the principles of legitimacy which come to be accepted. It is, in any case, only within the context of power relations that legitimacy becomes relevant at all.

From a governmentality point of view, it might be more appropriate to frame this in terms of the suggestion that broader power relations which work through freedom rely, in some form or another, on a range of legitimating mechanisms. Certainly, I agree with Clark that it is only within the context of power relations that legitimacy becomes relevant at all.

70   *C. Death*

This raises important political and ethical questions for an analysis of particular legitimating mechanisms. Steven Bernstein concludes his analysis of the forms of legitimacy represented by the Kyoto Protocol on climate change by noting that '[t]here is no necessary relationship between legitimacy and solving the world's environmental or social problems', and indeed forms of environmental governance like Kyoto 'can easily legitimate the very order the institution was ostensibly created to change' (2011: 43). Brassett and Tsingou also observe that '[m]atching standards of legitimacy to the various and ongoing practices of global governance only defers the deeper question of how far those practices are themselves implicated in relations of power that regard certain standards of legitimacy as appropriate' (2011: 3). For this reason an analysis of the role of legitimating mechanisms like environmental mainstreaming projects must include an appreciation of the broader context within which they are located, and ensures that scholars of governmentality cannot ignore questions of ethics and politics.

Environmental mainstreaming as a legitimating mechanism

It is now widely accepted by many practitioners and institutions that more legitimate forms of governance for sustainable development must include more deliberative mechanisms, participatory forms of governance and hybrid authority structures. Environmental mainstreaming is one such technique that draws heavily upon such understandings of procedural legitimacy. Such forms of liberal governmentality are now well-established in mainstream development discourse – particularly in the environmental sector – and despite recurrent concerns over their correlation with output legitimacy or effectiveness, they continue to be widely promoted. Given this, it is therefore quite surprising to hear a prominent research fellow at the Overseas Development Institute (ODI), and his team of researchers, proclaim that in developing countries

> democracy is a desirable long-term goal but not a reliable route to better public policies in the short and medium term; and citizen pressure is at best a weak factor and at worst a distraction from dealing with the main drivers of bad governance.
>
> (Booth, 2011: 2)

Their open scepticism toward concepts like transparency, openness and civil society ownership in the developing world, and the call for strong and centralised political leadership which may be unaccountable and hierarchical but which produces more effective development outputs, is at odds with most of the prevailing norms regarding good governance. (See also Cooksey, 2011a, 2011b. Cooksey and Kelsall, 2011.)

This chapter is not an in-depth engagement with the work, influences and impact of the *Africa Power and Politics* programme at the ODI, although there is more to their argument than simply prioritising output legitimacy (effectiveness) over input legitimacy (democratic procedures).[2] Rather, I take their

Legitimacy and governmentality in Tanzania   71

argument as a provocation to study the relationship between politics, governance and legitimacy in the context of one of their core cases: Tanzania. Tanzania's experiences with environmental mainstreaming seem to be exactly the sort of interventions that Booth and others critique; governmentality scholars have also been critical of similar interventions like Poverty Reduction Strategy Papers (Abrahamsen, 2004; Harrison, 2004). But do these two critiques reach similar political conclusions? The conclusion to this chapter returns to this question.

Environmental mainstreaming is about including environmental concerns (natural resource management, a safe and healthy living environment, conservation of ecosystems, etc) within broader government policy-making and development planning. The primary form environmental mainstreaming has taken in the developing world is through National Strategies for Sustainable Development (NSSDs). These can be seen as a form of good governance which are designed at least in part to improve the legitimacy of policy-making from an environmental point of view (Dalal-Clayton and Bass, 2009; DSD, 2009; George and Kirkpatrick, 2006; Meadowcroft, 2007). Integrating the principles of sustainable development into country policies and programmes is one of the targets (7a) in the Millennium Development Goals (Dalal-Clayton and Bass, 2009: 26), and in 2002, at the World Summit for Sustainable Development in Johannesburg, states were urged not only to take immediate steps to make progress in the formulation and elaboration of NSSDs but also to begin their implementation by 2005. In 2009, 106 Member States of the UN were implementing an NSSD (DSD, 2009).

NSSDs have much in common with a whole range of other so-called 'new governance' mechanisms that became increasingly prevalent in a range of policy contexts in the 1990s and 2000s (Bäckstrand *et al.*, 2010; Conca, 2005; Karkkainen, 2004). In particular they dovetail closely – both in conceptual design and often in practice – with Poverty Reduction Strategy Papers (PRSPs) (Abrahamsen, 2004; Fraser and Whitfield, 2009; Geoghegan, 2007; George and Kirkpatrick, 2006; Gould and Ojanen, 2003; Harrison, 2004: 103–107). Indeed, developing countries already devising a PRSP (required to access debt relief and international lending) have been encouraged to 'mainstream' environmental issues into the PRSP and use this as their NSSD (George and Kirkpatrick, 2006: 147). As I have discussed elsewhere, PRSPs are a particularly fruitful mechanism for governmentality approaches to study, as they involve rationalised attempts to conduct the conduct of free subjects, within particular fields of visibility and mobilising particular forms of knowledge and practical techniques (Death, 2013b: 778–781).

Similarly, NSSDs can be treated as governmental technologies which function (at least in part) as legitimating mechanisms. There are a number of reasons for this: they are designed to convince a number of audiences or political constituencies (particularly the scientific and NGO communities) that states are capable of playing a constructive role in 'greening'; they seek to promote forms of deliberative democratic 'input' or procedural legitimacy which have become the norm for environmental governance, such as public participation, accountability, transparency, subsidiarity and decentralisation of authority; and they are underpinned by the assumption (or at least the hope) that they might promote 'output' or substantive forms of legitimacy, such as more effective environmental policies and ecological protection, alongside social and economic objectives, in the pursuit of sustainable development.

The central goal of the NSSD is the promotion of sustainable development, usually defined as 'development which meets the needs of the present without comprising the ability of future generations to meet their own needs' (Brundtland, 1987: 43), which is measured through environmental, social and economic indicators. Subsidiary goals to be promoted through the NSSD include: public participation and involvement of affected parties and major groups, country ownership, subsidiarity, accountability and transparency (Dalal-Clayton and Bass, 2009: 76; George and Kirkpatrick, 2006; Meadowcroft, 1997: 181–182). A UNCSD document on NSSDs produced for the Johannesburg Summit in 2002 described them as 'a cyclical and interactive process of planning, participation and action in which the emphasis is on managing progress towards sustainability goals rather than producing a "plan" as an end product' (in Meadowcroft, 2007: 154).

The sustainable development vision can in part be seen as an attempt to persuade developing countries that the environmental agenda was not incompatible with achieving development or tackling poverty (Meadowcroft, 1997: 169). From this perspective, NSSDs are therefore also a practice of legitimacy within international society (Clark, 2005), aimed primarily at the developing world, with the intention of building consensus around a form of sustainable development acceptable to both developed and developing nations. Moreover, by taking the form of national strategies, they also invoke a language and tradition of national planning and state-led development which carries considerable historical and political resonance for many state elites in the developing world. For example, one review of the Tanzanian NSSD observed, a little euphemistically perhaps, 'that Tanzania's famed planning expertise – in part a legacy of President Nyerere's goal of self-reliance – has truly come of age' (Assey et al., 2007: 11). This is despite the fact that the form of state planning that NSSDs typically promote is quite different to older command-and-control models (George and Kirkpatrick, 2006; Meadowcroft, 1997, 2007). In any case, the promotion of NSSDs is an explicit recognition that states have a crucial role to play in initiating and facilitating national planning for sustainable development, in some form.

In all these ways, therefore, NSSDs and the broader practices of environmental mainstreaming of which they are part can be seen as legitimating mechanisms, between states and non-state constituencies and between developed and developing states. The next section of this chapter explores what this means in Tanzania in more detail, and seeks to assess both the relative success of these legitimating mechanisms (from an empirical and sociological point of view, i.e. to what degree have they been accepted by their target audiences and constituencies), and the broader critical implications of these practices from the perspective of state-society relations, developed-developing country relations, as well as environmental impacts.

Environmental mainstreaming in Tanzania

Tanzania is a useful case study because it has been often lauded as an outstanding example of a developing country which has mainstreamed environmental considerations into development planning, through successive country-owned and nationally-driven poverty reduction strategy papers and sustainable development strategies, within a broader context of a harmonised and productive relationship with international donors (Fraser and Whitfield, 2009; Geoghegan, 2007; Nord *et al.*, 2009). Indeed it has become 'a common reference point for donors who are speaking about the continent more generally' (Harrison *et al.*, 2009: 295). In 2007 a report by the International Institute for Environment and Development (IIED) recorded 'an ambitious and unprecedented Tanzanian initiative to integrate environmental issues into development policy and practice', which concluded it was 'largely very positive' and 'offers an iconic and enduring (and perhaps rather rare) example of a nationally developed policy process which delivers – in practice – what the World Bank's Poverty Reduction Strategy principles describe in theory' (Assey *et al.*, 2007: iv; see also Dalal-Clayton and Bass, 2009; Rutasitara *et al.*, 2010: 27). Given the context of the previous history – and considerable tensions – between Tanzania and the international community over governance issues, this suggests that these new forms of governance mechanism have been quite successful as legitimating practices. It is therefore a prominent example of the apparently successful deployment of an NSSD as a legitimating mechanism. How exactly did this happen, however?

Governmental practices

The NSSD process in Tanzania has been closely tied to a broader and more highly contested PRSP process. Tanzania's first National Poverty Eradication Strategy in 1997 was rejected by the World Bank, and a more intimately donor-driven Poverty Reduction Strategy was agreed in 2000 (Abrahamsen, 2004; Gould and Ojanen, 2003; Harrison, 2001). At around the same time a coalition emerged within Tanzanian politics calling for environmental issues to have a higher priority within government planning. Building on the launch of the National Environment Policy in 1997, a DFID and UNDP-sponsored review of the environmental implications of the first PRSP was conducted in 2003 (Assey *et al.*, 2007: 7 and 13). In a bid to address concerns raised, including rather narrow public participation and the limited attention given to environmental issues, a new PRSP – this time called the National Strategy for Growth and the Reduction of Poverty (NSGRP), or in Swahili, *Mkakati wa Kukuza Uchumi na Kupunguza Umaskini Tanzania* (MKUKUTA) – was developed in 2005 (Assey *et al.*, 2007: 11–13; Bojö and Reddy, 2003: 14; interviews with Manyama, Cheche, Ekingo, Rutasitara and Howlett). It was scheduled to run for five years, at which point it was succeeded by MKUKUTA II. These MKUKUTA strategies have been accepted by the UN's Division for Sustainable Development as Tanzania's NSSD (DSD, 2009).

74   *C. Death*

A great deal of attention, both national and transnational, was devoted to the environmental mainstreaming of MKUKUTA, which has been held up as an 'inspiration to other developing countries, especially in Africa' (Assey *et al.*, 2007: iv). Reviewers of the environmental mainstreaming process optimistically concluded that 'with the environment established as central to the MKUKUTA, Tanzania's development is now following a more secure and sustainable path', whilst admitting there was still a significant 'implementation gap' (Assey *et al.*, 2007: 2). The first MKUKUTA strategy included 15 directly 'environmental' targets (out of 108 targets in total) which are quantitative and measurable through specific national indicators, and the strategy was motivated by a broader vision of sustainable development, in line with *Vision 2025*, Tanzania's national development strategy.

One of the features of the organisational forms promoted through the environmental mainstreaming process has been an expansion of the number of actors involved in Tanzanian governance. The mainstreaming of environmental concerns in the MKUKUTA process was achieved with substantial support and assistance from donor and international actors, primarily DFID and UNDP (Assey *et al.*, 2007: 1; Rutasitara *et al.*, 2010: 5–7; interviews with Manyama, Mongula, Cheche and Howlett). Although the mainstreaming process was driven by the Tanzanian Vice President's Office (VPO), their key Integrating Environment Programme was funded by a diverse range of actors including DANIDA, DFID, the UNDP Poverty Environment Initiative, the UNEP Poverty Environment Programme and the Royal Norwegian Government through the UNDP Drylands Development Centre (Assey *et al.*, 2007: 17; UNDP-UNEP, 2010). The MKUKUTA drafting team was chaired by the VPO, and included individuals from government and the private sector, CSOs, and academic and research institutions, and it was predominantly Tanzanian, with only three non-Tanzanian residents and (unusually) no foreign consultants. Despite the absence of foreign consultants, the impact of pervasive global technologies of development planning, such as the ubiquitous logical framework approach (or 'logframe'), were clearly evident (Assey *et al.*, 2007: 15; Fraser and Whitfield, 2009: 78–80; Gould and Ojanen, 2003: 85–86; Green, 2003: 135–136; interview with Rutasitara). Through a range of participatory and consultative processes many civil society and local organisations also engaged with formulating government policy, and this has been regarded as one of MKUKUTA's biggest institutional innovations and legacies for Tanzanian governance (Assey *et al.*, 2007: 36–37; United Republic of Tanzania, 2005: chapter 3; 2010).

These practices of environmental mainstreaming encapsulated in the NSSD/MKUKUTA can be seen as part of a broadly successful legitimating mechanism for Tanzania's relationships with the rest of international society in two ways. First, during the 1980s and 1990s the relationship between Tanzania and its donors was often tense and fractious (Gould and Ojanen, 2003: 39; Harrison, 2004: 29–33). The degree of foreign involvement in Tanzanian policy-making was resented by Tanzanian elites and, combined with economic tensions caused by the imposition of Structural Adjustment Programmes, working relationships were reaching breaking point. A period of negotiation and reform of the donor–recipient aid relationship (including provision of a five month 'quiet period' each year during which donor visits are discouraged in order to allow the Tanzanian government space for policy formulation) eventually led to a more consensual (and hence broadly legitimate) relationship (Assey *et al.*, 2007: 23; Harrison *et al.*, 2009: 278–281). The processes through which the PRSPs and NSSD were designed, implemented and monitored are good examples of this new relationship in practice, characterised (at least in theory) by 'harmonisation, alignment and joint assistance' (Assey *et al.*, 2007: 1). The official view of this process can be summed up as follows:

> In the case of the MKUKUTA in general, and its environmental mainstreaming work in particular, the more overt aspects of donor dominance have now dissipated. Indeed, we might say there has been a resurgence in Tanzanian self-reliance, and good examples of donor alignment behind Tanzanian interests.
>
> (Assey *et al.*, 2007: 24)

For this reason Tanzania is now seen as a shining model of effective, transparent partnerships between donors and developing countries (Fraser and Whitfield, 2009: 80–81; Geoghegan, 2007; Gould and Ojanen, 2003: 14; Harrison, 2004: 39–40; Nord *et al.*, 2009: 5).

Second, the success of this legitimating mechanism can be evidenced by the widespread praise for Tanzania's environmental mainstreaming process by a wide range of environmental NGOs and international commentators. Tanzania has always held a special place for the international conservation and development communities – the Serengeti was the first national park in British colonial Africa (Neumann, 1998, 2001), and development agencies such as Oxfam were enamoured with Julius Nyerere's promotion of self-sufficiency and rural development in the 1960s and 1970s (Jennings, 2002) – but the widely perceived success of the environmental mainstreaming process has led to renewed plaudits for Tanzania's commitment to sustainable development (Assey *et al.*, 2007; Dalal-Clayton and Bass, 2009; Geoghegan, 2007). In particular, the MKUKUTA strategy was praised for highlighting the positive role sound environmental management can play in national development – rather than conceiving the environment either negatively (as a constraint on development) or as separate from development issues (Assey *et al.*, 2007: 5; Dalal-Clayton and Bass, 2009: 37). This has led to the emergence of what the IIED report referred to as a more 'legitimate environmental narrative' in Tanzania (Assey *et al.*, 2007: 35).

Governmental rationalities

The success of the NSSD as a legitimating mechanism is also attributable to the presence of a number of key governmental rationalities within the environmental mainstreaming process. They include a mixture of what Kronsell and Bäckstrand

76 *C. Death*

(2010) refer to as administrative, economic and deliberative rationales, each of which played their part in appealing to particular political constituencies.

The most deeply embedded rationale underpinning the NSSD process in Tanzania is administrative, and is characterised by a hunger for more and better data. Much of the focus of MKUKUTA I and II has been on improving capacity for data monitoring, analysis and evaluation (United Republic of Tanzania, 2010: 22). Donors have sought to improve standards of data collection, analysis and assessment processes, and evaluation and reporting systems (Jansen, 2009: 12; UNDP-UNEP, 2010; interviews with Cheche, Ekingo and Ladislaus). An official in the MKUKUTA Secretariat claimed that there have been significant improvements in terms of Tanzania's capacity to monitor and evaluate data on the measurable indicators (even if the indicators themselves are not always met), and there is now a 'coherent and harmonised monitoring system' (interview with Ekingo). Moreover, the 2011 five-year development plan promises that 'elaborate mechanisms will be put in place to improve data collection and data flow mechanisms to ensure quality, validity and accuracy of data' (United Republic of Tanzania, 2011: 79).

This flood of data, arising from surveillance, surveys and monitoring, is driven by and reciprocally fuels the proliferation of reviews, plans, strategies and policies that are required from developing countries like Tanzania. These include National Environmental Plans, State of the Environment reports, National Biodiversity Strategies and Actions Plans, sustainable land management plans, climate change vulnerability and capacity assessments, environmental impact assessments, integrated development plans, rural and urban land planning frameworks and many more, each with demands for quantifiable, verifiable data (Dalal-Clayton and Bass, 2009: 56 and 94–95).

A secondary governmental rationality identifiable in some parts of the environmental mainstreaming process is a market-based rationality. This is more limited in Tanzania than elsewhere, given a continuing suspicion of market mechanisms and foreign capital from both government and the broader public (a legacy of Tanzania's particular history of state planning and African socialism) (Chachage, 2010: 9; Cooksey, 2003, 2011b; Cooksey and Kelsall, 2011: 11–12), but recent governments have stressed the role of the private sector and the market in delivering sustainable development. Despite little direct private sector involvement in the MKUKUTA process, the private sector is increasingly a dominant and driving force in agricultural development, food security, carbon finance and energy supply (Assey *et al.*, 2007: 47; Bofin *et al.*, 2011: 72; Chachage, 2010; Igoe, 2005). Development discourse in Tanzania is becoming even more clearly orientated towards the private sector, and MKUKUTA II declared that though it 'builds on its predecessor's strategy, it is oriented more towards growth and enhancement of productivity ... and calls for more active private sector participation' (United Republic of Tanzania, 2010: ix). The Tanzanian government's *Kilimo Kwanza* (Agriculture First) strategy is committed to attracting foreign investment, and the 2006 *State of the Environment* report confirmed that 'the government is promoting and encourages participation of private investments in large-scale agriculture' (United Republic of Tanzania, 2006: 146; see also United Republic of Tanzania, 2010: 43; interview with Cooksey).

Finally, and in a rather more limited way, it is possible to identify more democratic and deliberative rationalities at work in the NSSD and environmental mainstreaming processes, which have become 'more holistic, consultative and driven by stakeholder demands' (Assey *et al.*, 2007: 1). The first MKUKUTA strategy featured the largest ever exercise in public consultation on environmental issues in Tanzania, meeting 18,000 participants in 168 villages (four in each of 42 districts), 1000 CSO participants, 25,000 completed questionnaires from the public, environmental NGOs and parliamentarians (Assey *et al.*, 2007: 25–28). It defined the key actors for its implementation as follows:

> Central government ministries and LGAs, independent departments and agencies (MDAs), private sector, Civil Society Organizations (CSOs) and Communities. Parliament will play an oversight role over the government in the implementation process. Likewise, the Development Partners (DP) will play a supportive role in the implementation.
>
> (United Republic of Tanzania, 2005: 55)

A multi-stakeholder Environment Working Group was established to provide consultation and deliberation on the mainstreaming process, and consisted of 'government sectors including representation of Local Government Authorities, NGOs, CBOs, private sector actors and donor technical leads' (Assey *et al.*, 2007: 18).

Moreover, these processes have also sought to build upon existing attempts to decentralise natural resource management, and involve local village authorities more directly in environmental governance (Brockington, 2008; Lecoutere, 2011; Ribot, 2003). On the one hand such processes could be seen as the Tanzanian state encouraging the principle of subsidiarity in environmental governance, and thus as evidence for more democratic and deliberative forms of governance. On the other hand, it is doubtful whether such processes necessarily result in increased accountability and transparency. Some empirical evidence suggests that they may in fact entrench local and gendered power relationships, rather than challenging them (Bofin *et al.*, 2011: 19; Brockington, 2008: 112; Cooksey and Kelsall, 2011: 41; Dill, 2009; Lecoutere, 2011: 255; Nelson, 2007; Ribot, 2003: 56). Furthermore, most accounts suggest that these decentralisation efforts have been quite limited in both their scale and effectiveness so far (Assey *et al.*, 2007: 10; Lange, 2008; Luttrell and Pantaleo, 2008: 33; Mniwasa and Shauri, 2001; Sunseri, 2005: 632).

As such it would be a misrepresentation to suggest that the NSSD/MKUKUTA process has been entirely successful in legitimating either Tanzanian development policies or international environmental discourse to the broader local population. Decentralisation of authority, and greater participation in governance, are often regarded cynically (as an opportunity to participate in lucrative workshops) or suspiciously (as an attempt to 'buy-off' civil society

78   *C. Death*

support) (Dill, 2009; Gould and Ojanen, 2003; Green, 2003; Igoe, 2005). On the other hand, several sources do note a more active press, a more combative Parliament, and an increasingly vibrant civil society sphere in Tanzania, at least in part due to the proliferation of more deliberative and participatory new modes of governance (Assey *et al.*, 2007: 8–9, 13; Luttrell and Pantaleo, 2008: 10; Norrington-Davies and Thornton, 2009: 31). The overall assessment that emerges from the preceding analysis, however, is that the environmental mainstreaming process has been a highly successful legitimating mechanism for the Tanzanian state and its cooperative civil society partners to international audiences; whereas domestically the reception has been rather more mixed.

The implications of NSSD in Tanzania and beyond

As the previous section suggested, the NSSD process in Tanzania has been a qualified success in its function as a legitimating mechanism, particularly internationally. It has been part of a broader evolution of an apparently more consensual and cooperative relationship between the Tanzanian state and its international donors. It has won plaudits from international environment and development organisations, and has been described as an 'inspiration to other developing countries, especially in Africa' (Assey *et al.*, 2007: iv). Part of the reason for this has been its combination of administrative, market-based and democratic governmental rationalities. However, there is still some scepticism in many quarters – particularly amongst critical local commentators – over the degree to which Tanzanian environmental governance is variously administratively competent, committed to free market competition, or actively pursuing democratic deliberation.

What are the political implications of this? In this section I suggest that what is being legitimated in Tanzania through mechanisms like NSSD are forms of hybrid authority structure which are complex, opaque and not particularly democratic or deliberative, and which continue to have groups of elites who straddle state and non-state, public and private domains, at their heart (Cooksey, 2011b: 92). The implications of the NSSD are not negligible, moreover, but rather are part of a broader transformation of the character of Tanzanian power relationships.

The complexity and opacity of these hybrid authority structures in Tanzania are evident to even a cursory examination. Researchers from the Overseas Development Institute (ODI) note a lack of clarity about what is meant by 'the environment' in Tanzania, meaning that 'the question of who is in charge of protecting the environment and through what methods is it done is not a straightforward one in the Tanzanian case' (Luttrell and Pantaleo, 2008: 34–35). Drawing a clear map of the competencies and levels of authority between the President, the Vice President's Office (containing the Division of Environment), the National Environmental Management Council, the Ministry of Finance, parliament and the judiciary, competing line departments (each of which are supposed to have their own environmental unit), regional authorities and village authorities is almost impossible (for one recent and partial attempt, see Rutasitara *et al.*, 2010: 13).

To further complicate matters, the pervasive presence of donor, NGO and university/Third Sector advisors and authorities within state governance structures runs deep. Gould and Ojanen's study of the poverty reduction strategy process in Tanzania concluded that the process led to a select group of locally based NGOs and transnational agencies being invited to 'merge in the circle' of the national policy-making elite – in effect to become part of the state itself (2003: 13). Harrison argues that through such processes 'the national-international boundary has been rendered so much more porous by a historically embedded "mutual assimilation" of donor and state power and ideas' (2001: 661). There is a further profusion of authorities and actors in terms of the actual implementation of environmental projects 'on-the-ground', including the donor sector, international NGOs, externally funded national or local NGOs, community organisations, transnational capital (with their own murky networks of fund managers, investment advisors, contractors and sub-contractors, etc) and personal patronage links. Research by NGOs and local activists reveals a wide range of cases of conflict, characterised by shady business relationships, unknown investors, unclear lines of political accountability and responsibility, contested land ownership and contradictory accounts of village meetings (Chachage, 2010; Chachage and Mbunda, 2009; Cooksey, 2011b; Igoe, 2005; interview with Baha). Indeed, this degree of opacity is one way in which the system 'works' for those skilled enough to negotiate it, and as Gould and Ojanen note, 'the higher echelons of decision-making authority are buffered against the direct influence of non-state actors (or "the poor") by an ambiguous and multi-staged chain of bureaucratic reporting procedures' (2003: 72).

Whilst complex and opaque structures of authority are by no means new in African politics (see Booth, 2011: 3; Cooksey, 2011b; Cooksey and Kelsall, 2011; Hyden, 1980: 18; Ruitenbeek and Cartier, 2008), so-called 'new' governance mechanisms in sectors like environmental management and development can enable them to continue to flourish. The mining sector in Tanzania, for example, has been described as 'a matter of loose and rival informal coalitions competing for control of the state apparatus through opportunistic rent-seeking and state plunder' (Cooksey, 2011a: 90). Complex networks of powerful individuals, local and international private companies, political parties and state institutions have contributed to what appears to be endemic and apparently 'long-term private sector "capture"' of the Department of Wildlife in the Ministry of Natural Resources and Tourism, producing an overall picture of 'uncoordinated and collectively dysfunctional rent-seeking' in Tanzania's natural resource sectors (Cooksey, 2011b: 66 and 84). In these sectors rents are channelled through 'ad hoc alliances of politicians, officials (including members of the armed forces), and private brokers' (Cooksey and Kelsall, 2011: 85; see also Bofin *et al.*, 2011; Ruitenbeek and Cartier, 2008). In most of these cases the sheer opacity of business relationships and practices prevents easy identifications of clear hierarchies of governance.

80 *C. Death*

Overall, therefore, the organisational forms of environmental governance in Tanzania – to which the NSSD process contributed – have created a complex and hybrid authority structure. However, contrary to some claims in the environmental or 'new' governance literature (e.g. Karkkainen, 2004) these are not strictly non-hierarchical, as the Tanzanian state is reluctant to formally cede authority in any area. Rather, the existence of a plethora of authority structures – ranging from international norms and laws, donor state influence, international NGO penetration, the local 'neo-patrimonial' state, to the blurring of the public and the private spheres – mean that environmental governance is characterised by what might be termed neo-hierarchy, or multiple hierarchies (Death, 2013a: 9). This agglomeration of multiple hierarchies incorporates what Dan Brockington has termed an 'environmental-conservation complex', consisting of the national and local state, international agencies and NGOs, political parties, and business and private interests (2006: 102–106). This complex is not confined to the conservation arena, however, but rather encompasses a diverse range of actors straddling all areas of environmental governance.

How should we understand this complex and hybrid authority structure? As should be clear, it does not have a simple underlying logic or function; it is not simply a form of domination nor of emancipation. It is not best characterised simply as neoliberal hegemony (Bernstein, 2004: 157–158), nor as entrenched neo-patrimonialism (Cooksey and Kelsall, 2011), nor as ecological modernisation (Mol and Buttel, 2002: 7–8), although elements of all of these can be discerned. In terms of the *longue durée* of African state–society relations, one could interpret it in terms of an evolving and dynamic set of power relations between the central state bureaucracy and the rural population.[3] The establishment of conservation and resource management policies under colonialism were an attempt to secure more state control – over valuable resources and territory – beyond the urban and coastal regions (Levine, 2002; Nelson, 2007; Neumann, 1998). Nyerere's rural development policies of *ujamaa* sought to extend statist penetration and control over the 'uncaptured peasantry' (Hyden, 1980; Scott, 1998; Shao, 1986). Environmental discourses of land degradation, over-grazing, conservation, food security and resource management have always been, and continue to be, deployed to justify closer state management of tensions between settled and pastoralist communities (Brockington, 2006: 109; Igoe, 2005; Neumann, 2001; Sunseri, 2005). Michael Sheridan's research on North Pare has revealed that 'most farmers now say that the Kiswahili term *hifadhi* (conservation) really means government ownership and mismanagement' (2009: 91). Contemporary environmental governance has been characterised by an intensification of state monitoring, evaluation, auditing and surveillance over the Tanzanian natural environment and rural population. Sometimes this has even involved direct violence, such as the attacks by state forces against villagers living in or near conservation areas and forests in 1997 and 1998 (Shivji, 2006: 243–247; Sunseri, 2005: 609–610). Brockington claims he found that 'from the point of view of Tanzanian peasants, the local state was most prominent in their day-to-day experience for the varieties of violence it perpetrated' (2008: 112).

Legitimacy and governmentality in Tanzania 81

This tendency for environmental governance to mean, in practice, greater state control and penetration over rural populations can be seen in two very different examples. The first is the Tanzanian government's latest policy for agricultural development – *Kilimo Kwanza*. This policy has identified large tracts of under-utilised 'virgin land' in Tanzania, which is being made available for agribusiness and biofuel investment, inspired by visions of mechanised farms in Iowa (United Republic of Tanzania, 2006: 39; interview with Baha). In reality of course there is very little 'under-utilised' or 'virgin' land in Tanzania, and pastoralists, Burundian refugees, and 'out-of-place' villagers and 'squatters' are being removed. As such the agricultural sector has been characterised by what Brian Cooksey described in 2003 as 'the recent recrudescence of statist legislation, policies and practices', albeit in alliance with favoured private investors (2003: 67). Local activists' perception of these processes is that 'the state, at the central government level in collaboration with centralised appendages at the local governments' level, has continued to exert its statist arms in managing agriculture, albeit, through privatization rather than nationalization' (Chachage and Mbunda, 2009: 95). Such trends are a central part of what has been termed the phenomenon of 'land-grabbing' or the 'new scramble for Africa' (Carmody, 2011).

The second example of the intensification of statist control over land and territory, through processes of environmental governance, comes from the monitoring and data analysis dimensions of the MKUKUTA process itself. As discussed above, this administrative rationality has led to the proliferation of coding, monitoring, analysis, and evaluation mechanisms, through countless reviews, audits, surveys and innumerable datasets. This reflects the increasing dominance of what is sometimes referred to as the 'new managerialism' of development aid (Abrahamsen, 2004: 1459; Broch-Due, 2000: 36–38; Gould and Ojanen, 2003: 14; Green, 2003: 137). This trend is being driven by the international development institutions, such as the World Bank, which desires 'quantified, time-bound, costed, realistic targets and indicators relating to environment' (Bojö and Reddy, 2003: 2; see also Harrison, 2004). What this tends to achieve in practice – given the dominance of Dar es Salaam-based state institutions such as the Ministry of Finance over data collection and analysis – is the reinforcement and deeper penetration of central state power over rural areas and non-state actors. Environmental governance in Tanzania is therefore characterised by the extension of state control throughout the national territory, including into areas which it has only irregularly penetrated.

This recrudescence of the state is a very different process, however, to earlier colonial and post-colonial command-and-control statist dynamics. The nature of the state is fundamentally changing, as donors, civil society groups and private actors in effect become 'part of the state itself' (Harrison, 2001: 669). Even the proper function of the state in environment and development planning and management is changing (Abrahamsen, 2004; Conca, 2005: 195–196; Mol and Buttel, 2002: 6). The 2009 Poverty and Human Development report stated that 'Tanzania's Vision is to achieve a vibrant, developed market economy, which implies that the role of the state is facilitative rather than directive' (United

82 *C. Death*

Republic of Tanzania, 2009: 172). This shift – frequently described as moving from 'rowing to steering' – is best described in MKUKUTA II:

> The private sector has an important and critical role to play in achieving poverty reduction outcomes because of its central role as the engine for economic growth. The government is reducing its role to core functions of policy formulation, economic management, provision of economic and social infrastructure, and legal and regulatory framework, maintenance of law and order as well as selected areas of public-private sector partnership.
> (United Republic of Tanzania, 2010: 107)

As such, the Tanzanian state is not the only 'winner' through processes of capacity-building for environmental governance – so too are the international donor agencies, consultants and analysts who fund, support, deliver training and assess results. So too are those civil society organisations who are willing to be supportive partners, to be 'consulted' and 'empowered' in the proper manner, and to act as a conduit (or replacement) for involving and representing broader local communities (Dill, 2009). So too are the private sector actors who gain legitimacy and policy influence, as well as access to lucrative natural resources.

Conclusion

The NSSD process in Tanzania – comprising the environmental mainstreaming of the country's poverty reduction strategy – has been broadly regarded as a success. One enthusiastic review concluded that 'these are exciting times in Tanzania. The MKUKUTA has leaped vigorously across a "planning gap" – offering a more holistic, inclusive, operationally relevant strategy than any previous national plan. It has good public support' (Assey *et al.*, 2007: 39). It can therefore be considered a successful legitimating mechanism in several ways. Donor-state relationships have improved and Tanzania is seen as a responsible exemplar of environmental mainstreaming in the eyes of international society. International and local civil society partners, including some private sector actors, have been 'legitimated' and enabled through their engagement with the environmental mainstreaming process. It is through such legitimating mechanisms that forms of development governmentality are able to secure the consent of the governed.

However, actual environmental and development improvements 'on the ground' are less obvious or inspiring. Tanzania is unlikely to achieve the Millennium Development Goal targets for poverty reduction, food security, maternal mortality or access to potable water (United Republic of Tanzania, 2008: iii). In 2008 33 per cent of the mainland population was still below the basic needs poverty line; 60 per cent of under-5s were underweight or stunted from lack of food; and 43 per cent of the rural population lacked access to potable water (ibid.). Food security is further threatened by predictions that climatic changes will result in a 33 per cent fall in maize yields nationally, and up to 84 per cent in central regions (United Republic of Tanzania, 2007: 7). This has become a highly charged political issue linked to allegations of 'land-grabbing' by foreign companies for biofuels and agricultural exports, with activists alleging state investment-friendly policies are 'cultivating hunger' (Chachage and Mbunda, 2009: 96; see also Chachage, 2010; Kamanga, 2008). Allegations of chronic mismanagement, rent-seeking and pervasive corruption in the forestry, fisheries and wildlife conservation sectors further contribute to substantial doubts over the efficacy of the much-lauded environmental mainstreaming, as well as belying claims that what is happening in Tanzania is the straightforward extension of neoliberal free market policies (Cooksey, 2003, 2011a, 2011b; Cooksey and Kelsall, 2011).

Some might interpret this disjuncture as implying that the NSSD are 'essentially symbolic exercises' (Meadowcroft, 2007: 159), or that sustainable development more broadly is simply 'polite meaningless words' (Middleton and O'Keefe, 2001: 31). In contrast, this chapter has suggested that much of the international praise for the Tanzanian experience works actively and quite effectively to legitimate (in the eyes of key constituencies) the ways in which vested interests are entrenching their control over natural resources, and new power relationships are emerging between global and local capital, the Tanzanian state and civil society, and the international donor industry. Neither is it evident that transformations in environmental governance are generating impressive improvements in ecological sustainability and food security in Tanzania. Perhaps some of the praise for the legitimacy of new forms of governmentality such as NSSDs and environmental mainstreaming – indicative of the successful operation of these practices as legitimating mechanisms – itself works to divert attention from the inequitable and unjust power relationships which structure Tanzanian society. This raises important questions for the role of critical academic research on the legitimacy of global governance. As Brassett and Tsingou question in a different context: '[w]hat if by engaging in a framework assessment of the basis of legitimate global governance we inadvertently condone – or at least leave unquestioned – the ongoing constitution and/or normalization of certain practices?' (2011: 11; see also Green, 2003).

It is concerns similar to these that may well have motivated the critiques set out by David Booth and his colleagues. The work of the *Africa Power and Politics* researchers suggest that openness, transparency and civic participation are all a waste of time, and that we should 'abandon the polite fiction that the politicians in charge of most poor developing countries are really committed to development' (Booth, 2011: 4). I am not convinced, however, that the answer lies in the promotion of 'developmental patrimonialism' and autocratic leaders who can 'get things done' (Booth, 2011: 3). Rather, a critical focus on the implications and power relations behind widespread and influential legitimating mechanisms, and drawing attention to cases where new forms of governance appear to legitimate forms of politics apparently inimical to their broader aims, is surely a challenge to develop alternative legitimacy games which work to promote alternative power relations and empower different sets of social actors.

84   C. Death

Notes

1 This chapter is based upon a paper presented at a workshop at the Department of Political Science, Lund University, 7–8 May 2012, entitled 'The Legitimacy and Legitimation of Transnational Governance'. I am very grateful to the participants and organisers for the opportunity to discuss these ideas, and for the feedback received. Helpful advice was also received from Clive Gabay. The chapter is primarily conceptual, but draws upon reviews of Tanzanian planning and strategy documents, informed by a trip to Dar es Salaam in August 2011 which was supported by the British Institute in Eastern Africa. Semi-structured elite interviews and follow-up emails were conducted with 12 government officials, academics, donors and civil society activists. A discussion of environmental governance in Tanzania from a rather different theoretical perspective is available in Death (2013a).
2 For more details, see www.institutions-africa.org, as well as Booth (2011); Cooksey (2011a, 2011b); Cooksey and Kelsall (2011).
3 Such an argument has many similarities to James Ferguson's claims about the workings of the development 'anti-politics machine' in Lesotho (1994). For a discussion of Ferguson's argument and its bearing on Tanzanian politics, see Green (2003: 125–127) and Igoe (2005: 138).

Interviews

Baha, Bernard. Senior Programme Officer Research Publication and Documentation, Land Rights and Resources Institute (HakiArdhi). Dar es Salaam, 12 August 2011.

Banasiak, Magdalena. Climate Change and Environment Adviser in DFID Tanzania. Dar es Salaam, 9 August 2011.

Cheche, Blandina. Poverty-Environment Officer in the Division of Environment in the Vice-President's Office. Dar es Salaam, 9 August 2011.

Cooksey, Brian. Independent researcher. Dar es Salaam, 12 August 2011.

Ekingo, Magembe. Senior Economist, MKUKUTA Secretariat, Ministry of Finance. Dar es Salaam, 11 August 2011.

Howlett, David. DFID. Telephone interview, 9 January 2012.

Ladislaus, Kyaruzi. Climate Change desk officer at Vice President's Office in the Division of Environment in the Vice-President's Office. Dar es Salaam, 9 August 2011.

Manyama, Amon. Senior Assistant Resident Representative Pro-Poor Policy and Wealth Creation, UNDP. Dar es Salaam, 11 August 2011.

Mongula, Benedict. Institute of Development Studies, University of Dar es Salaam. Dar es Salaam, 15 August 2011.

Ndaki, Patrick. Senior Education Officer in the Division of Environment in the Vice-President's Office. Dar es Salaam, 9 August 2011.

Rutasitara, Longinus. Institute of Development Studies, University of Dar es Salaam. Dar es Salaam, 16 August 2011.

References

Abrahamsen, Rita (2004) 'The power of partnerships in global governance'. *Third World Quarterly*, 25, 8: 1453–1467.

Assey, Paschal, Stephen Bass, Blandina Cheche, David Howlett, George Jambiya, Idris Kikula, Servacius Likwelile, Amon Manyama, Eric Mugurusi, Ruzika Muheto and Longinus Rutasitara (2007) *Environment at the Heart of Tanzania's Development:*

Lessons from Tanzania National Strategy for Growth and Reduction of Poverty (MKUKUTA). London: International Institute for Environment and Development.

Bäckstrand, Karin, Jamil Khan, Annica Kronsell and Eva Lövbrand (eds) (2010) *Environmental Politics and Deliberative Democracy: Examining the promise of new modes of governance*. Cheltenham: Edward Elgar.

Bernstein, Steven (2004) 'Legitimacy in global environmental governance'. *Journal of International Law and International Relations*, 1: 139–166.

Bernstein, Steven (2011) 'Legitimacy in intergovernmental and non-state governance'. *Review of International Political Economy*, 18, 1: 17–51.

Bofin, Peter, Marie-Lise du Preez, André Standing and Aled Williams (2011) *REDD Integrity: Addressing governance and corruption challenges in schemes for Reducing Emissions from Deforestation and Forest Degradation (REDD)*. Bergen: Chr. Michelsen Institute.

Bojö, Jan and Rama Chandra Reddy (2003) *Status and Evolution of Environmental Priorities in the Poverty Reduction Strategies: An assessment of fifty Poverty Reduction Strategy Papers*. Washington D.C.: World Bank.

Booth, David (2011) *Governance for Development in Africa: Building on what works*. London: ODI.

Brassett, James and Eleni Tsingou (2011) 'The politics of legitimate global governance'. *Review of International Political Economy*, 18, 1: 1–16.

Broch-Due, Vigdis (2000) 'Producing nature and poverty in Africa: an introduction', in *Producing Nature and Poverty in Africa*, eds. Vigdis Broch-Due and Richard A. Schroeder, 9–52. Uppsala; Nordiska Afrikainstitutet.

Brockington, Dan (2006) 'The politics and ethnography of environmentalism in Tanzania'. *African Affairs*, 105, 418: 97–116.

Brockington, Dan (2008) 'Corruption, taxation, and natural resource management in Tanzania'. *Journal of Development Studies*, 44, 1: 103–126.

Brundtland, Gro Harlem (1987) *Our Common Future: World Commission on Environment and Development*. Oxford: Oxford University Press.

Carmody, Pádraig (2011) *The New Scramble for Africa*. Cambridge: Polity.

Chachage, Chambi (2010) *Land Acquisition and Accumulation in Tanzania: The case of Morogoro, Iringa and Pwani regions*. Research paper commissioned for Pelum Tanzania. Available at www.commercialpressuresonland.org/sites/default/files/110406_Land_Acquisition_Tanzania.pdf (accessed 3 October 2011).

Chachage, Chambi and Richard Mbunda (2009) *The State of the then NAFCO, NARCO and Absentee Landlords' Farms/Ranches in Tanzania*. Dar es Salaam: HakiArdhi.

Clark, Ian (2005) *Legitimacy in International Society*. Oxford: Oxford University Press.

Clark, Ian (2007) *International Legitimacy and World Society*. Oxford: Oxford University Press.

Conca, Ken (2005) 'Old states in new bottles? The hybridization of authority in global environmental governance', in *The State and the Global Ecological Crisis*, eds. John Barry and Robyn Eckersley, 181–205. Cambridge, MA: MIT Press.

Cooksey, Brian (2003) 'Marketing reform? The rise and fall of agricultural liberalisation in Tanzania'. *Development Policy Review*, 21, 1: 67–91.

Cooksey, Brian (2011a) *The Investment and Business Environment for Gold Exploration and Mining in Tanzania*. London: ODI.

Cooksey, Brian (2011b) *Public Goods, Rents and Business in Tanzania*. London: ODI.

Cooksey, Brian and Tim Kelsall (2011) *The Political Economy of the Investment Climate in Tanzania*. London: ODI.

86 C. Death

Dalal-Clayton, Barry and Steve Bass (2009) *The Challenges of Environmental Mainstreaming: Experience of integrating environment into development institutions and decisions*. London: IIED.

Dean, Mitchell (2007) *Governing Societies: Political perspectives on domestic and international rule*. Maidenhead: Open University Press.

Death, Carl (2013a) 'Environmental mainstreaming and post-sovereign governance in Tanzania'. *Journal of Eastern African Studies*, 7, 1: 1–20.

Death, Carl (2013b) 'Governmentality at the limits of the international: African politics and Foucauldian theory'. *Review of International Studies*, 39, 3: 763–787.

DFID Tanzania (2011) *Operational Plan 2011–15*, May. Available at www.dfid.gov.uk/ Documents/publications1/op/tanzania-2011.pdf (accessed 3 October 2011).

Dill, Brian (2009) 'The paradoxes of community-based participation in Dar es Salaam'. *Development and Change*, 40, 4: 717–743.

DSD (2009) 'National sustainable development strategies'. Available at www.un.org/esa/ dsd/dsd_aofw_nsds/nsds_index.shtml (accessed 17 April 2012).

Ferguson, James (1994) *The Anti-Politics Machine: 'Development', depoliticization and bureaucratic power in Lesotho*. Minneapolis: Minnesota Press.

Foucault, Michel (2007) *Security, Territory, Population: Lectures at the Collège de France 1977–1978*. Ed. M. Senellart, trans. G. Burchell. Basingstoke: Palgrave Macmillan.

Foucault, Michel (2008) *The Birth of Biopolitics: Lectures at the Collège de France 1978–1979*. Ed. Michel Senellart, trans. Graham Burchell. Basingstoke: Palgrave Macmillan.

Foucault, Michel (2010) *The Government of Self and Others: Lectures at the Collège de France 1982–1983*. Ed. Frédérick Gros, trans. Graham Burchell. Basingstoke: Palgrave Macmillan.

Fraser, Alastair and Lindsay Whitfield (2009) 'Understanding contemporary aid relationships', in *The Politics of Aid: African Strategies for Dealing with Donors*, eds. Lindsay Whitfield, 74–107. Oxford: Oxford University Press.

Geoghegan, Tighe (2007) *Making Aid Work Better for Recipients, and Improving National Planning Processes for Sustainable Development in the Bargain*. London: IIED. Available at http://pubs.iied.org/pdfs/11069IIED.pdf (accessed 8 August 2011).

George, Clive and Colin Kirkpatrick (2006) 'Assessing national sustainable development strategies: strengthening the links to operational policy'. *Natural Resources Forum*, 30: 146–156.

Gould, Jeremy and Julia Ojanen (2003) *'Merging in the Circle': The politics of Tanzania's Poverty Reduction Strategy*. Helsinki: Institute of Development Studies, University of Helsinki.

Green, Maia (2003) 'Globalizing development in Tanzania: policy franchising through participatory project management'. *Critique of Anthropology*, 23, 2: 123–143.

Harrison, Graham (2001) 'Post-conditionality politics and administrative reform: reflections on the cases of Uganda and Tanzania'. *Development and Change*, 32, 4: 657–679.

Harrison, Graham (2004) *The World Bank and Africa: The construction of governance states*. Abingdon: Routledge.

Harrison, Graham and Sarah Mulley with Duncan Holtom (2009) 'Tanzania: a genuine case of recipient leadership in the aid system?', in *The Politics of Aid: African Strategies for Dealing with Donors*, ed. Lindsay Whitfield, 271–298. Oxford: Oxford University Press.

Hyden, Goran (1980) *Beyond Ujamaa in Tanzania: Underdevelopment and an uncaptured peasantry*. London: Heinemann.

Igoe, Jim (2005) 'Power and force in Tanzanian civil society: the story of Barabaig NGOs in the Hanang Community Development Project', in *Between a Rock and a Hard Place: African NGOs, Donors and the State*, eds. Jim Igoe and Tim Kelsall, 115–146. Durham, NC: Carolina Academic Press.

Jansen, Eirik G. (2009) *Does Aid Work? Reflections on a natural resources programme in Tanzania*. Bergen: Chr. Michelsen Institute.

Jennings, Michael (2002) '"Almost an Oxfam in itself": Oxfam, Ujamaa, and development in Tanzania'. *African Affairs*, 101: 509–530.

Kamanga, Khoti Chilomba (2008) *The Agrofuel Industry in Tanzania: A critical enquiry into challenges and opportunities*. Dar es Salaam: HakiArdhi.

Karkkainen, Bradley C. (2004) 'Post-sovereign environmental governance'. *Global Environmental Politics*, 4, 1: 72–96.

Kimani, Nicholas (2007) *Reinvention of Environmental Governance in East Africa: Explanatory and normative dimensions*. Unpublished PhD thesis, Australian National University.

Kronsell, Annica and Karin Bäckstrand (2010) 'Rationalities and forms of governance: a framework for analysing the legitimacy of new modes of governance', in *Environmental Politics and Deliberative Democracy: Examining the promise of new modes of governance*, Karin Bäckstrand, Jamil Khan, Annica Kronsell and Eva Lövbrand (eds), 28–46. Cheltenham: Edward Elgar.

Kulindwa, K., R. Lokina and A. Hepelwa (2010) *Poverty-Environment Policy Analysis*. Dar es Salaam: Ministry of Finance and Economic Affairs.

Lange, Siri (2008) 'The depoliticisation of development and the democratisation of politics in Tanzania: parallel structures as obstacles to delivering services to the poor'. *Journal of Development Studies*, 44, 8: 1122–1144.

Lecoutere, Els (2011) 'Institutions under construction: resolving resources conflicts in Tanzania irrigation schemes'. *Journal of Eastern African Studies*, 5, 2: 252–273.

Levine, Arielle (2002) 'Convergence or convenience? International conservation NGOs and development assistance in Tanzania'. *World Development*, 30, 6: 1043–1055.

Luttrell, Cecilia and Innocent Pantaleo (2008) *Budget Support, Aid Instruments and the Environment: The country context, Tanzania country case study*. London: Overseas Development Institute.

Meadowcroft, James (1997) 'Planning, democracy and the challenge of sustainable development'. *International Political Science Review*, 18, 2: 167–189.

Meadowcroft, James (2007) 'National sustainable development strategies: features, challenges, reflexivity'. *European Environment*, 17: 152–163.

Middleton, Neil and Phil O'Keefe (2001) *Redefining Sustainable Development*. London: Pluto Press.

Mniwasa, Eugene and Vincent Shauri (2001) *Review of the Decentralization Process and its Impact on Environmental and Natural Resources Management in Tanzania*. Dar es Salaam: Lawyers Environmental Action Team.

Mol, Arthur P. J. and Frederick H. Buttel (2002) 'The environmental state under pressure: an introduction', in *The Environmental State under Pressure*, eds. Arthur P. J. Mol and Frederick H. Buttel, 1–12. Oxford: Elsevier.

Nelson, Fred (2007) *Emergent or Illusory? Community wildlife management in Tanzania*. London: International Institute for Environment and Development.

Neumann, Roderick P. (1998) *Imposing Wilderness: Struggles over livelihood and nature preservation in Africa*. Berkeley: University of California Press.

88 *C. Death*

Neumann, Roderick P. (2001) 'Africa's 'last wilderness': reordering space for political and economic control in colonial Tanzania'. *Africa*, 71, 4: 641–665.

Nord, Roger, Yuri Sobolev, David Dunn, Alejandro Hajdenberg, Niko Hobdari, Samar Maziad and Stéphane Roudet (2009) *Tanzania: The story of an African transition*. Washington, D.C.: International Monetary Fund.

Norrington-Davies, Gemma and Nigel Thornton (2009) *Climate Change Financing and Aid Effectiveness: Tanzania case study*. Paris: OECD.

Ribot, Jesse C. (2003) 'Democratic Decentralisation of Natural Resources: Institutional choice and discretionary power transfers in Sub-Saharan Africa'. *Public Administration and Development*, 23: 53–65.

Ruitenbeek, Jack and Cynthia Cartier (2008) *Putting Tanzania's Hidden Economy to Work: reform, management and protection of its natural resource sector*. Washington, D.C.: World Bank.

Rutasitara, Longinus, Razack B. Lokina and Fredrick Yona (2010) *Mainstreaming Environment into MKUKUTA II Process: Interim report*. University of Dar es Salaam, Department for Economics.

Scott, James C. (1998) *Seeing Like a State: How certain schemes to improve the human condition have failed*. New Haven: Yale University Press.

Shao, John (1986) 'The villagization programme and the disruption of the ecological balance in Tanzania'. *Canadian Journal of African Studies*, 20, 2: 219–239.

Sheridan, Michael (2009) 'The environmental and social history of African sacred groves: a Tanzanian case study'. *African Studies Review*, 52, 1: 73–98.

Shivji, Issa G. (2006) *Let the People Speak: Tanzania down the road to neo-liberalism*. Dakar: CODESRIA.

Sunseri, Thaddeus (2005) ' "Something else to burn": forest squatters, conservationists, and the state in modern Tanzania'. *Journal of Modern African Studies*, 43, 4: 609–640.

UNDP-UNEP (2010) *Poverty and Environment Initiative (PEI), PEI Country Fact Sheet Tanzania*, February. Available at www.unpei.org/PDF/tanzania-country-sheet.pdf (accessed 28 October 2011).

United Republic of Tanzania (2005) *National Strategy for Growth and the Reduction of Poverty (NSGRP)*. Dar es Salaam: Vice President's Office.

United Republic of Tanzania (2006) *State of the Environment Report 2006*. Dar es Salaam: Vice President's Office, Division of Environment.

United Republic of Tanzania (2007) *National Programme of Adaptation (NAPA)*. Dar es Salaam: Vice President's Office.

United Republic of Tanzania (2008) *Millennium Development Goals Report: Midway evaluation 2000–2008*. Dar es Salaam: Ministry of Finance and Economic Affairs.

United Republic of Tanzania (2009) *Poverty and Human Development Report 2009*. Dar es Salaam: Ministry of Finance and Economic Affairs.

United Republic of Tanzania (2010) *National Strategy for Growth and Reduction of Poverty II*. Dar es Salaam: Ministry of Finance and Economic Affairs.

United Republic of Tanzania (2011) *The Tanzania Five Year Development Plan, 2011/12–2015/16, Unleashing Tanzania's Latent Growth Potentials*, draft. Dar es Salaam: President's Office, Planning Commission.

Part II
Building communities

5 Business and the uses of 'civil society'

Governing Congolese mining areas

Jana Hönke

Introduction

Not only development agencies, international organisations and international non-governmental organisations (NGOs) intervene in postcolonial societies, but also multinational companies (MNCs).[1] These companies are today expected to promote the building of liberal states and civil societies. Some of them in fact do engage in activities that follow this demand and engage in participatory community development and capacity building. In some areas in Africa, they are in fact amongst the most active promoters of what some refer to as 'global liberal governmentality' (Sending and Neumann 2006). These are business spaces, and in particular areas of extraction that have received investment by large multinational mining companies, such as the Niger Delta in Nigeria or the Copperbelt in the Democratic Republic of the Congo and Zambia. These companies often refer to the people living adjacent to their operations as 'their communities' and in engaging with them draw on the discourse of civil society.

This chapter analyses companies' practices in adjacent communities, using the case of mining companies in copper and cobalt-rich Southern Katanga in the Democratic Republic of Congo (DRC). It looks at large and medium-sized multinational companies that have committed themselves to standards of corporate social responsibility. These are for this chapter the American company Freeport MacMoRan, Canadian First Quantum and Australian Anvil Mining. Examining the everyday practices of these companies allows us to show ambiguous uses and effects of the idea of civil society and participatory community engagement.

Drawing on case studies from the early twentieth century and the post-2000 period, this chapter shows, first, that companies have always been comprehensively involved in ordering practices in adjacent communities. However, the participatory management of today is different from the coercive and disciplinary paternalism used to control local communities a century ago. Nevertheless, despite this shift to a new liberal governmentality (Rose 1999), which emphasises the participation of the population in its own governance, there are also striking similarities between early colonial and contemporary corporate ordering attempts. Participation operates in concert with powerful techniques of coercion

92   *J. Hönke*

and indirect rule. While dominating official discourse, calling on self-responsible citizens coexists with fortress protection and older practices of paternalistic cooptation and indirect rule (Hönke 2013). In addition, participatory community engagement and recourse to the discourse of liberal civil society takes place selectively. Technocratic problem-solving-oriented cooperation and service-delivery is encouraged whilst other, contentious activity is silenced. The liberal claim of self-determination is in fact compromised by the recourse to indirect rule and coercion in order to secure stable working conditions, as well as managerial approaches to participation.

After an exploration of the literature on participatory community development and corporate-community relations, the chapter analyses continuities and changes in corporate community practices in the early twentieth century and the post-2003 period in Katanga, DRC. It examines how Western donor agencies join in with companies in building a service-oriented 'civil society' while excluding more critical voices. It also criticises the lack of sustainability of corporate participatory community programmes such as in times of economic crisis.

Foreign companies, local ordering and the community

In the context of an ongoing re-assemblage of local and transnational order (Agnew 2009; Abrahamsen and Williams 2010; Engel and Nugent 2010), MNCs have become important governors. There is a large literature on corporate social responsibility (CSR), which focuses on companies' contribution to development and security at the local level (e.g. Hamann *et al.* 2008, Börzel *et al.* 2012). Corporate security practices have been discussed with regard to conflict and conflict prevention, yet this literature has been mainly interested in voluntary regulation and potential business contributions to collective goods provision (Haufler 2001; Deitelhoff and Wolf 2010). These studies emphasise that companies engage with local communities and NGOs and sometimes even build up new civil society structures.[2]

In contrast to this literature, other studies point to the dark sides of corporate activities in and effects on local communities. Companies do use coercive force in order to protect their installations and shield them off from adjacent communities (Frynas 2001; Drohan 2004; Hönke 2010). In addition, companies' participatory community engagement gives rise to new forms of exclusion or sometimes simply maintains old hierarchies to achieve stability (Watts 2004b; Zalik 2004; Welker 2009). Developmental approaches often remain piecemeal, cause conflict within adjacent communities and remain insulated from broader society (Ferguson 2005; Soares de Oliveira 2007: 103–122, Hönke with Thomas 2012). A few studies look at how companies react to community protest and their use of development approaches to prevent conflict with and attacks from communities and local militias (Watts 2004a; Zalik 2004). Looking at governance by companies from the 'bottom-up' perspective, these studies show that company practices are far from emancipatory forms of community participation and do not lead to meaningful redistribution of benefits.

Business and the uses of 'civil society' 93

How can we make sense of these parallel observations of corporate developmental engagement in communities on the one hand, and exclusionary and coercive practices on the other? How do we understand appeals to civil society and self-determination alongside paternalist and coercive practices? Governmentality provides an analytical tool to better understand the ensemble of these contemporary ordering practices and is particularly useful for making sense of them in non-state governance. Company activities have also rarely been studied from a perspective of ordering or policing.[3] However, by understanding corporate community policies as part of a policing – or ordering – project, I hold, we gain a better understanding of governance by companies. This perspective is inspired by Mark Duffield's work on the merging of security and development in Western interventions in the Global South (Duffield 2001, 2007). It is striking – and largely unexplored – to what extent this merging characterises ordering regimes in business spaces such as extraction enclaves.[4]

One of the key techniques of contemporary 'advanced liberalism' (Rose 1999) has been described as 'governing at a distance': states, companies and community leaders involve intermediary groups (citizen groups, professionals, voluntary associations, social partners and private firms) in their own governance. Such a logic of governing at a distance works through responsible and self-governing entities (Sorensen and Torfing 2007: 6). It is characterised by governing through market mechanisms and the promotion of individual responsibility and entrepreneurial values. Ownership, participation and self-determination are key principles.[5]

The underlying logic of such 'govern[ing] through freedom' (Rose 1999; Krasmann and Volkmer 2007) is, however, one of risk management. Managing security risks is less about causes and more about pre-emptively acting upon potentially problematic zones and groups of people (Rose 1999). Feeley and Simon (1992) have observed a 'new penology' in which security governance shifts focus towards proactively 'producing' law-abiding citizens and making them participate in their own policing. Yet at the same time, potential offenders and entire places defined as uncertain are excluded, sealed off and managed in a more restrictive way, before any crime has been committed, in order to prevent future harm to others (Jones 2007). By so 'making up governable spaces' (Rose 1999), liberal governmentality redefines spaces of in- and ex-clusion.

Participatory approaches to community development promoted by companies' CSR departments follow such logic. Strategies of including 'responsible communities' in transnational governance hence coexists with forms of indirect rule and coercion. Activating modes of governance are seemingly contradicted, yet also complemented, by their interrelation with sovereign and disciplinary modes of power in local practice. As has been argued for other cases, it is the interplay of these different modes of governing that characterises liberal governance (Valverde 1996; Hindess 2001). There are double standards and paradoxes within liberal political thinking: illiberal practices of governing are part and parcel of the liberal tradition, for those unable to govern themselves as well as those opposed to liberal market order. This is reflected in company community

94   *J. Hönke*

management. Parallel logics and double standards characterise the practice of securing commercial extraction (Hönke 2012, 2013). In consequence, a depoliticised understanding of participation limits the participatory measures themselves (Cleaver 1999; Cooke and Kothari 2001; Dill 2009).

The following sections reconstruct the ordering practices of mining companies. Two questions stand out in guiding the analysis: First, what is actually new about 'new' community practices? And, second, what is the regime of practices within which participatory community engagement takes place? In other words, what are the (contradictory) dynamics around contemporary corporate community policies?

Before I turn to my empirical case, a brief discussion of what might be considered 'new' about external actors' community engagement is due. Mamdani (1996) for instance discusses 'old' colonial and 'new' postcolonial forms of indirect rule. He describes colonial domination as based on a system of indirect rule in which subjects depended on the absolute powers of a local chief acting between them and the colonial government. His model of 'decentralised despotism' is based on evidence from rural areas. Companies in early industrial ventures partly relied on such repressive, indirect arrangements of control, while at the same time establishing their own bubble of semi-private governance in which they had far-reaching powers based on delegated authority from the colonial administration. From the early twentieth century, companies increasingly governed this bubble according to a biopolitical logic (Foucault 2004 [1979]) aimed at creating an industrial workforce. Despite an overall rationality of 'commandment' – according to Mbembe (2001) the exercise of arbitrary and little conditioned power based on racial distinctions – industrial enclaves in Africa were constructed as islands of modernity (Ferguson 1999) in which 'advanced liberal' – if disciplinary-paternalist – modes of governing prevailed.

'Indirect private government', described by Mbembe as a new manner of ruling contemporary spaces in the peripheries, shares some important characteristics with governance in the early colonial period. Indirect private government is characterised by privatised sovereignty within 'more or less autonomous pockets' (Mbembe 2001: 80) within states in which market logics prevail. I agree that such forms of ruling have become more important in current processes of de-/re-territorialisation in Africa (Hönke 2010). However, despite a return to more private government, such as in the era of business empires of the eighteenth and nineteenth century, how companies seek to produce order today is different from the past. It does not always entail increased violence and coercion, as is the case in the war economies of extraction Mbembe (2001: 79) refers to. New technologies of governing used by multinational companies aim at reducing direct, physical violence and instead promote development and participation. Companies selectively engage in governing localities in order to ensure production and engage in developmental schemes of 'improvement' (Murray Li 2007).

Contemporary 'schemes of improvement' share some similarities with colonial ideas of betterment and techniques of indirect rule (Cooke 2003). However, participatory engagement with communities today is embedded in the more activating logics of advanced liberalism than the paternalist discipline of the past. To some extent in contrast to Cooke, I hold that it is important to distinguish between community engagement that outsources local governance to chiefs and strong men – as described in Mamdani's decentralised despotism model – and participatory engagement with individuals and groups in the context of contemporary corporate risk management. In corporate ordering practices, techniques of indirect rule coexist with techniques of participatory engagement yet are clearly distinct from them (Hönke 2012, 2013).

In order to develop this argument I now turn to the case of mining companies in Katanga, starting with a discussion of company interventions in adjacent communities in the early twentieth century followed by an analysis of contemporary community interventions.

Between coercive and paternalist discipline – companies' ordering practices in the early twentieth century

The first industrial mining companies began operating in Sub-Saharan Africa in the last quarter of the nineteenth century. As elsewhere, setting up industrial extraction projects was closely related to colonial occupation and the establishment of direct control over African territory. In the Congo Independent State (the Belgian Congo from 1908), the Union Minière du Haut Katanga (UMHK) was founded in 1906 to explore what is today Katanga and to set up industrial copper extraction. Despite the difference of the colonial context, UMHK, like contemporary mining companies in the DRC, operated in an institutional context characterised by weak state capacities and plural authorities: no state monopoly of violence was in place and various actors competed over local power. Looking at UMHK's ordering practices reveals another striking similarity between the two periods: maintaining industrial production involved not only protecting private property with private force but also interventions in adjacent areas in order to create stable working conditions.

Integrating Katanga as a supplier of cobalt and copper into the world market, industrial mining profoundly shaped local social, political and economic structures. For our purposes, the early regime of governing extraction based on forced labour and coercion (see Higginson 1989) is of less interest than the increasingly paternalist, disciplinary logic of managing the company and its workforce introduced by the UMHK management from the 1920s. As a new mode of exercising power, disciplinary practices revolved around the idea of transforming subjectivities in order to build a mass labour force that was cheap but fit for modern industrial extraction. The company changed from governing through corporal punishment to more indirect and productive modes of power. It got deeply involved in workers' lives and thus in the labour settlements that it simultaneously sought to isolate from the 'traditional', 'pre-modern' world surrounding them (Hönke 2013, chapter 6).

Liberal theories conceptualise private property as the natural domain of private governance. In the period from the 1880s to the 1920s this domain

96   *J. Hönke*

consisted of an extended, semi-private area. UMHK controlled a closed realm extending from the workplace to entire labour settlements in which workers lived with their families. The company encouraged monogamous marriages and provided workers with such families with accommodation, food rations, healthcare and schooling (for a description, see Dibwe dia Mwembu 2001). '[A]n army of agents from helping professions and missionary societies' (Higginson 1989) were sent into the labour camps, not only with medicine but also with moral visions of how African workers and families should behave. In the spirit of a new rationality of governance that Michel Foucault describes for Europe as a regime of discipline and biopolitics, the control and (re)production of life became the focus of interventions aimed at the production of a permanent class of wage labour (Stoler and Cooper 1997: 31f).

The colonial administration and the UMHK 'sought to reach further under the workers' caps while tying their hands faster to new pacesetting machinery' (Higginson 1988: 2). The virtues of the new industrial discipline were punctuality, temperance and sexual restraint. In the workshops, priests from the Benedict Fathers and African auxiliaries were supposed to teach apprentices respect and passivity in the face of superior European civilisation. They were also expected to educate workers in European ways of life and turn them away from 'backward African customs' (Higginson 1988: 6f). In a way the camps were the colonial version of the *cités ouvrières* built in Europe in the nineteenth century to (re) produce, cater for and control a new, disciplined industrial labour force (Peemans 1997: 37). It was not the company alone that maintained this extractive order. The company, Catholic Church and, with time, increasingly the colonial state ran a regime of coercive paternalism in extended pockets of territory: the mines and the labour settlements in their direct vicinity. In the settlements, two authorities maintained a totalitarian subculture: 'the compound head, responsible for discipline maintenance, and the [Catholic] teacher-preacher responsible for morals and learning' (Vellut 1983). The colonial state appeared as a tax collector and as a punishing agent of last resort.

What emerged at the end of the 1920s around the mines of Katanga was thus a regulatory regime of discipline as known from early labour cities in Europe, yet in a more coercive and exclusive form (for other cases, see Mitchell 1991; Legg 2007). Isolating the bubble of industrial, disciplinary order established in the labour camps from an environment perceived as hostile and more disorderly (Dibwe dia Mwembu and Kalaba Mutabusha 2005: 62), the disciplinary regime within the extended fortress of the mine was, however, in sharp contrast to the scope of disciplinary regimes observed in Europe that targeted entire populations within state territories. UMHK rarely got directly involved in governing the communities and urban areas outside the extended zone of semi-private governance described above, such as the new mining cities of Elizabethville (Lubumbashi), Jadoville (Likasi) and Kolwezi (Fetter 1976).

Alongside coercion, which according to Legg (2007) and Mbembe (2001) were characteristic for colonial governmentality, in the restricted territory of the workplace and the workers' compounds, whose boundaries were closely policed, the company increasingly adopted a rather paternalistic style of governing. However, there was no recourse to the notion of civil society nor was participation and self-determination an important feature of the workforce-focused corporate community policies of the past. What we find, instead, is a territorial bubble of semi-private governance in which disciplinary power became the dominant mode of governing the workforce.

Between participatory community engagement and indirect rule, post-2000

How do these paternalist techniques of securing production – by transforming subjectivities and building and growing labour communities – differ from today's new concern about communities? Companies have been increasingly exposed to social and political conflicts that emerge from the environment in which they operate. In contexts in which host states are not able to provide stable working conditions and protect industrial extraction, security managers have become increasingly concerned with managing security risks that they believe emanate from local communities. Managing volatile social and political environments, companies have become involved in securing extraction through selected engagement in adjacent communities.

A managerial approach to risk governance, which characterises the new liberal governmentality, was first developed in the business sector (Johnston and Shearing 2003: ch. 3). Since the 1990s, larger and more visible companies started to turn to less reactive and more pre-emptive modes of dealing with potential issues of insecurity. Security managers complement reactive punishment with acting on risks pre-emptively. What has been described for policing, which since the 1980s has turned to a kind of 'actuarial risk management' (O'Malley 1996), has therefore travelled to remote business spaces in the South. Security governance now works more through managing particular risk groups, issues and spaces.

In the policing literature, such techniques have been well described so far with regards to urban phenomena, such as shopping malls and gated communities. Here, the 'good community' – the inhabitants of the middle-class neighbourhood, the consumers – are invited to use and help protect these spaces. However, physical barriers, but also cameras, patrols and spatial design exclude those with supposedly 'threatening' behaviour: potential 'criminals', hawkers and non-consumers (see, for example, Jones, 2007).

With companies in Katanga we find similar patterns. Corporate security strategists see security risks to mining companies as increasingly emanating from adjacent communities. Companies in Katanga refer to these communities ambiguously as both their most immediate threat and a potential belt of protection for operational security.[6] Therefore they complement their traditional 'fortress mentality' (Johnston and Shearing 2003), which made them concentrate on protecting the narrow space of private property through fencing-off, deterrence and surveillance, with flexible engagement in the 'community belt', trying to make

98 *J. Hönke*

these communities partners in policing the enclave. I term 'community belt' the space that companies refer to as their communities and theatre of operation (Hönke 2012, 2013). Sometimes this is geographically defined by companies as, for instance, the communities within a particular distance or as the host administrative unit. What is important about the new rationale of managing order within this belt is, however, that companies no longer take on direct territorial control over these areas, such as was the case with the extended labour camps run by UMHK in the early colonial period. While there are still small labour compounds for a limited number of expatriate and more senior employees, the 'community belt' refers to the inhabited space around mining operations into which new forms of participatory community engagement flexibly and selectively stretch out.

Conflicts with communities erupt over access to land, over relocation and, more generally, over who has to bear the costs of mining and how the benefits of extraction should be distributed. In addition to frequent violent confrontations with artisanal miners, there are other examples of how communities turn to confrontational methods in Katanga in order to make such claims. In a settlement formerly run by state-owned mining company *Gécamines* close to Kolwezi, for instance, inhabitants organised protests and took a mine manager hostage to pressure the Canadian company FQML to repair the local sewage system.[7] Firms thus complain that they are under pressure to take on more and more social functions.[8]

The phenomenon is not specific to Katanga. Situated at the bottom of a transnational, asymmetric field of struggle, indigenous communities stage conflicts at the very local level of transnational economic ventures to claim rights and redistribution of benefits of natural resource extraction (see Szablowski 2007). In more and more places, these conflicts are no longer repressed or mediated by host state governments. In addition, communities link up more easily with transnational INGOs or media and thus are more likely to effectively damage companies' reputations.[9]

As a result, local security governance has changed:

> Security has evolved over the years and many people think [...], see security as a main guarding function, iron gates, securing an office complex or mine complex against theft or wrongdoing. [...] In a broader context, certainly, the industry has evolved over the last 10 years ... security moved on. It's much more of a risk management role we now fulfill.[10]

This view is supported by the observation of an NGO project manager working with another mining company. He saw 'more and more interest to really link the agendas of security and social development [...] in the last two years with a lot of the major internationally listed companies' in Katanga.[11] The extent to which the trend of merging security and development in liberal global governance that Mark Duffield (2001, 2007) has described for the field of peace operations is striking, and aid is also evident in the field of commercial security governance.

Business and the uses of 'civil society' 99

In protecting commercial extraction, multinational mining companies in Katanga now also draw on techniques of dialogue and participatory development management in order to make adjacent communities partners in policing the extraction enclave. A social and community manager describes how, through dialogue with communities and education, his company was trying to make people accept its mining operations in their midst as '*patrimoine de leur environment*': as a property and valuable part of their environment that they want to protect.

In his account, the exclusive, island-like character of the 'community belt' becomes evident. The idea is to make the poor village communities adjacent to the mine partners of the company's private, for-profit endeavour. Once communities perceive their own well-being and prosperity as linked to that of the company, according to the approach's rationality, they will socially sanction theft from the mine and help to denounce illegal intruders and thieves.[12]

Companies consider communication a key technique for preventing insecurity. They have established regular consultations with communities in the neighbouring ex-Gécamines cities, as well as in villages. These are also supposed to dissolve grievances by giving people the opportunity to express complaints and demands without resorting to violence.

However, the liaison officers can also be interpreted as an extended arm of in-house intelligence, as they are informants placed within communities and provide local information.[13] This makes community engagement an ambivalent endeavour. Liaison officers formally have a social mandate, but can be seen as additional important set of 'eyes and ears' for the company in the mining communities.[14] In this logic they are part of the intelligence services, an early warning system that should increase awareness of risks.

Another aspect of this new form of community engagement is strategic philanthropy, or investments in communities in order to placate critics or improve a companies' reputation which have no clear relationship to the negative externalities and thus responsibilities a company has for the effects of its core business practices. Such social investment might do 'good' in that it might improve collective goods provision in local communities. Contracted by Anvil Mining, the NGO Pact, for instance, introduced new participatory procedures around Anvil's operations. Pact sought to form local development committees to represent communities better vis-à-vis the company. Companies thus call on those living around mining sites to represent 'the' local communities. Those representatives then make up community development committees that have at least two functions. Those organised by the NGO Pact decide – from a set of potential options – what to spend the companies' social investment on. Through these committees, the company also asks community members to take responsibility for local security – and thereby the protection of company assets.[15]

Such involvement, however, has important indirect effects on local politics and the distribution of power and authority in the local arena. The committees mentioned above are part of a company procedure that is represented as apolitical and functionally specific. However, these institutions and the selection of

100   *J. Hönke*

those supposed to represent 'the community' in them is highly political. Social investment usually benefits some but puts other people in a locality at a disadvantage.[16] Such unequal distribution of corporate social investment is created through the fabrication of forums that include those in alliance with the company but excluding others who raise critical issues.[17] In fact, companies create political institutions parallel to existing state and customary political structures at the local level. These might call local political hierarchies into question and introduce (democratic) change.

However, in the eyes of companies, democratic participatory community engagement can easily contradict private security interests. Instead of contributing to the companies' overall goal of achieving stable working conditions, these may undermine social and political stability. Therefore, firms steer clear of too progressively intervening in local social and political hierarchies, and often steer clear of engaging with critical NGOs or marginalised groups. On the contrary, they often rely on clientelistic, stability-oriented arrangements of indirect rule – sometimes under the cover of CSR – by working with the strongest and officially recognised local authority regardless of that person's legitimacy in the eyes of the local population (Hönke, with Thomas 2012; Hönke 2013; Geenen and Hönke forthcoming). Anthropologist Marina Welker (2009) has shown this for mining company Newmont's community programmes in Indonesia, which it introduced after being criticised for partnering with the regime and not working enough with local communities. She demonstrates how the company nurtures existing patrimonial networks through CSR and sides with incumbent, conservative chiefs against environmental activists to maintain stability.

Hence community forums can theoretically be used in order to raise concerns. However, because of a biased selection process and asymmetric power relations, this is not often the case. Practices of clientelism and co-optation coexist with the participatory development engagement described above.

This co-optation model is in the long tradition of indirect rule. It consists of supporting chiefs and local big men to guarantee local order. As chiefs are legally '*pas important, mais indispensable*'[18] in local politics in the DRC, they have been set up as privileged contacts and partners of mining companies. While mining legislation officially deprives them of their land rights, they have an important role in local governance: local administration, if there is any, depends on chiefs and without them, nothing works.[19] Local government in the DRC has not been elected since the 2006 adoption of a new constitution calling for local elections. Decentralisation, also enacted in the new constitution, has still not been implemented, either at provincial or district and lower levels. Local elections have not taken place and the lower tiers of state administration are built on 'traditional chiefs' and local power structures (Young and Turner 1985). While the Congolese constitution and mining code attribute both mineral and surface rights to the state, concentrating the politics of mining in the hands of central government, traditional authorities are the main de facto authorities at local level.

This is evidenced by the capacity of chiefs to mobilise communities in favour of or against companies. In mid-2008, for instance, a confrontation between the company TFM and local communities on the issue of employment appears to have been orchestrated by one of the local chiefs.[20] In another case of violent attacks against Anvil Mining in early 2008, these seem to have been organised by the local chief in reaction to his conflict with the company.[21] In the mining regions, therefore, a clientele pattern of firm-chief interaction goes far beyond customary forms of paying tribute to local authorities. Chiefs have been put on company payrolls and receive strategic investments in their jurisdiction in exchange for social peace.[22]

The security manager of a multinational company in Katanga puts this pragmatic approach to managing security through indirect rule as follows: 'We are stuck to those who are legally in power. There is no purpose in lamenting about the authorities. You want that copper? Deal with it.'[23] With regard to the host state, the rentier state literature and others have described at length how this logic strengthens unaccountable political regimes (Reno 1997). With regards to company–state relations, I have argued elsewhere (Hönke 2010) that the increasing role of corporate entities in security governance can be understood as a new form of indirect discharge, used by external governments and, in the case of Katanga, by the Kabila government. They quasi-outsource policing functions to mining companies.

In addition, participatory engagement is limited in itself. Due to a discursively predetermined setting, the set of policies that communities can actually decide about and implement is limited. Liberal economic institutions and a global CSR discourse set clear boundaries within which self-determination is possible. Investors' property and mining rights, for instance, usually trump customary land rights and customary artisanal mining rights. Certain forms of claim making are delegitimised as undemocratic, or even criminalised. Local residents and artisanal miners in the Kolwezi area in Katanga, for instance, do not channel their protest through community forums. They do not have access to them, or consider them as ineffective in attaining their goals. They are an expression of a managerial approach to participation that often serves as another technique of control rather than helping emancipation (Cooke 2001; see also Cruikshank 1999). If people turn to alternative strategies, such as demonstrations, blockades or trespassing, these are treated as illegitimate and are met with repression (Hönke 2013).

To summarise, the case of mining companies' ordering practices in Katanga shows that contemporary participatory management is different from the coercive and disciplinary paternalism companies used to control local communities in the past. While multinational companies engage beyond the fortress of the mine in adjacent communities – as in early colonialism, and much more than in the intervening years – the contemporary rationality of ordering is considerably different. It is less territorial and more activating in how it calls on individuals and communities to take responsibility for maintaining order around the mines. However, while companies promote participatory engagement and civil society to some extent, they also stick to powerful local actors who are crucial for stability. This poses a constraint to alternative, more representative political

102 *J. Hönke*

structures and emancipatory policies that participatory engagement could potentially encourage (see, for example, Hickey and Mohan 2005). Companies are conservative forces in the sense that they side with those in power for legal and de facto physical security (Reno 2004). Apart from their growing importance in local ordering, this importance of indirect rule shows striking similarities with the early colonial period.

Donors, 'good' and 'bad' civil society and the global economic crisis

Two additional points will be raised in this final section. The first relates to how *external governments* perceive and police civil society in the field of extractive industries in the DRC. The second is about the slowdown in demand for copper and cobalt in the context of the global economic crisis and how this has affected corporate community policies.

First, it is striking that, similar to multinational mining companies, donor agencies that work on resource governance in Katanga, such as the British DfID (Department for International Development) and the American USAID, also have a selective take on 'legitimate' protest and 'good' (as well as 'bad') civil society. Representatives of both agencies only consider service-providing, problem-solving oriented NGOs collaborating with companies as 'good' and legitimate parts of civil society. By contrast, they criticise watchdog NGOs, which observe and denounce companies' security and human right practices, as useless and problematic.[24] These are not mere personal points of views by individuals in Katanga. This distinction has practical effects in that donors fund service-oriented NGOs such as Pact Congo, but not critical observers, such as Global Witness or ACIDH. However, the public shaming of multinational mining companies by the latter has been crucial in making companies engage in participatory community engagement.

Second, the rise in commodity prices and the subsequent investment boom that took place in Katanga from 2004 to 2008, during which most of the material presented above was collected, was followed by a bust from late 2008 onwards. As a consequence, mining companies cut back on their activities in the region or even closed down (Mthembu-Salter 2009). This has had tremendous effects on corporate community engagement policies, which points to further limitations of corporate civil society policies. Besides cutting back on core business activities, companies have cut back even more on participatory community engagement. NGO Pact Congo, for instance, had run the community programme for Anvil Mining and other companies before the crisis. It had also developed and implemented an integrated development and security programme in the Kolwezi area, the Kolwezi Artisanal Mining Project, which was to an important extent financed by mining companies that operate in this region.[25] A core component of these programmes was the empowerment of the local population that was negatively affected by industrial mining and in conflict with companies and/or government officials. They sought, for instance, to build stakeholder forums in which local residents and artisanal miners got together with mining company representatives and government in order to prevent conflict and develop alternative development options. These programmes were closed down because mining companies withdrew their funding in the wake of the bust. Eventually, Pact closed down its offices in Katanga.[26] These consequences of the economic crisis underline that in addition to their selectivity and hybridity, corporate participatory community engagement also lacks sustainability.

Conclusion

In recent years, multinational companies have emphasised more and more that they were contributing to preventing conflict, and to building states and civil societies in Africa. This chapter has shown that engagement in African societies by firms is not entirely new. Companies operating in the early colonial period intervened in adjacent communities. These interventions were, however, driven by a disciplinary logic and focused on neatly delimited territory. Their major goal was to produce a mass labour force. The UMHK in Katanga created an extended bubble of semi-private governance largely shut off from its larger environment.

Contemporary strategies of participatory development and CSR are no longer concerned with disciplining and transforming people. However, they are problematic in their own right. In order to strategically manage security risks that may potentially emanate from adjacent communities, the 'community belt' has become a space in which firms concentrate selective interventions. In contrast to the enclaves of the past, this 'belt' is less territorial. It has no fixed demarcations and remains a social space with flexible borders. Community engagement within this belt is, however, hybrid and has exclusionary and depoliticising effects.

Despite the emphasis on the population's role in its own governance, there are in fact striking similarities between early colonial and contemporary corporate ordering attempts in the postcolonial world. In everyday practice, for instance, old techniques of cooptation and indirect rule persist. Whereas a new liberal governmentality dominates the discourses of development, state-building and corporate community engagement, companies police adjacent communities with recourse to indirect rule and coercion as well (see also Hönke 2012, 2013). While multinational companies are expected to, and increasingly do, engage in participatory community development, there are thus ample reasons for critically (re)examining governance interventions by profit-oriented actors such as multinational companies.

However, such critical engagement is not only apt in the case of private for-profit actors. It is striking to what extent companies refer to the same discourses as states and international organisations. The rationalities of new liberal governmentality are widely shared and transcend supposed boundaries between profit and not-for-profit, state and non-state spheres. However, the liberal claim to self-determination and democratic procedures in these governance interventions is compromised by managerialism and the recourse to indirect rule and coercion in order to ensure stability.

104 *J. Hönke*

Notes

1 I would like to thank two anonymous reviewers and the editors of this volume for their comments on earlier versions of this paper. I acknowledge generous support for field research by the Research Centre SFB 700 Governance in Areas of Limited Statehood and the German Research Foundation. This chapter is an expanded and revised version of an article published as Jana Hönke, 'Multinationals and Security Governance in the Community: Participation, Discipline and Indirect Rule', *Journal of Intervention and Statebuilding*, 6, 1 (2012): 57–73.
2 See, however, Börzel and Hönke 2012 and Zalik 2004.
3 See, however, Hönke 2010 and 2012, and Abrahamsen and Williams 2010.
4 Exceptions are the case studies by Welker 2009 and Zalik 2004. See also Soares de Oliveira 2007: 107ff.
5 For a discussion of these principles and their paradox effects in development and state-building interventions, see Cleaver 1999, Kühn 2010 and Jahn 2007.
6 Interview with company manager security and development, 21 November 2008, Kolwezi; Interview with Pact Congo, October 2007 and November 2008, Lubumbashi.
7 Interview with company security manager, 22 November 2008, Kolwezi.
8 Interview with manager community relations and social development, 3 October 2007, Johannesburg.
9 See, for instance, the transnational campaigns against Anvil in Katanga and Anglogold Ashanti in Ituri (Börzel and Hönke 2012).
10 Interview with ex-group security manager, 26 October 2007, Ndola.
11 Interview with Pact representative, 17 October 2008, Lubumbashi. This refers to the period before the world economic crisis. See the last section of this chapter for the impact of the world economic crisis on the mining industry in Katanga and hence the community engagement of companies.
12 Interview with company social development manager, 15 November 2008, Lubumbashi.
13 Interview with company security manager DRC, 22 November 2008, Lubumbashi.
14 Interviews with company security and social development managers, 15 and 21 November 2008, Lubumbashi.
15 Interviews with Pact Congo in November 2007 and 2008, DRC; Interviews with security and community managers of Anvil Mining, November–December 2008, DRC.
16 For development management it has been shown that 'participation' often reproduces existing inequalities and hierarchies (Cooke and Kothari 2001).
17 For a pertinent case in this regard in Eastern DRC see Geenen and Hönke (forthcoming). Michael Watts (2004b) shows how oil companies in the Niger Delta create new communal identities and divisions.
18 Interview with World Bank Extractive Industries Programme, 29 October 2008, Kinshasa.
19 The Constitution 2006 and the new Mining Code 2002 attribute both mineral and surface rights to the state. Interview with CEO consultancy African Institute of Corporate Citizenship and former UNDP worker in the DRC, 7 October 2008, Johannesburg.
20 Interview with company social development and security managers, 7 November 2008, Lubumbashi; Dan 2008: All Mine, Dan Rather Reports (Transcript). HDNet. 23 September 2008.
21 Interview with advocate, 19 November 2008, Kolwezi; Interview with World Bank Extractive Industries Programme, 29 October 2008, Kinshasa.
22 See note 21; Interview with CEO consultancy African Institute of Corporate Citizenship and former UNDP worker in the DRC, 7 October 2008, Johannesburg; Interview with company manager security and development, 21 November 2008, Kolwezi.
23 Interview with ex-security manager, mining company, Ndola, 26 October 2007.

24 Interview with USAID country representative DRC, 29 October 2008, Kinshasa and conversations 4 November 2008, Lubumbashi; with DfID country representative, meeting in Kinshasa, and conversations 4 November 2008, Lubumbashi.
25 Interviews with Pact Congo representatives and with Anvil Mining representatives, October–November 2008, Lubumbashi.
26 Pact Congo: Status Update 2009, unpublished document, mimeo. Interviews with former Pact Congo staff in Lubumbashi, Kinshasa and Kolwezi, September and October 2012.

References

Abrahamsen, R. and Williams, M.C., 2010. *Security beyond the State: Security Privatization and International Politics*, Cambridge: Cambridge University Press.
Agnew, J., 2009. *Globalization and Sovereignty*, Lanham: Rowman and Littlefield.
Börzel, T.A. and Hönke, J., 2012. *Security and Human Rights: Mining Companies between International Commitment and Corporate Practice*, Baden-Baden: Nomos.
Börzel, T.A., Hönke, J. and Thauer, C., 2012. Corporate Responsibility, Multinational Corporations and the Nation State: Does it Really Take the State? *Business and Politics*, 14: 3, 1–34.
Cleaver, F., 1999. Paradoxes of Participation: Questioning Participatory Approaches to Development. *Journal of International Development*, 11: 4, 597–612.
Cooke, B., 2001. *From Colonial Participation to Development Management*, IDPM Discussion Paper Series, Working Paper 63, Manchester.
Cooke, B., 2003. The New Continuity with Colonial Administration: Participation in Development Management. *Third World Quarterly*, 24: 1, 47–61.
Cooke, B. and Kothari, U. (eds), 2001. *Participation: The New Tyranny?* London: Zed Books.
Cruikshank, B., 1999. *The Will to Empower: Democratic Citizens and Other Subjects*, Ithaca, NY: Cornell University Press.
Deitelhoff, N. and Wolf, K.-D. (eds), 2010. *Corporate Security Responsibility?* Basingstoke: Palgrave.
Dibwe Dia Mwembu, D., 2001. *Bana Shaba Abandonnés Par Leur Père: structures de l'autorité et histoire sociale de la famille ouvrière au Katanga, 1910–1997*, Paris: L'Harmattan.
Dibwe Dia Mwembu, D. and Kalaba Mutabusha, G., 2005. Lubumbashi: Des lieux et des personnes, in D. De Lame and D. Dibwe Dia Mwembu (eds), *Tout passe. Instantanés populaires et traces du passé à Lubumbashi*, Tervuren: Musée royale de l'Afrique centrale.
Dill, B., 2009. The Paradoxes of Community-based Participation in Dar es Salaam. *Development and Change*, 40: 4, 717–743.
Drohan, M., 2004. *Making a Killing: How and why Corporations Use Armed Force to do Business*, Guilford, CT: Lyon's Press.
Duffield, M., 2001. *Global Governance and the New Wars: The Merging of Development and Security*, London, New York: Zed Books.
Duffield, M., 2007. *Development, Security and Unending War: Governing the World of People*, Cambridge: Polity.
Engel, U. and Nugent, P. (eds), 2010. *Respacing Africa*, Leiden: Brill.
Feeley, M.M. and Simon, J., 1992. The New Penology: Notes on the Emerging Strategy of Corrections and its Implications. *Criminology*, 30: 4, 449–474.

106 *J. Hönke*

Ferguson, J., 1999. *Expectations of Modernity: Myths and Meanings of Urban Life on the Zambian Copperbelt*, Berkeley, CA: University of California Press.

Ferguson, J., 2005. Seeing Like an Oil Company: Space, Security, and Global Capital in Neoliberal Africa. *American Anthropologist*, 107: 3, 377–382.

Fetter, B., 1976. *The Creation of Elizabethville, 1910–1940*, Stanford: Hoover Insitute Press.

Foucault, M., 2004 [1979]. *Geschichte der Gouvernementalität II: Die Geburt der Biopolitik*, Frankfurt am Main: Suhrkamp.

Frynas, J.G., 2001. Corporate and State Response to Anti-Oil Protests in the Niger Delta. *African Affairs*, 100: 398, 27–54.

Geenen, S. and Hönke, J. (forthcoming). 'Land Grabbing' by Mining Companies: State Reconfiguration and Local Contentions in South-Kivu, DRC, in A. Ansom (ed.), *Land Grabbing in the Great Lakes Region of Africa*, Woodebridge: James Currey.

Hamann, R., Woolman, S. and Sprague, C., 2008. *The Business of Sustainable Development in Africa: Human Rights, Partnerships, Alternative Business Models*, New York: United Nations University Press.

Haufler, V., 2001. *A Public Role for the Private Sector: Industry Self-Regulation in a Global Economy*, Washington, D.C.: Carnegie Endowment for International Peace.

Hickey, S. and Mohan, G., 2005. Relocating Participation within a Radical Politics of Development. *Development and Change*, 36: 2, 237–262.

Higginson, J.E., 1988. Disputing the Machines: Scientific Management and the Transformation of the Work Routine at the Union Minière du Haut-Katanga, 1918–1930. *African Economic History*, 17, 1–21.

Higginson, J.E., 1989. *A Working Class in the Making: Belgian Colonial Labor Policy, Private Enterprise, and the African Mineworker, 1907–1951*, Madison, WI: University of Wisconsin Press.

Hindess, B., 2001. The Liberal Government of Unfreedom. *Alternatives*, 26: 1, 93–111.

Hönke, J., 2010. New Political Topographies: Mining Companies and Indirect Discharge in Southern Katanga (DRC). *Politique Africaine*, 120, 105–127.

Hönke, J., 2012. Multinationals and Security Governance in the Community: Participation, Discipline and Indirect Rule. *Journal of Intervention and Statebuilding*, 6: 1, 89–105.

Hönke, J., 2013. *Transnational Companies and Security Governance: Hybrid Practices in a Postcolonial World*, London: Routledge.

Hönke, J., with Thomas, E., 2012. *Governance for Whom? Capturing the Inclusiveness and Unintended Effects of Governance*. Berlin: Working Paper Series Research Centre for Governance No. 31.

Jahn, B., 2007. The Tragedy of Liberal Diplomacy: Democratization, Intervention, Statebuilding (Part I). *Journal of Intervention and Statebuilding*, 1: 1, 87–106.

Johnston, L. and Shearing, C., 2003. *Governing Security: Explorations in Policing and Justice*, London, New York: Routledge.

Jones, T., 2007. The Governance of Security: Pluralization, Privatization, and Polarization in Crime Control, in M. Maguire, R. Morgan and R. Reiner (eds), *The Oxford Handbook of Criminology*, Oxford: Oxford University Press, 841–865.

Krasmann, S. and Volkmer, M. (eds), 2007. *Michael Foucaults 'Geschichte der Gouvernementalität' in den Sozialwissenschaften. Internationale Beiträge*, Bielefeld: Transcript.

Kühn, F., 2010. *Sicherheit und Entwicklung in der Weltgesellschaft: Liberales Paradigma und Staatsaufbau in Afghanistan*, Wiesbaden: VS Verlag für Sozialwissenschaften.

Legg, S.I., 2007. *Spaces of Colonialism: Delhi's Urban Governmentalities*, Malden, MA, Oxford: Blackwell Publishing.

Mamdani, M., 1996. *Citizen and Subject: Contemporary Africa and the Legacy of Late Colonialism*, Princeton, NJ: Princeton University Press.

Mbembe, A., 2001. *On the Postcolony*, Berkeley, CA: University of California Press.

Mitchell, T., 1991. *Colonizing Egypt*, Berkeley, CA: University of California Press.

Mthembu-Salter, G., 2009. *Natural Resource Governance, Boom and Bust: The Case of Kolwezi in the DRC*. Occasional Paper No. 35, South African Institute of International Affairs.

Murray Li, T., 2007. *The Will to Improve Governmentality, Development, and the Practice of Politics*, Durham: Duke University Press.

O'Malley, P., 1996. Risk and Responsibility, in A. Barry, T. Osborne and N. Rose (eds), *Foucault and Political Reason: Liberalism, Neo-Liberalism, and Rationalities of Government*, Chicago, IL: Chicago University Press, 189–208.

Peemans, J.-P., 1997. *Le Congo-Zaïre au gré du XXième siècle: état, économie, société, 1880–1990*, Paris: L'Harmattan.

Reno, W., 1997. African Weak States and Commercial Alliances. *African Affairs*, 96: 383, 165–185.

Reno, W., 2004. Order and Commerce in Turbulent Areas: 19th Century Lessons, 21st Century Practice. *Third World Quarterly*, 25: 4, 607–625.

Rose, N., 1999. *Powers of Freedom: Reframing Political Thought*, Cambridge: Cambridge University Press.

Sending, O.J. and Neumann, I.B., 2006. Governance to Governmentality: Analyzing NGOs, States, and Power. *International Studies Quarterly*, 50: 3, 651–672.

Soares de Oliveira, R., 2007. *Oil and Politics in the Gulf of Guinea*, London: Hurst and Columbia University Press.

Sorensen, E. and Torfing, J. (eds), 2007. *Theories of Democratic Network Governance*, Houndmills: Palgrave.

Stoler, A.L. and Cooper, F. (eds), 1997. *Tensions of Empire: Colonial Cultures in a Bourgeois World*, Berkeley, CA: California University Press.

Szablowski, D., 2007. *Transnational Law and Local Struggles: Mining Communities and the World Bank*, Oxford: Hart Publishing.

Valverde, M., 1996. 'Despotism' and Ethical Liberal Governance. *Economy and Society*, 25: 3, 357–372.

Vellut, J.-L., 1983. Mining in the Belgian Congo, in D. Birmingham and P.M. Martin (eds), *History of Central Africa*, London: Longman, 126–162.

Watts, M.J., 2004a. Resource Curse? Governmentality, Oil and Power in the Niger Delta, Nigeria. *Geopolitics*, 9: 1, 50–80.

Watts, M.J., 2004b. Antinomies of Community: Some Thoughts on Geography, Resources and Empire. *Transactions of the Institute of British Geographers*, 29: 2, 195–216.

Welker, M.A., 2009. Corporate Security Begins in the Community: Mining, the Corporate Social Responsibility Industry, and Environmental Advocacy in Indonesia. *Cultural Anthropology*, 24: 1, 142–179.

Young, C. and Turner, T., 1985. *The Rise and Decline of the Zairian State*, Madison, WI: University of Wisconsin Press.

Zalik, A., 2004. The Niger Delta: 'Petro Violence' and 'Partnership Development'. *Review of African Political Economy*, 101, 401–424.

6 Connecting state, citizen and society?

The externalised context of community groups in Zambia

Karen Treasure

Introduction

Civil society has been promoted by development actors in Africa ostensibly to complement the move to formal multi-party democratic systems of governance which took place in the 1990s. Civil society actors are commonly associated with a number of traits which are deemed to bolster the value of democracy, by representing the public in a more direct and active sense than the infrequent ballot of elections, and by holding governments accountable for policy choices. Approaches to the promotion of civil society have differed significantly, adapting to critiques of methods used and trends in the evaluation of impacts. In line with broader changes in development strategies, recent projects have focused on targeting African societies at the local, community scale, in order to encourage bottom-up and grassroots participation in processes of development and social change (Long 2001). This attempt to localise civil society rhetorically promises to empower African communities to participate more effectively in the democratic processes which govern them. Community groups, or 'Community-Based Organisations' (CBOs), are understood as social groups constituted by, and therefore representative of, the communities they serve. They are generally assumed to be motivated by issues that are considered significant within those same communities, and to act as ideal agents of civil society, providing political space outside of the state model and encouraging citizen action.

Such an uncritical normative framework, however, has been demonstrated to have serious flaws in other areas of development analysis and international relations more broadly. Not only are communities 'imagined' (Anderson 1983) to some extent, as boundaries are not obviously assigned, but they are also riven by their own hierarchies and power relations (Mohan and Stokke 2000), encouraging self-interested action on the part of individuals or specific groups within communities and thus often working against broad local interests (Dill 2009). Moreover, the provision of international resources to fund projects in African communities distorts the very basis on which civil society, and more broadly community action, is predicated and justified as a useful and effective force to resist the over-arching power of the African state. Donor incentives and rewards for civil society, which require latent competition for ongoing funding

Connecting state, citizen and society? 109

and external control over targets, means that much of the focus of community groups motivated this way is external to the communities they are supposed to represent.

This chapter draws on research conducted in the Southern Province of Zambia to illustrate this externalised context of so-called community groups. Community groups function as associational formations, bringing people together in communities and promoting communication. Such groups are often very successful in bringing about limited changes to local conditions, but their motivation, *raison d'etre* and focus is derived from international-scale actors, resources and processes. By definition, this agenda is externally prioritised and insecure. Rather than reflecting organically generated local objectives, it is reproducing the global neoliberal discourse directly at the local scale in African communities. There are two bases on which such reflections challenge assumptions regarding the role of civil society as an essential arbiter of democracy in African states. First is the recognition that community-based organisations are essentially active only at international and local scales, being relatively powerless to influence the former sphere and often creating changes to power relations in the latter, with no security (and very little capacity) in any new developmental landscape. Thus, the creation of this kind of civil society provides no effective challenge to current parameters for action, and at best stabilises existing forms of agency and the global structures they respond to. Second, by focusing on local self-reliance and community-scale resource generation, these groups actively deter national democratic participation, embracing the reality that national level politics is an unproductive arena to pursue greater capacity. This disengagement from national level politics prevents scrutiny of the political process and thus also prevents the hope of holding leaders or ministers to account domestically.

As such then, community groups may actually be creating an increasingly favourable environment for a neo-patrimonial state (see Chabal and Daloz 2005; Erdmann and Engel 2006; Taylor and Williams 2008) to act with impunity. Rather than building a more open state with improved mechanisms of accountability and participatory politics, community groups may actually be deterring effective national level participation. According to the ensuing analysis, both of these arguments contribute to an understanding of African community groups as reinforcing existing power balances in international relations. It should be noted that this analysis specifically refers to community-based forms of civil society whose activities are directed as identified here, that is emphasising self-reliance and small-scale resource generation. It is not meant to advocate such sweeping conclusions across other forms of civil society groupings in Zambia or across Africa.

This chapter proceeds in four sections. Various understandings and modes of conceptualising civil society are discussed first, to establish a theoretical framework for the ensuing discussions. Here the rhetorical benefits of civil society in the 'good governance' agenda will be outlined, as well as modes of theorising civil society at community scale in Zambia. Second, the context of communities in Zambia, and southern Africa more broadly, is explored. How development

110 K. Treasure

opportunities are framed is central to this analysis, and this is not affected as much by the policies of the Zambian state as by the structural realities of global markets and living in 'global shadows' (Ferguson 2006). Third, the empirical case study of community groups in the Southern Province of Zambia is detailed. Particular attention is given to the manner in which groups fulfil (or not) their assumed role as civil society, and their capacity to change the dominant frameworks of opportunity in African communities. The final section draws together the argument that community groups are neither providing increased democratic accountability nor meaningful pluralism in Zambia. They are, however, providing increased resilience to current patterns of global inequalities through stabilising neoliberal structures and discourses in African communities.

Civil society for Zambians, and in theory

Mahmood Mamdani insists on studying 'actually existing civil society' because he is concerned with 'its actual historical formation, not programmatically' (1996), but in this chapter the ensuing study of community groups seeks rather to interrogate the label of civil society that has been assigned to particular actors. The rhetoric of civil society within the international promotion of a 'good governance' agenda, since the 1990s, promotes an understanding of civil society as an essential strand of democratic development. Thus, this research considers how community groups in Zambia are, or are not, fulfilling this ideal role of civil society. The analysis has a greater focus on the 'unintended consequences' (Ferguson 1990) of the international promotion of civil society. Here the approach rejoins Mamdani, by endorsing recognition of all exchanges of power relations, from local to global scale, as equally necessary in the effort to know Africa and African civil society. Such a perspective recognises the 'exceptionalism' (Fowler 2012) of African constructs given the specific nature of the African context, namely differences in modes of formal/informal networks, patronage, voluntarism, and so on.

The following sections outline the normative and theoretical frameworks for this research. First, there is a review of the role of civil society in the 'good governance' agenda and global development discourses more broadly. Second, the notion of community-based civil society is discussed to find a working theoretical position.

Civil society: the African 'development' view

Civil society is often deterministically linked to processes of democratisation (Bratton 1994) and 'good governance'. Particularly since the wave of democratisation during the 1990s, African development has been framed as a political problematic which requires better governance to solve. 'Within this framework civil society is held to be an inherently democratic and democratising sphere wherein private actors and institutions can flourish' (Mercer 2003: 747). A free and independent civil society is recognised as a key component of the 'good governance' agenda, underpinning a free media and judiciary and the decentralisation of government. These mechanisms are deemed to move away from the fiercely centralised power of 'big man' politics which was/is so prevalent in post-colonial Africa. Civil society, by providing a link between public and private spaces, is presumed to increase participation of the public in holding governments to account and maintaining scrutiny on domestic politics.

This framework is linked to a broader notion of increasing 'participatory governance' which has been embraced by donors in their policies across the developing world, a narrative which is recognised to have had an impact but to be limited in scope (Speer 2012). Abrahamsen's research shows that the 'main effects of the good governance discourse, despite all its proclamations in favour of democracy, is to help reproduce and maintain a world order that is essentially undemocratic' (2000: 147). Indeed, studies in other regions have also shown that the effects of civil society actors can be highly distorting to patterns of governance, for example in India where 'civil society' organisations have been recognised to improve service delivery, yet at the same time being responsible for the 'constricted political space available to people' (Roy 2008). Thus, the grand claims associated with the formation of civil society require further scrutiny, particularly in respect of community-based action.

Theorising community-based civil society in Africa

Community-based actors represent a specific type of civil society in theoretical terms. The role of civil society within liberalism is discussed in more depth in Chapter 2 of this volume, so this section will focus on the potential of community-based organisations to act as effective civil society actors. Community-scale groups are often assumed to represent the community directly and authentically, but an extensive literature points to the barriers to participation for those who are disadvantaged or marginalised. During field research for this project, a bystander summed this up:

> It is not for the community, it is just for them in the groups. [The NGO] should help us all if they help them, some of them here have enough but we are hungry.
>
> (Woman in Sinalulongwe village, November 2009)

Recognition of this factor means that the problems associated with the definition of what, where and who the community is are put into perspective: communities have arbitrary and abstract boundaries. They do not operate as distinct and cohesive entities. Interests represented by community-based organisations therefore cannot be considered to be an accurate representation of the entire community. Furthermore, the representations made by community-based organisations are often framed by the kinds of activities donors are willing to fund (Mosse 2001; Mercer and Green 2012), despite claims that communities are free to identify their own agendas. Accepting these imperfections in the terminology, the label

112   K. Treasure

of community-based organisations remains useful in signifying that group members belong to the community that will be affected by any intervention.

Links between a community-based perspective and classical civil society literatures exist in a number of guises. For Tocqueville, associational practices were considered pluralist by definition, providing a diversity of sources of power in society and therefore acting as a check on state power (Tocqueville 1835). Such an interpretation of civil society means that community-based organisations hold great potential, representing as they do the most extensive range of pluralism possible. However, as Gramsci noted, such formations do not necessarily represent pluralistic positions if they emerge from the existing society and culture. Structure and agency in society are not formed independently but rather are constantly reproducing and reflecting one another. In his theorisation of the concept of hegemony, Gramsci argued that the bourgeoisie had potential to convince the masses that they had an interest in maintaining a system which in fact exploited them. Social organisations, therefore, hold potential for counter-hegemonic struggle through dissent, but they can also contribute to the overarching power of hegemonic discourses if they do not meet this 'potential' (1971). From this perspective it is implied that social movements do have the power to change the dominant discourse, not by opposing existing structures of power on their own terms, but by creating space to develop new ways of thinking which critique exploitative or oppressive power relations in all their forms.

Developing this line of thinking, Gramsci was followed by theorists from the Frankfurt school, notably Habermas (1979, 1984, 1987) and Marcuse (1972). These critical theorists advocated the loosely defined notion of 'emancipation' to inhibit the dangers of an imperial or hegemonic philosophy. Habermas (1979, 1984, 1987) insisted that communicative action was essential to counteract the dominant/dominated dichotomy. Marcuse (1972) forwarded the notion of a 'one dimensional society', arguing that 'the masses' were so absorbed into the capitalist mindset that they were unable to even identify, or therefore conceive of change to, the overarching structure of capitalist culture, thereby underlining the power encompassed in that form of structure.

Community-based organisations which assume the discourse of civil society actors can therefore be seen to have two possible, and diametrically opposed, effects. Cox has thus defined two types of civil society:

> in a 'bottom-up' sense, civil society is the realm in which those who are disadvantaged by the globalisation of the world economy can mount their protests and seek alternatives.... In a 'top-down' sense however, states and corporate interests influence the development of this current version of civil society towards making it an agency for stabilising the social and political status quo.
>
> (Cox 1999: 10–11)

Where civil society actors are formed in harmony with existing dominant structures of power, they can serve to deepen the exploitative forces which result from the superstructure. When such organisations are created at community scale, the impact of this is to develop and embed the hegemonic discourse, thus reducing the capacity, or at least the likelihood, of counter-hegemonic potential. Research shows that as community-scale participation in development projects orchestrated by donors has become more popular, 'more radical thinking and action toward "empowerment" and "liberation" of the people is becoming marginalised' (Rahman 1995: 26).

On the other hand, members of rural communities are those who are furthest from the mantras of neoliberal hegemony and therefore those who could potentially hold the greatest access to alternative intellectual spaces and interpretations. It is the ability to maintain this distance, to such an extent that autonomy is upheld, which is indicative of the potential to act as effective agents of civil society (Hearn 2001: 44). However, autonomy from structures and discourses of power may mean that effective forms of civil society cannot be recognised as such, so different are they from expected forms or sources of dissent. It has been argued that civil society in Africa is a fluid force which may be structurally unrecognisable to outsiders (Bayart 1986), and this is congruent with the counter-hegemonic potential recognised in the Gramscian perspective. Conformity to accepted modes of engagement for civil society actors (and thus the modes in which they are recognised and characterised) acts as a severe barrier to the preservation of autonomy. This brings into question the likelihood that international donors can create effective forms of civil society, coterminous as their interests are with the hegemonic forces of international political economy which affect African communities. As Lewis (2002: 582) succinctly puts it,

> [w]hile the prescriptive strengthening of civil society is strongly associated with the ideological dominance of neo-liberalism, there is the paradox that contestation by civil society organizations and social movements can also constitute a means through which such orthodoxies are challenged and resisted.

Indeed, under conditions of neoliberalism it is noted that sites of collective association are narrowing in general (Ferguson 2003).

Community-based civil society thus holds the potential to offer people a space to affect structures which become dominant and exploitative in their lives, but the label alone does not reflect this role. It requires a will to define a counter-hegemonic position by the people and the energy with which to propagate such a force as a movement, resisting or dissenting from the constraints of hegemonic discourses and dominant power relations. Community-based organisations are more disconnected from hegemonic interests than many other forms of civil society actors and therefore could have greater potential to create free sites of collective association. The context of community groups in Zambia is now explored to analyse their capacity to produce counter-hegemonic ideas or action with emancipatory potential.

114 *K. Treasure*

Frameworks of opportunity in rural Zambia

Several rural communities across the Southern Province of Zambia were the focus of field research informing this analysis. In each area visited, a community group had been established with the assistance of a Zambian non-governmental organisation (NGO) Women for Change, whose work was primarily funded by DanChurchAid, a Danish international non-governmental organisation (INGO). The groups studied were promoting gender equality, but the philosophy of donors was that gender equality was being prioritised as the best route to wider developmental progress. This study did not interrogate the effectiveness of the groups to promote gender equality but rather the wider effects of community group creation and their resulting value as civil society actors. Members of community groups were interviewed according to a semi-structured methodology to identify their time and space specific perceptions on the most pressing needs of the community. Data from these interviews was valued for the richness of the knowledge of those in the community, and was therefore analysed in its original form. The context was provided by secondary research, observations of conditions and constraints on action in the community. Thus, the following section explores how community groups within the project were formed and on what basis they were deemed to have a role as civil society. The context of rural Zambia is then briefly outlined, illustrating the contextualised frameworks of opportunity outlined by members of community groups and their hopes and aspirations for social change.

Constructing community groups and district associations

Community groups, in the cases studied, were created with the primary focus of addressing gender inequality in rural Zambia. The focus of Women for Change was largely to promote equality of gender relations, the absence of which is seen as a central constraint to developmental progress in many rural areas of Zambia. Their key message was that men and women should be equal partners in community groups. The chairperson of these community groups was required to be female as a direct and immediate rebalancing of gender power, but all other roles were assigned without reference to gender. Community groups were formed across small localities, and were encouraged to have around 30 to 40 members. Increased demand for groups was ostensibly addressed by the formation of more groups, all requiring support, guidance and resources from Women for Change.

The philosophy of funders and 'field animators', representatives in the field whose purpose was to animate the community rather than work for it, was that the creation of community groups served a number of purposes considered advantageous in dominant development trajectories. Community groups were considered to provide a sustainable outcome to the project, given that groups ran themselves without direct or constant support and were anticipated to be able to continue doing so beyond the project time-frame. Women for Change provided resources to initiate ventures for community groups pertaining to income

Connecting state, citizen and society? 115

generation, community facilities and so on, only after the group had identified their own objectives and demonstrated they had done all they could towards achieving such goals on their own. Many inputs were required to be multiplied, for example with livestock or poultry, and then paid back, usually in practice by passing on the original input to another local group. Desired objectives were identified through a process of 'self-realisation' which required community members to recognise that they had the skills necessary to operationalise object-ives. Community groups were also encouraged to be reliant on local resources rather than relying on insecure chains of external distribution. In this way, com-munity groups were deemed not to create dependency on aid provision, as so many development interventions have been considered to do in the past. The increased communication induced by community action, forming a group, was also considered to have empowerment potential, requiring social exchanges which were considered to be lacking previously. The NGO also provided skills training opportunities so that community members could reflect on their expand-ing skillset with hope for a changed future. This emphasis on self-help and com-munity confidence was central to the justification for community groups as a development strategy. They argued that as the confidence of the community increased, so the community would be better able to represent its own interests and thereby aspire to a better future.

To this end, once around ten groups had been formed across an area, they were encouraged to join together and form an Area Association. Multiple Area Associations in a particular region were encouraged to join and form a District Level Association (DLA), ascribed with facilitating a broad-sharing of best prac-tice for community groups and their associated skills. They were also considered to be suitable to formalise into an NGO in their own right, which would enable them to apply for funding to accomplish goals independently.

> When Area Associations have the skills to manage themselves there is no reason why they cannot apply for funding. That way they can identify their worst problems and put a proposal to get funding for that project. So they can be registered as their own organisation.
> (Interview, NGO District Co-ordinator, October 2009)

District Level Associations were also assumed to constitute civil society actors, primarily for their role in community advocacy. These organisations were relat-ively new at the time of field research, so it was too early to assess advocacy functions empirically. However, a conclusion can be drawn about the potential for these actors given that the notion of advocacy is based on collective repres-entation and on access to the power structures that frame opportunity. Given that these groups neither represent their communities holistically nor participate effectively in the global structures which direct development constraints, it can be assumed that they will be relatively ineffective in terms of advocacy. The next section discusses the governance – in its broadest sense – of rural Zambia, to provide a lens by which to assess the contribution of DLAs (and by

116   *K. Treasure*

association their constituent community groups) to counter-hegemonic struggle as civil society.

Constraints to opportunity and the focus of community change

Dominant discourses hold that Zambia is a multi-party democracy, which has generally held free and fair elections (at least since the end of Kaunda's one-party state in 1991) (Rakner 2003). Legitimate access to power for Zambian citizens, therefore, is through formalised democratic state politics (Simon 2005). While many flaws in the democratic culture of Zambia are accepted, hegemonic discourses continue to reinforce the legitimacy of the multi-party democratic Zambian state as the authority by which Zambians are governed (Simon 2005). This means the right of Zambian citizens to a legitimate voice in the construction of international discourses is mediated by the state.

There are a number of key flaws, additional to those implied in the 'good governance' agenda outlined above, to this presentation of a right to power and representation for Zambian people. First, many have argued that the Zambian state does not seek to pursue equitable rights for all its citizens (Rakner 2003; Simon 2005). In common with other African examples, the post-colonial state has maintained a so-called neo-patrimonial regime, which is resource seeking and maintains political loyalty through patronage (see Taylor and Williams 2008). Such regimes cannot be disconnected from the historical narratives which have produced them: the need to gain legitimacy in the immediate postcolonial era; impositions of democratic governance; inclusion in the liberalised global market from an uncompetitive position; to name but a few.

Second, in the communities studied, the presence of the state is largely invisible. These areas are not favoured by any particular political figure or party, and there are no judicial or social services of any kind provided by the state for considerable distances from the villages studied. Traditional leadership structures, chiefs and headmen, for example, have authority on matters of wrong-doing and land tenure. Although cases of criminality may be assumed to provoke recourse to the state, community members referred exclusively to local forms of authority to resolve disputes. Moreover, the local roads to most villages are impassable in the wet season and other infrastructure is largely absent, with the exception of some basic schools and medical facilities in some villages, which are generally significantly under-resourced. This brief illustration is to emphasise the disengagement of the state from the lives of most community members in the areas visited. Such a level of disengagement means the theoretical social contract between governed and government is largely obsolete, arguably creating a self-fulfilling prophecy of state withdrawal from governance functions. Thus, without ignoring the importance of the state in constructing the broad framework of meta-narratives for development opportunities, recognition of these factors means that the state is not the primary arbiter of relations in the communities studied.

Third, and inherently connected to the last two issues, the main constraints to action in the community are arguably invoked by processes operating at global

Connecting state, citizen and society? 117

scale, primarily the global market and international development policies. To give one example in detail, community members consistently complained that their key problem in subsistence was that they had insufficient resources to grow maize and insufficient access to water for drinking. The costs of maize seed, and the additional inputs required for credible yields, are set by the global market. The state of Zambia is limited in the changes it can make to these conditions, given their lack of resources, and the demands of the liberalised markets dictated by Structural Adjustment Programmes (Simon *et al.* 1995; Gunnell 2004). Opportunities for even basic subsistence are thus created, and constrained, by the unequal and unfair mantle of 'free trade' in the global economy which allows for extreme distortions, for example, the significant subsidies of European farmers in the form of the Central Agricultural Policy despite its constant reformation (Nordic Africa Institute 2009). The so-called 'green revolution' has tied small-scale African farmers to global prices for agricultural supplies, which need to be purchased annually given that seeds from hybrids will not reproduce, and this has priced them out of the market. Put simply, it is the pursuit of profit by global agri-business corporations, justified by the apparent logic of neo-liberalism, that constrains access to agricultural seeds, and thus subsistence, for some Zambians (see Shiva 2001).

As well as access to clean water, other problems self-identified in the area were the lack of educational opportunities for families who could not afford to contribute to education and the lack of healthcare. All such provisions may come, or not, to the community through external funding and programming. So ingrained is the recognition of disengagement of the state from these roles that community members recognise the need to represent their needs directly to NGOs rather than government.

> Government cannot look after people here – they are not here on the ground and they do not understand the issues [people are facing] – only NGOs are there to do that. Area politician did visit once to check on the maize marketing in the area but has not come again. Politicians do not represent communities – only NGOs are present on the ground, and they are the only ones making a difference.
>
> (Chairperson, Chizwamundi B AA, October 2009)

The politician referred to in this quote took office 18 months before this interview. Although there is often a risk of interviewees presenting pro-NGO views to interviewers, this research was conducted after several weeks living in the community and was thereby largely disconnected from association with the NGO.

As such, the demands for changes needed most urgently by members of community groups focus upon two categories of international 'actors', namely the global market and the global development regime. Such discourses are beyond the role and power of the state to directly control and in this way the state should be recognised as an ineffective analytical category when assessing the platform

118   *K. Treasure*

for counter-hegemonic struggle implied in the concept of civil society. To illustrate this point further, even state-sponsored programmes for example the subsidised provision of agricultural inputs are confined to a neoliberal logic, as they target larger-scale farmers and those who can contribute to the scheme, leaving those who are most in need of social change unassisted. Studies have shown that the profitability of maize in Zambia is more dependent on conditions often associated with small-scale farming in Zambia than on fertiliser application rates (Xu *et al.* 2009). Yet, despite this, the Government of Zambia have continued to subsidise fertiliser to ever greater degrees with the extension of the Fertilizer Support Program which has run since 2002, having been planned only as a two-year project, and giving it a budget of ZMK150 billion for fiscal year 2007–2008 (World Bank 2010). The state should therefore be analysed as a single layer or actor in the creation of these global structures, contributing to the vagaries of neoliberalism in the international system but not in control of them. The following section will explore more deeply the role of these community groups, and their scaled-up Associations, to represent community interests and the nature of the platforms they can access to represent themselves, create dissent or provide advocacy as civil society.

Community groups as civil society?

Analysis of these community groups, within the frameworks of opportunities outlined above, problematises their labelling as civil society actors. The argument has two central strands. One is that the operation and impact of community groups is at the local and international levels. At local scale, the groups create new forms of community action and new hierarchies, or the extenuation of existing ones. At international level, new NGOs that are formed in the name of civil society and as a product of community-based organisations, operate from a position of relative powerlessness in the race for funding and therefore resources for action. By deduction, the second theme recognises that the level of community disengagement from the state, both in terms of the lack of direct interaction with state policies and the logic of neo-patrimonial rule, cannot bolster the culture of democracy that is so uncritically assigned to the formation of community groups in development policy circles. Such actors are neither creating effective resistance to state power nor are they fostering a more mature democratic culture for citizens. Indeed, by providing better coping strategies for communities within the constrained framework of opportunities provided by global neoliberal dominance, such groups may actually be deepening the hegemonic structures which perpetuate extreme poverty. This section addresses these strands of the argument in turn.

Community groups as local- and international-scale actors

At the local scale, the impact of community groups was perceived by their members to be significant. Many interviewees expressed similar sentiments to the following:

The lives of the children will be different – they will have the knowledge when they are young. It is hard to change for the old people, but for the young it is good. They will treat each other better and co-operate.

(Member of Kaksense Group, November 2009)

Such reported perspectives are important in and of themselves, signalling the positive attitudes that can be created through community communication and cooperative action. Indeed, it may be considered that such aspirations are fundamental to the creation of social movements and in this way the groups may provide a glimpse of an important aspect of non-hegemonic relations, leading some to conclude in other contexts that they hold potential for the development of new forms of citizenship (Gaynor 2010). However, a more detailed understanding of the roles played by these actors is necessary to clarify their potential in altering hegemonic discourses.

The activities of groups vary considerably. All are run by a committee structure and there are regular meetings in most areas. Most attempt to generate collective options for income generation, including vegetable gardening, clay pot making, bee keeping, poultry or livestock breeding. Groups, or some members, are invited to attend training sessions organised by the implementing NGO, and it is understood that such knowledge will be shared throughout the group. Foci of training sessions include leadership abilities, report writing, accounting and so on. Many groups run community seed-banks, which aim to decrease the cost of hybrid agricultural seed by paying for the certification of a couple of farmers to produce seeds with permission from patent holders. Seed-banks store the seed to be distributed the following season, and all members of the group share their harvest with the seed-producing farmer in return. In many areas, groups have contributed to building community facilities (generally a meeting hall), under the direction of the NGO.

There is no doubt that these activities inspire hope and an aspiration for a better future amongst community members, as shown above. But there are several reasons to problematise their capacity to make meaningful changes to frameworks of opportunity or for counter-hegemonic potential. Seed-banks fail to provide sufficient seed for a subsistence harvest for most farmers/households, primarily because those households are not able to contribute enough in the first place. They do create a limited safety net, which guarantees some access to seed, but they also perpetuate the relationship of exploitative dependence with the seed corporation. Training sessions are aimed at constructing successful community groups and civil society, and thus focus on skills that are only necessary in the context of NGO formation and operation. It is reflective of the current socio-economic status of remote Zambian communities that NGOs are a necessary feature of life. But NGOs, funded as they are through complex motivations of distant observers, are both a symbol of and a stabiliser to current community conditions. Many studies have shown that formalised African NGOs create a range of impacts at local scale, and many of these patterns are evident here. For example, many accounts identify that NGO action is largely commercialised and

120   *K. Treasure*

disconnected from the priorities of communities (Lewis and Opoku-Mensah 2006). Dill (2009), through a study in Tanzania, has identified that modern forms of civil society can bear little resemblance to the collective associations that built the reputation of civil society as grassroots, non-governmental representation for the people, as increasingly there is status and wealth involved in being part of a successful civil society actor. The notion of indigenous NGOs forming a 'comprador class' (Hearn 2007) is thus becoming increasingly well-established.

Moreover, income generation, while clearly a priority for community members, given their impoverished economic status and understanding of how to improve their access to essential resources, contributes to the further embedding of inequalities. Illustrating this, informal communications with market traders in Sinalulongwe village market revealed that Coca-Cola sells for the same price as the locally produced traditional maize drink with the maize producers making only a scant profit. Thus local production, and thereby also the potential for reliable forms of income, is constrained by the competition of imported goods rather than by a lack of capacity to produce.

Bolstering the income generating capacity in the community can reduce the immediate and direct effects of poverty. However, as one interviewee noted,

> Incomes are better now, there is just enough food with the group – but not all the children can go to school. That is still too much money for us.
> (Chairperson, Kabanda group, November 2009)

Thus group members remain within a system that determines a significant level of poverty for communities disadvantaged within the dominant global framework of power relations. This is incompatible with a fundamental challenge to existing discourses, as the creation of community groups itself was a construction of this same discursive framework. Emanating from the international development regime, the objectives of this project required approval by that same hegemonic logic in order to operate. Despite the emphasis on 'self-realisation', 'self-reliance' and localism, 'in practice the reverse happens, as local civil society sectors play an interstitial role connecting national and international development priorities to local places' (Mercer and Green 2012: 7).

It is also noted by Mercer and Green that needs identified as most pressing in rural communities 'were not taken up by the local civil society sector, because they do not chime with the kinds of activities that development donors are willing to fund, at least not through the civil society sector' (2012: 7). Their specification that funding would not come from the civil society sector is undoubtedly true, but Mercer and Green fail to note that all sectors of donor funding remain exclusionary to 'local' African NGOs for a variety of reasons. In order to compete effectively for funding, it has been found that organisations need to be professional and accessible with an urban base (Scholte 2012: 191). This trend is also noted in the sporadic nature of activity by African local NGOs, as they are unable to function without being successful in the international competition for funding. Some authors have concluded that '[r]ather than thinking of

Connecting state, citizen and society? 121

CSOs as permanent organisations, it is more accurate to think of them as dormant organisations which come to life periodically when they win donor funds for a specific project' (Mercer and Green 2012: 5).

These factors point to the relative powerlessness of constructed community-based organisations in the global development regime, as has been highlighted in the general relationship between Africa and international institutions (Payne 2010; Scholte 2012). This highlights two extreme flaws in the assumption that rural community-based organisations can represent themselves and provide advocacy effectively. Not only is there a challenge to match genuinely self-generated priorities with those generated externally at global scale, but there are also significant barriers to their effective participation as competitive actors in this arena. Such conclusions are borne out by a significant number of studies which show that while donor funded civil society organisations may have capacity in affecting immediate conditions in African communities, there is little evidence that they are effecting the kind of changes to governance implied by the good governance discourse described above. Moreover, if African NGOs are successful in gaining funding from the international development regime it is only by adjusting their priorities, approaches and ethics to fit with existing hegemonic structures, in opposition both to any counter-hegemonic potential and the very understanding of 'local'. Such exclusion from effective power at international scale, and the lack of potential for the types of local action promoted to change frameworks of opportunity, means that civil society actors formed through these processes do not hold potential to fulfil the role of civil society with emancipatory potential.

Disengagement from 'legitimate' power networks

The analysis above leaves one important issue unexplored: what role do these actors play in improving the national discourses of democratic culture, as implied by international donors and the good governance agenda? This is an important angle of analysis, because it problematises the discourse which constructs 'local' civil society actors as significant in the deepening of liberal democratic culture. Indeed, dominant Western understandings of the Westphalian state system imply that there is a legitimate demand for all citizens to be represented in, or at least not excluded from, the generation of state policy, discourses and culture. Thus, access to 'legitimate' power for citizens within states is deemed to be at state level. According to the dominant discourse then, effective civil society has two pathways. One dictates a need to build stronger relations, sometimes symbolised as a 'bridge' between state and citizens in order for citizens to claim their legitimate voice. The other, deemed necessary where a state is unresponsive to citizens, is through dissent and struggle against state policies and injustices. These two perspectives are discussed below, with reference to the effectiveness of the actors studied to fulfil these roles.

The notion of civil society as a 'bridge' between African governments and citizens is problematic in the current context as the types of organisations formed are not incentivised to engage with the state in any way. They are excluded from

122　*K. Treasure*

discussion with formal national associations, largely on the same basis as is outlined above with reference to exclusion from the international development regime. Many such organisations exist in Zambia, and the argument here is not meant to suggest that there can be no influence on the state by NGOs. However, the focus on broadly based national participation in donor-supported development strategies, particularly Poverty Reduction Strategy Papers, has tended to be analysed as relatively ineffective at creating more broadly based country ownership (Gould 2005). Thus, despite an increasing rhetorical focus on incorporating 'local' values into development assistance, the local community groups studied here do not, and arguably cannot, contribute effectively either to international discourses of development which affect the state, nor directly to the state itself.

Indeed, the notion of civil society as a 'bridge' relies on the understanding that the state has a duty to be responsive to citizens. But this constitutes a severe misunderstanding of the neo-patrimonial logic of the Zambian state. Access to power in Zambia, as across many southern African states, largely depends on access to national resources to maintain political loyalties. In 2011, the Patriotic Front won the election ahead of the Movement for Multiparty Democracy which had ruled the country since 1991. Despite this change in political leadership there remains strong evidence to support portrayal of the state as resource seeking, clientelistic and neo-patrimonial. Indeed, the historical and external construction of the state increases the likelihood of a continuation of these same patterns. This is not so much in terms of a stagnant structural analysis of the state, more in recognition of the relative capacity of both the state and rural communities. Rural communities are excluded by low levels of education and infrastructure, which deter possibilities for national political engagement. The Zambian state is also excluded from possibilities of effective engagement to some extent, being dependent on externally targeted donor interventions for the ordering of development objectives (Moyo 2009) and on the false construction of incentives and policy outcomes through foreign aid exchanges (Wrong 2009). If the state is unresponsive to engagement, then increasing pluralism requires dissent. But the 'pluralist paradox' (Rakner 2001) has demonstrated that under conditions of multi-party democracy, opposition is effectively silenced unless it constitutes formal political competition. The barriers to effective engagement outlined above equally apply to mounting effective opposition in formal terms.

This said, Gramscian notions of dissent refer rather to strategies of extraversion, non-compliance or dislocation from existing structures of power, thus essentially implying a disengagement from dominant frameworks of power. While in conventional analysis such frameworks are set by the state, it has been established earlier that this is not the case for the communities studied, whose opportunities are more practically framed by the global market and the global development regime. It is these frameworks of power that largely dictate access to essential resources and services as well as the construction of hegemonic discourses. Therefore, effective dissent for counter-hegemonic potential requires resistance to these structures, but the strategies used by community groups do not tend to offer such possibilities. By creating coping strategies within the terms

Connecting state, citizen and society? 123

of engagement between communities and the global market, in seed banks for example, community groups are arguably stabilising existing inequalities and this is noted by community members.

> The best thing ... is that we can get seed. But how can I feed my family with only five bags of seed? I have seven children and we can farm, but five bags is nothing.
>
> (Member, Kamucheba Group, October 2009)

A similar argument can be made for the ineffectiveness of income-generation as constituting dissent to dominant frameworks, notwithstanding its value as short-term relief for economically impoverished households. The pursuit of skills which are largely inapplicable within local communities must, by definition, be motivated by the engagement with external discourses of power. Indeed, they must be directed at increasing the embedded nature of this discursive framework and advancing competitiveness within it, and therefore cannot be considered as resistance. As well as temporarily resisting the conditions of local impoverishment for some community members, such actions can be seen to deter the likelihood of demands for more radical, perhaps counter-hegemonic, change. These relations can also be seen to hinder progress for political development at national level, where a claim to legitimate power as citizens is strongest.

Conclusion: community-based civil society in southern Africa

Community groups in Zambia, and the associations derived from them, are failing to fulfil the role of civil society ascribed to them both by dominant development narratives and the Gramscian vision of counter-hegemonic potential. In the first place, these groups cannot be seen to improve the democratic culture or system. They operate largely without reference to the state, providing neither a 'bridge' between government and citizens, nor a credible platform for dissent to state policies. In the second place, activities promoted by groups embrace the neoliberal doctrine, in order to be successful at gaining funds from international sources, by adapting to the structural prerogatives presented. The notion of such groups as community-based is particularly problematic. Due to the dominance of the hegemonic discourse, they respond as sensitively, if not more so, to externally generated global development discourses than to 'local' concerns.

Many of the relationships identified in this analysis have been identified elsewhere, often with reference to more formal organisations. The present analysis provides a deeper understanding of the politics of 'community-based' civil society organisations in rural southern Africa. This research and the conclusions drawn here are important because of the possibility of 'doing more harm than good' (Anderson 1999) despite the rhetoric of assistance. Throughout this analysis it has been noted that the inclusion of communities, through civil society, in global discourses may only offer further entrenchment of current global inequalities. This phenomenon has been identified elsewhere in the scholarship on civil society in Africa. Hearn has concluded that donors use formal '"civil society" as a vehicle for stabilising the existing order' (2001: 52), by narrowing the focus of funds available to include only recognised tasks and priorities. Additionally, it is noted that 'localism diverts attention from the structural causes of poverty and feeds into the belief that market-based globalisation can and should be harnessed to work for the poor' (Mohan 2002: 150). Elsewhere, Mercer finds that the 'focus on participation and good governance obscure a more covert and insidious expression of power which simultaneously empowers and normalises the actions of development partners' (2003:759), and as such is indeed the very antithesis of counter-hegemonic action. Such conclusions reinforce the arguments presented here and demonstrate that, despite the relief that community groups and other embodiments of local civil society actors may provide, if they are 'successful' according to mainstream doctrine then they must, albeit paradoxically, be working against prospects for self-realisation of development trajectories in remote African communities by reproducing, reinforcing and strengthening the very discourses which construct current global power inequalities.

References

Abrahamsen, R. (2000). *Disciplining Democracy: Development Discourse and Good Governance in Africa*. London, Zed Books.

Anderson, M. (1999). *Do No Harm: How Aid Can Support Peace or War*. London, Lynne Reinner Publishers.

Anderson, P. (1983). *Imagined Communities: Reflections on the Origins and Spread of Nationalism*. London, Verso.

Bayart, J.-F. (1986). 'Civil Society in Africa', in P. Chabal. *Political Domination in Africa*. New York, Cambridge University Press.

Bratton, M. (1994). *Civil Society and Political Transition in Africa*. IDR Reports, Volume 11, Number 6. Institute for Development Research.

Chabal, P. and J.-P. Daloz (2005). *Africa Works: Disorder as Political Instrument*. Bloomington, IN, Indiana University Press.

Cox, R. (1999). 'Civil Society at the Turn of the Millenium: Prospects for an Alternative World Order'. *Review of International Studies* 25(1): 3–19.

Dill, B. (2009). 'The Paradoxes of Community-Based Participation in Dar es Salaam'. *Development and Change* 40(4): 717–743.

Erdmann, G. and U. Engel (2006). *Neopatrimonialism Revisisted: Beyond a Catch-All Concept*. Working Paper No. 16. Hamburg, GIGA (German Institute of Global and Area Studies).

Ferguson, J. (1990). *The Anti-Politics Machine: Development, Depoliticization and Bureaucratic Power in Lesotho*. Mineapolis, MN, University of Minnesota Press.

Ferguson, J. (2003). 'Stillborn Chrysalis: Reflections on the Fate of National Culture in Neo-Liberal Zambia'. *Global Networks* 3(3): 271–297.

Ferguson, J. (2006). *Global Shadows: Africa in the Neoliberal World Order*. Durham, NC, Duke University Press.

Fowler, A. (2012). 'Measuring Civil Society: Perspectives on Afro-centrism'. *Voluntas* 23: 5–25.

Gaynor, N. (2010). 'Between Citizenship and Clientship: The Politics of Particpatory Governance in Malawi'. *Journal of Southern African Studies* 36(4): 801–816.

Gould, J. (ed.) (2005). *The New Conditionality: The Politics of Poverty Reduction Strategies*. London, Zed Books.

Gramsci, A. (1971). *Selections from the Prison Notebooks of Antonio Gramsci*. Q. Hoare and G. N. Smith (eds). London, Lawrence and Wishart.

Gunnell, B. (2004). 'A Conspiracy of the Rich'. *New Statesman* 133: 27–28.

Habermas, J. (1979). *Communication and the Evolution of Society*. London, Heinemann Educational.

Habermas, J. (1984). *Theory of Communicative Action*. Volume One. London, Heinemann Education.

Habermas, J. (1987). *Theory of Communicative Action*. Volume Two. London, Polity Press.

Hearn, J. (2001). 'The 'Uses and Abuses' of Civil Society in Africa'. *Review of African Political Economy* 28(87): 43–53.

Hearn, J. (2007). 'African NGOs: The New Compradors?' *Development and Change* 38(6): 1095–1110.

Lewis, D. (2002). 'Civil Society in an African Context: Reflections on the Usefulness of a Concept'. *Development and Change* 33(4): 569–586.

Lewis, D. and P. Opoku-Mensah (2006). 'Moving Forward Research Agendas on International NGOs: Theory, Agency and Context'. *Journal of International Development* 18: 665–675.

Long, C. (2001). *Participation of the Poor in Development Initiatives: Taking Their Rightful Place*. London, Earthscan Publications.

Mamdani, M. (1996). 'Indirect Rule, Civil Society and Ethnicity: The African Dilemma'. *Social Justice* 23(1–2): 145–150.

Marcuse, H. (1972). *One Dimensional Man*. London, Abacus.

Mercer, C. (2003). 'Performing Partnership: Civil Society and the Illusions of Good Governance in Tanzania'. *Political Geography* 22(7): 741–763.

Mercer, C. and M. Green (2012). 'Making Civil Society Work: Contracting, Cosmopolitanism and Community Development in Rural Tanzania'. *Geoforum*, in press.

Mohan, G. (2002). 'The Disappointments of Civil Society: The Politics of NGO Intervention in Northern Ghana'. *Political Geography* 21(1): 125–154.

Mohan, G. and K. Stokke (2000). 'Participatory Development and Empowerment: The Dangers of Localism'. *Third World Quarterly* 21(2): 247–268.

Mosse, D. (2001). 'People's Knowledge, Participation and Patronage: Operations and Representations in Rural Development', in B. Cooke and U. Kothari. *Participation: The New Tyranny?* London, Zed Books.

Moyo, D. (2009). *Dead Aid: Why Aid is Not Working and How There is Another Way for Africa*. London, Penguin Books.

Nordic Africa Institute (2009). *The Impact of the Common Agricultural Policy (CAP) Reform on Africa-EU Trade in Food and Agricultural Products*. Special issue on the EU Africa Partnership Strategy. Available at: www.nai.uu.se/publications/series/notes/978-91-7106-653-4.pdf.

Payne, A. (2010). 'How Many Gs are there in "Global Governance" after the Crisis? The Perspectives of the "Marginal Majority" of the World's States'. *International Affairs* 86(3): 729–740.

Rahman, M. A. (1995). 'Participatory Development: Towards Liberation or Co-optation?', in G. Craig and M. Mayo. *Community Empowerment: A Reader in Participation and Development*. London, Zed Books.

126   K. Treasure

Rakner, L. (2001). 'The Pluralist Paradox: The Decline of Economic Interest Groups in Zambia in the 1990s'. *Development and Change* 32: 521–543.

Rakner, L. (2003). *Political and Economic Liberalisation in Zambia 1991–2001*. Uppsala, Sweden, Nordiska Afrikainstitutet.

Roy, I. (2008). 'Civil Society and Good Governance: (Re-)Conceptualizing the Interface'. *World Development* 36(4): 677–705.

Scholte, J. A. (2012). 'A More Inclusive Global Governance? The IMF and Civil Society in Africa'. *Global Governance* 18(2): 185–206.

Shiva, V. (2001). 'The World Trade Organisation and Developing World Agriculture', in E. Goldsmith and J. Mander. *The Case against the Global Economy and for a Turn towards Localisation*. London, Earthscan Publications.

Simon, D., W. Van Spengen, C. Dixon and A. Narman (eds) (1995). *Structurally Adjusted Africa: Poverty, Debt and Basic Needs*. London, Pluto Press.

Simon, D. J. (2005). 'Democracy Unrealized: Zambia's Third Republic under Frederick Chiluba', in L. A. Villalón and P. VonDoepp. *The Fate of Africa's Democratic Experiments: Elites and Institutions*. Bloomington, IN, Indiana University Press.

Speer, J. (2012). 'Participatory Governance Reform: A Good Strategy for Increasing Government Responsiveness and Improving Public Services?'. *World Development* 40(12): 2379–2398.

Taylor, I. and P. D. Williams (2008). 'Political Culture, State Elites and Regional Security in West Africa'. *Journal of Contemporary African Studies* 26(2): 137–149.

Tocqueville, A. de (1835). *Democracy in America*. Republished in 2003. London, Penguin Books.

World Bank (2010). Zambia – Impact Assessment of the Fertilizer Support Program: Analysis of Effectiveness and Efficiency. Available at: https://openknowledge.worldbank.org/handle/10986/2878.

Wrong, M. (2009). *It's Our Turn to Eat: The Story of a Kenyan Whistle Blower*. London, Fourth Estate.

Xu, Z., Z. Guan, T. S. Jayne and J. R. Black (2009). 'Factors Influencing the Profitability of Fertilizer Use on Maize in Zambia'. *Agricultural Economics* 40(4): 437–446.

Part III

Resistance and the everyday

7 Informality and the spaces of civil society in post-apartheid Johannesburg

Alex Wafer

Introduction

When, in late 1999, the City of Johannesburg ordered the forced removal of informal street traders from the area surrounding what is now the Metro Mall traders market in order to facilitate construction of the new municipal market, it precipitated violent (albeit short-lived) protests between informal traders and Metro police (Mngoma 2010; Skinner 2008; Tissington 2009). As a result of the removals, many traders lost their livelihoods and were forced to the city's precarious peripheries. These protests came at the end of a year of protracted protests between traders and police in response to the increased by-law enforcement against informal trading as part of a policy to relocate traders into purpose-built markets (see Johannesburg Transitional Municipal Council 1995). A number of socio-economic rights organisations in Johannesburg have criticised the municipality over the objectives and enforcement of the *informal trade* policy (see Cohen 2010; Peberdy and Rogerson 2003; Tissington 2009) and anyway the deadline has been constantly shifted back by the municipality (see Johannesburg Metro Council 2007). Yet other than the voices from what might be termed *formal* civil-society organisations (notably the Centre for Applied Legal Studies, the Socio-economic Rights Institute and the Inner City Resource Centre), there is very little organisational capacity among street traders, and no broad coalition has emerged. This is despite the high-profile emergence of what have been termed the *service delivery* protests during the same period (Ballard *et al.* 2006), when social movement organisations such as the Soweto Electricity Crisis Committee (SECC) gained national and even international profile for their opposition to the so-called 'neoliberal' restructuring of municipal government in 1999 (see Bond 2001; Ngwane 2003; Sparks 2001). In the decade since, there have been dozens of service delivery protests every year across the city (Death 2010); by comparison, informal traders in Johannesburg have been (and remain) notoriously fragmented (Motala 2002; Tissington 2009; Wafer 2010).

Carl Death (2010), reflecting on the emergence of the service delivery protests in particular, suggests that the South African state's repression of protest traces a broader reorientation of the spatiality of state power, congruent no longer (if ever) with sovereign territoriality but rather with discontinuous coalescences of

130   *A. Wafer*

state annunciation. Death speaks of an emergent geography of power as 'fractured and overlapping spaces of highly governed localities and international institutions, and increasingly ungovernable hinterlands, [forming] complex and heterogeneous networks and spaces of rule' (2010: 557). Death's conceptual rubric closely parallels Legg's (2007) reference to the 'tight and intense archipelago of institutions [of power]' in colonial Delhi (2007: 23). I suggest that both conceptualisations re-figure in more spatial terms Chatterjee's (2001) distinction between *civil* and *political* society, and are broadly consistent with an emergent literature on the *anthropology of the state*, in which state power is understood as only one, contingent, effect of social order (see Agrawal 2005; Corbridge 2005; Gupta 1995; Secor 2007 among others). State power, in this rubric, functions through the constitution of spaces (and moments) where particular configurations of bodies are constituted as citizens, while others remain excluded.

This chapter proceeds from such a rubric, taking seriously the assertion that the geography (and temporality) of state power after apartheid functions through a series of 'fractured and overlapping' coalescences. Using the lens of the Metro Mall market facility – considered here as one such coalescence of state power – the chapter argues that the encounter between fractured archipelago and 'ungovernable hinterlands' is not necessarily one of conflict but rather of (mis) recognition. I argue that the Metro Mall represents not simply an attempt to discipline urban space, but to deliberately implicate informal traders into a relationship with the post-apartheid state – that is, into *civil* society. In other words, in the context of constructing a postcolonial (and post-apartheid) state project, *civil* society is not always (intentionally) an exclusionary space, but one which must be actively constituted through the everyday practices of the institutions of state (see Agrawal 2005). While it is important to recognise the often violent processes of dispossession that accompany the construction of state spaces such as the Metro Mall, it is equally important to be attentive to the modes of citizenship that might emerge in this process.

Informality and apartheid urban order

Informal trading in Johannesburg, as in many other cities in the global South (Cross 1998; Hunt 2009), has long been associated with urban disorder and anxiety. Interventions by the municipality to control and manage informal street trading date as far back as the proclamation of the city in 1886, but was particularly pursued with the designation of land to establish Market Square (now Library Gardens) in the heart of the newly established settlement in 1893 (Beavon 2004). Initially, Market Square was designated as a space of free trade to all race groups, but increasing restrictions on the movements and economic practices of black South Africans meant that the market became dominated by white traders. Black market traders were pushed into more survivalist trade on the peripheries of the market and in the city streets surrounding Market Square. Nevertheless, trading formed an important aspect of urban livelihood for black

Informality and the spaces of civil society   131

South Africans in the early years of the gold-rush, contributing to the development of a significant black urban culture (Coplan 1994).

Colonial anxieties about congestion, poor hygiene and the presence of native bodies in the colonial city began to influence municipal planning and governance in the early twentieth century. In 1910 a new municipal market was planned for the neighbourhood of Newtown, on what was then the periphery of the City of Johannesburg – it was completed and opened in 1913 (Beavon 2004). The new market provided a much larger trading area, and improved transport links into and out of the rapidly growing city, but Beavon also suggests that the rationalities of efficiency must not distract from the other ambitions clearly at stake in the location of the new market. The Newtown neighbourhood was the site of some existing industrial activity at the time, including a tannery and other small textile industries, but importantly the area also housed a large multiracial community of working-class and poor families – most of whom were connected to either the tannery, low-paid service work in the city or petty trade in the municipal market. The new municipal market formed part of a major 'slum clearance' project of the neighbourhood, and marked the explicit implication of town planning ordinances and routine urban management in achieving a racially motivated urban governance agenda (Beavon 2004).

This implication of town planning and ordinances was not uncommon as a practice in colonial cities. Stephen Legg (2007) has demonstrated how urban planning in colonial India was implicated into the way in which native and colonial populations were governed. However, in the context of South Africa, it was also implicated into the twin projects of Afrikaner nationalism and industrial development (Posel 1991), leading to a very particular spatial configuration. In 1923 the Native (Black) Urban Areas Act was introduced in South Africa, which effectively abolished freehold rights for black South Africans and enforced their non-permanent residence in urban areas. The Act did permit for a limited amount of non-permanent informal street and market trading in the city, for which a permit was required, and this became one way through which unemployed black people could maintain a tenuous livelihood in the city without having to prove employment in mining or industry (Beavon 2004). And despite this and other severe restrictions designed to limit the licensing of black traders, a small community of black traders who operated legally developed within the new Johannesburg municipal market.

The apartheid municipality gradually succeeded in pushing all but a small pocket of informal black traders out of the central city in the pursuit of the apartheid dream of racially homogeneous cities. The use of town planning ordinances to control and manage the movements of designated groups of people in the city was evident again in 1972, when the municipality once again made the decision to move the Johannesburg Market away from the now-congested neighbourhood of Newtown (Gaule 2005). The Newtown site was closed down, and a wholesale market was planned for a site several kilometres south of the inner city. A new state-of-the-art market and distribution facility, based closely on the recently relocated New Covent Garden market in London, was opened in September 1974

132   A. Wafer

(Gaule 2005). Like other apartheid era infrastructure projects, the new market on the outskirts of the city served also to complement the segregationist rationality. The closure of the old market served as an effective strategy of foreclosing the severely limited opportunities at independent (i.e. non-contract labour) urban livelihoods for black South Africans, destroyed an emerging petty-bourgeoisie among black market traders, and simultaneously solidified the monopoly of the already powerful (and exclusively white) wholesale agents, who effectively control prices inside the market (Beavon 2004). Moreover, the location of the new Johannesburg Fresh Produce Market on disused industrial land to the south of the central city complemented the municipality's policy of building buffer-zones between designated white and designated black group areas (Beavon 2004).

The apartheid apparatus was of course never able to completely realise the dream of racial separation, and even at its height there existed incursions of black bodies into the white city – both tolerated and illicit. The figure of the domestic servant, for example, has always represented an anomaly in the apartheid ontology (Cock 1980), while high-density inner-city neighbourhoods such as Hillbrow were notoriously spaces where people could 'break the colour bar' (i.e. socialise outside of their race group) (Morris 1999). Already by the late 1980s a group of informal traders had established themselves around the designated 'black' entrance to the commuter railway station near Joubert Park in central Johannesburg, despite by-law restrictions on informal trading in the city (claims based on over 100 interviews with traders outside Park Station, 2006–2009). Nevertheless, it remained an activity largely confined to the peripheries and interstices of the city – regarded by authorities as the incursion of traditional practices into the white city (Beavon 2004). In fact, the political and economic significance of informal trading in the modern history of Johannesburg parallels the role of informal economic activities in other African cities (Hart 1973; Meagher 1990). In South Africa, as in other parts of the continent, informal trade was an important mechanism through which labour migrants were able to maintain a social, and therefore also a political, presence in the city.

Hart's (1973) seminal study on what he termed the *informal economy* in Ghana in the late 1960s, and later developments on this thesis (see Moser 1978), argue variously that informal urban activities: (a) were not in fact unproductive, but served to sustain the livelihoods of the (structurally) unemployed in urban areas; and (b) in so doing, these informal activities effectively 'subsidised' the formal economy, through lowering wage demands in the formal sector. Although informal economic activities (especially among the black population) were severely curtailed under apartheid, these practices sustained urban livelihoods during the period of falling real wages and rising unemployment in the late 1970s and 1980s (Gelb 1987). The political significance of this was that in the face of rising economic hardship, black South Africans were nevertheless able to contest apartheid rule from an urban base, making demands for urban services, and forcing the collapse of what has been termed the apartheid city, i.e. the litany of local ordinances and by-laws that together maintained urban segregation (Mabin 1992; Maylam 1995; Robinson 1992; Smith 1992; Tomlinson 1999).

The (spatial) governance of informality

An increasingly embattled apartheid state, needing to stem falling employment and real wages (which hit poor black South African households hardest), and mounting political violence in designated black neighbourhoods, passed the 1991 Business Act (among a string of other attempts to reform what was regarded as *petty* apartheid). The Act deregulated informal trading by black South Africans in urban areas, a tacit acknowledgement of its ubiquity and importance in sustaining household livelihoods. What was already a de facto urban practice in the townships and the urban peripheries was reluctantly allowed to encroach into the privileged (white) parts of the city. The (white controlled) City of Johannesburg municipality was left largely immobilised. Traditionally dominated by a liberal English-speaking business elite who were at best grudgingly oppositional to the predominantly Afrikaans-speaking apartheid Nationalist Party, the municipality attempted to project an image of Johannesburg as a non-racial city (Bremner 2000), but they were nevertheless caught in a liberal-modernist vision of urban government (Maylam 1990; Reid 2005; Tomlinson 1999). Confronted by a new constituency of urban users making demands for inclusion into the city yet who regarded white authority as illegitimate, the municipality avoided either enforcing the exclusionary laws of apartheid, or developing policies for including new users and new practices into the everyday life of the city (Reid 2005).

The initial policy recommendation was to designate specific areas across the city for trading, and to eventually build local market spaces; this would be enforced through anti-trading ordinances in areas where trading was deemed to be undesirable. The formal (i.e. white) business community and major landowners in the central city, through a public-private urban management committee called the Central Johannesburg Partnership (CJP), had supported such a policy – although they insisted on behalf of the business community that the municipality should incur any costs associated with building and maintaining the facilities (CJP employee, personal interview, April 2009). As a result of both municipal indecision and business mistrust, aside from a covered street-market in Hoek Street – planned in 1992 but completed in 1995, a year after the ending of apartheid – the strategy of locating traders into purpose-built market facilities was not effectively implemented, until the policy was reviewed in 1999. Instead, the CJP increased pressure on the municipality to allow for the establishment of Business Improvement Districts (BID), a popular model for urban management in British and North American cities in the 1980s (Peyroux 2007). In 1993 the CJP established the first voluntary BID in the inner city, despite the lack of any legislative framework for such an initiative. The BID relied on voluntary contributions from businesses within its demarcated area. It had no legal right to enforce anti-trading by-laws in the area of its remit, but it did provide a private security presence on the streets, which discouraged traders from establishing in the controlled area.

These competing claims over the spaces of the city – a right to trade vs. a desire for clean, ordered spaces – suggests something of what O'Malley *et al.*

134   *A. Wafer*

(1997: 509) call the 'messy actuality of rule' in (post-)apartheid Johannesburg. The business lobby is well resourced and represents a significant constituency within the central city – even if the interests of the post-apartheid municipality and the formal business sector are not commensurate. The CJP has continued to aggressively lobby for legislation on BID initiatives, for example, and in 1997 the Gauteng Provincial Legislature passed legislation, albeit within the less business-oriented language of City Improvement District (CID) (Gauteng Provincial Act No. 12 of 1997). Although community participation and engagement are required, the legislation effectively provides the framework for local property and businesses owners to take on some of the functions of municipal management – although by-law enforcement remains the jurisdiction of the Johannesburg Metro Police Department (JMPD) (Peyroux 2007: 8).

In contrast to the highly vocal and resourceful formal business community, Lipietz (2004) and Beall *et al.* (2002) have illustrated how the process of establishing partnerships for urban development with other constituents in the inner city involve often protracted and opaque politics – individuals who are active community leaders may suddenly cease to be involved, or disappear, or build alliances that undermine municipal projects. Beall *et al.* (2002) show, for example, how a large-scale public investment project involved an ultimately failed process of trying to identify community leaders and committed community members, in a context of perpetual demographic shifts, xenophobic suspicions and opaque networks of association. In a context where the municipality has struggled to identify – let alone forge working partnerships with – community representatives, the business lobby has been well resourced and highly visible.

There are nevertheless significant contradictions between the ambitions of the municipality and the interests of the CJP. Since the ending of apartheid, the informal economy has increasingly been seen as an important site for state intervention to support and integrate what it terms the 'second economy'. This commitment is based on ideological grounds (the proactive role of a transformative developmental state) as well as pragmatic grounds (the state's inability in the current global economy to ensure full employment) (du Toit and Neves 2007). Therefore, while there has arguably been a tendency amongst the business community to withdraw from investment in the inner city in the face of informality and the perception that by-law enforcement is being ignored, the municipal authorities have had a rather more nuanced attitude towards the presence of informal practices and modes of association in the inner city. Although there is no doubt that the municipality has been broadly supportive of the business community's attempts at managing certain functions in the inner city that the municipality itself is unable or unwilling to prioritise, the municipality nevertheless has a different political and social agenda to the business community:

> The state has an obligation to become involved. Some traders spend two hours setting up their stalls in the morning and two hours again in the evening taking it down. Traders are not able to leverage collective buying, or to coordinate waste management and security on their own. It is

Informality and the spaces of civil society   135

a notoriously fragmented industry, with intense trade emerging around commuter points and little management of the way in which people have access to this trade (...) so the state has a role to play in this industry, and in making sure that people have an opportunity to improve their lives.

(Municipal employee in strategic management, personal interview,
May 2009)

Contrary to the perception of the CJP, that the municipality has been unwilling to confront informality, at least since the mid-1990s the Office of the Mayor has been deeply concerned with informality, and the municipality's responsibilities in this regard. The link between informal trade and poverty alleviation is seen as a particular policy imperative:

The informal economy is an economy of poverty. It traps people and they struggle to get beyond it. For this reason the state needs to intervene.

(Municipal employee in strategic management, personal interview,
March 2009)

Or again:

[The informal sector] is a dysfunctional industry. There is no proper entry and exit, no labour laws, no protection. It is also filled with a whole host of survivalist traders, and it shows the failures of the welfare system. The apartheid attitude towards the informal sector was simply to abandon the poor. But who says that simply deregulating informal trade is a way to deal with the poor in this city?

(Municipal employee in development planning, personal interview,
April 2009)

The last of the above quotes suggests that the municipality is unclear exactly of its own mandate regarding the informal sector. There is a clear understanding that informal traders are constituents of a post-apartheid civil society, but this is also articulated as a failure not only of the formal economy to provide employment, but of the welfare state to prevent people becoming mere *survivalists*. The *Informal Trade Policy for the GJTMC Area* (1995) articulated this general interpretation of the role and function of informality within the post-apartheid city:

Having taken into account the characteristics of informal traders in the metropolitan area, and knowing that the informal sector plays a vital role in the future, the greatest challenge to local government is to promote and effectively manage informal trading. In order for informal trading to be promoted, and included in the city in a holistic manner, necessary control (legislation) and management (policy) needs to be developed, and initiated and implemented by the council.

(Johannesburg Transitional Municipal Council 1995, Introduction)

136 *A. Wafer*

The policy maintained a commitment to a *modernist* urban management regime of 'control' and 'management', articulating a consensus in policy circles that the best way to intervene into the lives of informal traders was to construct them as entrepreneurs, and to encourage them to aspire for formalisation – something that new markets could begin to provide. As Götz and Simone suggest in their assessment of municipal policy:

> If a sufficient number of markets could be built, and if they could be organized in a way which provided street traders incentives to keep stalls within them, the prohibition on *unorganised* street trading proper could be enforced with more vigour in the knowledge that a satisfactory alternative had been arranged.
>
> (Götz and Simone 2003, *emphasis added*)

Such a policy emphasis was in line with contemporary thinking in other cities of the South with regards informality (Cross 1998; De Soto 1990; Hunt 2009), and there is a notable consolidation of the entrepreneurial imperative in later policy formulations. The 2002 document titled *Informal Trading Development Program* clearly emphasis the construction of traders as entrepreneurs:

> There are two key elements to the [informal trade] policy. First, the policy seeks to remove traders from the streets and place them into markets, which have appropriate infrastructure and services to remove the negative consequences of street trading [...]. The second policy element is to develop informal trading into a more dynamic and commercially viable activity for those who earn their livings from such activities. The first element of the policy supports the second. The policy should be viewed as a developmental policy and not merely as a set of regulations – i.e., a policy to develop street trading and informal traders into a new mercantile class who operate in a semi-formal retail environment.
>
> (Johannesburg Metro Council 2002: 8.5)

Rather than governing urban space through the exclusion of informal activities from urban spaces – as the apartheid regime and colonial authorities attempted to do – the post-apartheid municipality in Johannesburg has articulated in policy (if not always in practice) an attempt to *include* informal urban activities such as street trading into the everyday life of the city. This is partly pragmatic, but must also be understood within a particular history of black urban livelihoods, as well as the more contemporary political valance of the so-called *second economy*. In an era of neoliberal urban development (Bond 2000a; Brenner and Theodore 2002; Ferguson and Gupta 2002; Williams and Taylor 2000) small-scale entrepreneurs have emerged as one imagination of the democratic citizen in many post-colonial societies (Brown *et al.* 2010; Meagher 2011). The implications of this for urban space in Johannesburg has been the preoccupation in policy with building an infrastructure of market halls into which traders can not only

Informality and the spaces of civil society 137

relocate their bodies and wares, but also their aspirations and self-imaginations, i.e. into which they can envisage their own citizenship. It is to these urban spaces – and the not always comensurate self-imaginations of citizenship – that I now turn.

Constructing spaces of citizenship

In 1997 the Inner City Office (ICO), a strategic development body within the municipality, was tasked with designing and building the first phase of market halls in the city. Given the scale of investment required, it was assumed that the project could most effectively and sustainably be achieved in partnership with local business and community partners. This was partly a strategic decision, but it was also a result of the increasing emphasis within municipal and national government on governance 'through partnerships', an element of an increasing *neoliberalisation* of urban government in the late 1990s within the municipality (Bond 2000b; Didier *et al*. 2013; Murray 2011).

The ICO adopted what Götz and Simone (2003) have termed a 'project approach' to establishing the conditions for effective governance in the inner city. This approach was deliberately opposed to the BID strategy of establishing order through by-law enforcement and visible policing. The reason for opting for this project approach were three-fold: first, it was believed to be more likely to attract funding from government and private-sector sources for one-off prestige projects, rather than for ongoing urban-management expenses. Second, in a context where workable partnerships appeared difficult to identify and sustain, especially among very vulnerable and fragile communities, strategic interventions were seen as the best hope of galvanising a very diffuse and fragmented urban population (Götz and Simone 2003). As Götz and Simone state:

> [A]gainst a 10,000 strong street trading population with no other means of livelihood, and with limited manpower and resources, a governmentality based on the principles of isolate, designate, assign, and individually permit or prohibit is simply not viable, or appropriate. Another solution to the problems as interpreted was needed.

Third, while the project approach was partly an intentional strategy, it also came about through the lack of institutional commitment and long-term budgeting within the municipality:

> Building facilities such as Metro Mall is very expensive. Nevertheless, capital budget is easier to get hold of than operating budgets. This forces a project management kind of approach, and makes it difficult to sustain projects (...). The state is willing to put resources into a single intervention and then wants to step back.
>
> (Municipal employee in strategic management, personal interview,
May 2009)

138   *A. Wafer*

This project approach faced criticism from community activists and NGOs working amongst inner city communities, on the one hand, and from the business lobby, on the other. It was argued that such prestige interventions would address real concerns faced by traders, and would simply become high-profile and expensive experiments. On the other hand, it was argued that this approach would not take account of the need to reintroduce order into the city by reinforcing the enforcement of by-laws. Nevertheless, it was hoped that through the building of the Metro Mall something of the dynamics of the informal economy might be learned, and generating new opportunities for individuals and groups to become involved. In short, the ICO was working on the assumption that rather than proscribing and disciplining the actions of individuals (an improbably complex task), traders could be invited into an encounter with state order through the market itself, and could thereby be induced to enact new forms of citizenship (Götz and Simone 2003).

The question of entrepreneurs as one imagination of a post-apartheid citizen was here seen in relation to another iteration of the post-apartheid citizens as the recipient of welfare (see, for example, Chipkin 2007):

> We knew in the process that many traders might lose their livelihoods, but we needed people to diversify, to move beyond just selling fruits and vegetables. We needed the informal economy to be viable for people (...). We have to help some traders to grow beyond the survivalist mode, and we also have to help formal business grow and prosper (...). Of course, some traders will always be survivalist, and maybe they need to be contained elsewhere in the social infrastructure.
>
> (Former Inner City Office employee, personal interview, April 2009)

The municipality has attempted to actively construct the informal sector as an object of government – to implicate traders into a particular kind of relationship with institutions of state power. The nature of this relationship is of course a less than coherent articulation of appropriate urban citizenship, manifest somewhere between anxieties about business investment in the city, more traditional urban management concerns, and – arguably – genuine social and political commitment towards what has historically been an excluded urban constituency. The picture that I am hoping to paint is one in which the state project, rather than simply a violent or parasitical imposition onto a population, is projected into the often opaque and messy actuality of everyday life, in the hope that it will resonate and take hold. What I will do in the next part is to show just how the state project does resonate, and how individuals and groups have been able to use the Metro Mall to make alternative claims about citizenship to those that the municipality would imagine.

Reclaiming the state-citizen nexus

Cross (1998) writing about informal traders in Mexico, and Simone (2004) writing about informality and associational life in a number of African cities,

Informality and the spaces of civil society 139

separately suggest that the ability to remain invisible and illegible is a resource that many individuals within the informal and illicit parts of the urban economy rely upon. Indeed, this largely corresponds with Chatterjee's discussion about the internal dynamics of *political society*: that it often exists as peripheral and clandestine. As we have discussed above, this fact has been a source of frustration for many (often well intentioned) state officials attempting to intervene into the sector, and to recast informal traders as entrepreneurial citizens.

In the past decade there has been no shortage of organisations claiming to represent traders. The following organisations are only a few that have emerged at various moments and in particular parts of the inner city claiming different mandates: African Council of Hawkers and Informal Businesses (ACHIB), Faith, Gauteng Hawkers Association (GHA), South African National Traders Alliance (SANTRA), Johannesburg Well of Development and Training (JOWEDET). In addition, there are innumerable ethnic and religious associations and local networks of association and cooperation, but these have no official membership. In a review of survey data on informal traders in South African cities, Motala (2002) confirmed a general pattern: in the period that the Metro Mall was being built, only 15 per cent of traders belonged to any form of political or civil-society association that claimed to represent traders' interests.

> The membership of those organisations that claim to represent traders swells at different times, most often when some problem arises. If any organisation claims to represent traders you have to ask: when and where? Certainly it seems that representing informal traders in the 1990s was a quick way to make money. Generally the groups are splintered.
>
> (Inner City Office employee, personal interview, April 2009)

One of the more visible organisations operating among traders during the period of field research (2009–2012) was the South African National Traders Alliance (SANTRA): out of over a hundred traders operating in Wanderers Street, less than 30 claimed to have even heard of SANTRA. Those who knew the organisation were either ambivalent or generally supportive, although none claimed to be a member of the organisation. According to a SANTRA spokesperson:

> There is no representation among traders. In the Johannesburg Fresh Produce Market there is a retailers forum, but the informal traders are not represented, even though we are the biggest client. [At Metro Mall] there is no proper committee as such, and the market has never been based on engagement and participation.
>
> (SANTRA spokeperson, personal interview, June 2009)

The organisation struggles to secure consistent support among traders, and it was admitted that membership figures are uncertain. Moreover, while SANTRA has a broad commitment to supporting and empowering informal traders, the organisation is not easily cast as political platform for traders. Rather, it functions as

140   *A. Wafer*

something of a micro business development NGO, concerned with making the informal sector a platform for building viable businesses. However, SANTRA dismiss the close association between their aims and those of the municipality:

> The plan for the market (...) was an attempt to shrink the informal traders. It was implemented by people who are against the advancement of poor black people. All these markets have never produced one successful businessman.
> (SANTRA spokesperson, personal interview, February 2010)

SANTRA regards the municipality as overly reliant on by-laws and restrictions, while ignoring the need for access to capital. In this way SANTRA claims to be a viable vehicle through which to invest in the informal economy – something that formal banks and government loan schemes have failed to do.

Yet despite general criticism of the municipality regarding the building of Metro Mall, the discourse of democratic citizenship remains a powerful and resonant one. In early 1999, some months after the opening of the first municipal market in the city (largely seen as a prototype for the much larger and more ambitious Metro Mall), a group of traders operating inside the new market submitted a memorandum of demands to the municipality. The memorandum effectively requested that traders be allowed to manage the facility themselves, based on a democratically elected traders' committee. In addition, the traders' committee would facilitate the formation of a number of cooperative groups from among themselves, which would be commissioned to undertake the services such as security patrols and the cleaning of the market. In the memorandum, the traders accused the municipally appointed management company of being undemocratic and unresponsive to the needs of traders, signalled by the outsourcing of the cleaning and security contracts to private companies. Instead, the traders argued, the municipality should acknowledge the existing capacities and knowledge that exists among traders themselves, and allow for the self-regulation of what is a public facility.

This was a powerful statement, and given the lack of social and political cohesion among traders that had characterised the negotiations leading up to the opening of the market, suggests that at the very least the market had achieved one of its intended outcomes: the market place as a material space had created the context for traders to imagine themselves as a coherent part of civil society – albeit not in the terms the municipality had envisioned. Here was a group of traders who clearly felt newly empowered to represent themselves as the rightful occupants of the market. Of interest, also, was the fact that the traders included both foreigners and South Africans, suggesting that the new market facility had the potential to constitute new subjectivities that overcome the *ethnic enclaves* that predominate within the informal economy in the city more broadly. The new market had apparently produced an organised and legible population of empowered traders who were able to speak in a shared voice, using official channels, to make claims about managing their own market.

So why then, given this obvious success, did the Executive Committee of the municipal council deny the memorandum of demands on 15 June 1999? If the

Informality and the spaces of civil society 141

building of market places was intended to create a point of encounter between the state and traders in the absence of more viable community partnerships, then it may seem counter-productive for the council to reject an autonomous attempt to achieve just that. Perhaps understandably, the municipality was reluctant to relinquish control of such an expensive new infrastructural asset, especially in a context where an apparently coherent trader organisation had not long previously proved to be far more complex. Yet there were also no overtures towards discussions on the memorandum. It gives some indication, therefore, that what had begun as an experiment in intervening into the informality of the inner city has emerged more recently as a mechanism for managing the distribution and activities of informal traders. Despite the commitment on the part of the municipality to create the conditions for traders to imagine themselves differently, this self-imagination on the part of the traders who submitted the memorandum clearly did not match the image that the municipality had of them.

So how do traders imagine themselves? What kind of citizenship do they claim, and what do they expect from the state project? The experience of another traders' organisation – the Johannesburg Well of Development and Training (JOWEDET) – is perhaps instructive here. In fact, JOWEDET is less of a traders' organisation and could be more accurately described as a kind of savings scheme structured around a Christian worship-group. The members of JOWEDET are mostly drawn from a particular part of the city, incorporating a small group of predominantly elderly women traders who have known each other for several years, trading on the streets together. The origins of the organisation shift depending who one speaks to, but by one account began with the donation in the early 1990s of a small caravan to a trader to use as a stall to sell cooked food. Recognising the need to support one another, he and a group of trader-friends decided to form an organisation. More recently, JOWEDET had been offered the use of a piece of land by an unnamed benefactor. As in the case of the caravan, the benefactor is not a trader; in this case he or she is connected to the group through a supplier at the Johannesburg Fresh Produce Market (JFPM).

> We have just been given access to three plots in Zuidbekom, near Soweto. The owner is working for City Deep [i.e. JFPM] so he is offering these three plots to JOWEDET to plough. [The municipality] doesn't know about this yet. We want them to be amazed when we show them what we can do [on our own].
>
> (ML, trader in Pritchard Street, personal interview, May 2009)

Like SANTRA, JOWEDET is not an organisation that claims to represent the interest of traders in a context of political agitation. It has a limited membership, and appears reluctant to share their networks beyond the group itself. JOWEDET represents a vehicle for securing and managing particular scarce resources that can offer its members an advantage – in this case, access to apparently lucrative benefactors in the form of either a caravan or a piece of land. Unlike SANTRA,

142 *A. Wafer*

JOWEDET is perhaps less immersed in a mythology of citizenship located in the expectations of the developmental state. Rather, members of JOWEDET tended to express a sense of the failure of these expectations. JOWEDET can be partly understood as a response to the failure of securing resources elsewhere, particularly from the state. Underlining the narratives of inclusion and exclusion that define JOWEDET is a sense of failure from elsewhere, a sense of resignation that things will have to be done without outside assistance:

> Everybody is tired of [the municipality]. If they have a meeting they can have it on their own (...) JOWEDET organised a big flea-market with all big companies who supply traders, but [municipality] and etcetera passed the buck. They stole the idea. (...) when we wanted to launch JOWEDET, we booked a big hall. They were supposed to pay, but again they passed the buck. These people are all bad.
>
> (ML, trader in Pritchard Street, personal interview, May 2009)

Yet despite this sense of disenchantment, ML's earlier statement – 'we want them to be amazed' – still suggests that there is some desire for recognition from the municipality. Clearly, both SANTRA and JOWEDET suggest a general disaffection with the role of the state in managing the informal sector in the inner city. But they also both use a language of inclusion and citizenship. It is the substance of that citizenship that is at stake.

Conclusion

In this chapter I have attempted to argue that the market place has provided a material context for a range of encounters that contain what Simone (2004) refers to as multiplicity of subject positions. Encounters between the state and citizens also occur in this space, the manifestation of mutual imaginations of each other. Begoña Aretxaga (2003) has argued that in the imagination of ordinary people the state is split, existing in the same moment as both good and bad state: 'triggering an imaginary of the state in which desire and fear are entangled in a relation of misrecognition from which one cannot be extricated' (2003: 407). Secor (2007) argues in a similar manner that these two imaginations of the state are always present, the relationship of citizen with state caught between what she calls *longing* and *despair* – between the good state that provides justice and belonging and the bad state that is uncaring and inflicts arbitrary punishment. The experience of the everyday state, for Secor, is best described as one of recoiling desire. In the everyday desire for justice, care and belonging, ordinary people imagine and call upon the good state. And yet, in the face of corruption and indifference people recoil in the moment of subjection: 'recognizing ourselves as subjects of an abstract guilt that is compounded through protests of innocence' (Secor 2007: 48). Hansen (2001) also makes a similar distinction, when talking about the state in postcolonial India, between what he calls the sublime and the profane, which both exist within the image of the state. That is, the state contains both the expectations of a better life, as well as the real experience of corruption, patronage and illegibility.

I suggest that Aretxaga (2003), Hansen (2001) and Secor (2007) are all attempting to make sense of something not dissimilar to the articulations of citizenship emerging from associations such as SANTRA and JOWEDET. That is, while individuals resist the obligations and disciplining of the state, they nevertheless make claims for inclusion within that state. The political project to establish the democratic post-apartheid state remains an incredibly powerful narrative in the popular imagination of many South Africans (Chipkin 2007). It is nevertheless confronted by a fractured landscape of social movement protests, religious organisations, informal networks of association and – in wealthy areas of the city – the progressive privatisation of modes of governance (see Benit-Gbaffou 2006; Dirsuweit 2006). Within this milieu, the municipal and provincial governments have struggled to assert more traditional practices of urban governance (e.g. by-laws, zoning, service provision), but remain very effective in terms of large infrastructure spending (Götz and Simone 2003). In this article I have focused on one specific example of the 'mutual imaginations' of state and citizen in the physical manifestation of the Metro Mall municipal market in Johannesburg. I suggested that the Metro Mall represented an attempt by municipal policy-makers to not only control, but to actually comprehend the otherwise opaque networks of informal street traders. Through the Metro Mall the municipality has attempted to actively constitute new forms of entrepreneurial citizenship. While this has been contested, the actual material space of the new market has constituted a political space through which traders have – albeit largely unsuccessfully – made alternative claims for democratic post-apartheid citizenship, which do not always correspond with those offered by the institutions of state order. I suggest, finally, that the Metro Mall might be therefore seen as constituting a part of an emergent spatiality of power after apartheid – one where the boundaries between 'the spaces of highly governed localities' and the 'ungovernable hinterlands' fracture, overlap and blur into far more complex and heterogeneous networks and spaces than the literature on civil society might contain.

References

Agrawal, A. 2005. 'Environmentality'. *Current Anthropology* 46 (2): 161–190.

Aretxaga, Begoña. 2003. 'Maddening States'. *Annual Review of Anthropology* 32: 393–410.

Ballard, Richard, Adam Habib and Imraan Valodia. 2006. *Voices of Protest: Social Movements in Post-apartheid South Africa*. University of KwaZulu-Natal Press.

Beall, Jo, Owen Crankshaw and Susan Parnell. 2002. *Uniting a Divided City: Governance and Social Exclusion in Johannesburg*. Illustrated edition. Earthscan.

Beavon, Keith. 2004. *Johannesburg: The Making and Shaping of the City*. 1st edn. Unisa Press.

Benit-Gbaffou, C. 2006. 'Policing Johannesburg's Wealthy Neighbourhoods: The Uncertain "Partnerships" between Police, Communities and Private Security Companies'. *TRIALOG* 89: 21.

Bond, Patrick. 2000a. *Elite Transition: From Apartheid to Neoliberalism in South Africa*. Pluto Press.

Bond, Patrick. 2000b. *Cities of Gold, Townships of Coal: Essays on South Africa's New Urban Crisis*. Africa World Press.

Bond, Patrick. 2001. 'Durban's Conference of Polluters, Market Failure and Critic Failure'. *Ephemera* 12: 42.

Bremner, Lindsay J. 2000. 'Post-apartheid Urban Geography: A Case Study of Greater Johannesburg's Rapid Land Development Programme'. *Development Southern Africa* 17 (1) (March): 87–104. doi:10.1080/03768350050003433.

Brenner, Neil and Nik Theodore. 2002. 'Cities and the Geographies of Actually Existing Neoliberalism'. *Antipode* 34 (3): 349–379.

Brown, Alison, Michal Lyons and Ibrahima Dankoco. 2010. 'Street Traders and the Emerging Spaces for Urban Voice and Citizenship in African Cities'. *Urban Studies* 47 (3): 666–683.

Chatterjee, Partha. 2001. 'On Civil and Political Society in Postcolonial Democracies'. In *Civil Society: History and Possibilities*, edited by S. Kaviraj and S. Khilnani. Cambridge University Press.

Chipkin, Ivor. 2007. *Do South Africans Exist? Nationalism, Democracy and the Identity of the People*. Wits University Press.

Cock, Jacklyn. 1980. *Maids and Madams: A Study in the Politics of Exploitation*. Ravan Press.

Cohen, Jennifer. 2010. 'How the Global Economic Crisis Reaches Marginalised Workers: The Case of Street Traders in Johannesburg, South Africa'. *Gender and Development* 18 (2): 277–289.

Coplan, David B. 1994. *In the Time of Cannibals: The Word Music of South Africa's Basotho Migrants*. University of Chicago Press. http://books.google.co.za/books?hl=en&lr=&id=Onpkh4_ozQgC&oi=fnd&pg=PR9&dq=david+coplan+you+have+left+me&ots=XBaV6r90_u&sig=iIPjNTM05BqUsgXq9Jpmt8EmBrA.

Corbridge, Stuart. 2005. *Seeing the State: Governance and Governmentality in India*. Cambridge University Press.

Cross, John Christopher. 1998. *Informal Politics: Street Vendors and the State in Mexico City*. Stanford University Press.

De Soto, H. 1990. *The Other Path: The Invisible Revolution in the Third World*. Harpercollins.

Death, Carl. 2010. 'Troubles at the Top: South African Protests and the 2002 Johannesburg Summit'. *African Affairs* 109 (437): 555–574.

Didier, Sophie, Marianne Morange and Elisabeth Peyroux. 2013. 'The Adaptative Nature of Neoliberalism at the Local Scale: Fifteen Years of City Improvement Districts in Cape Town and Johannesburg'. *Antipode* 45 (1): 121–139.

Dirsuweit, T. 2006. 'Security, Citizenship and Governance: An Introduction'. *Urban Forum*, 17: 295–300.

Du Toit, A. and D. Neves. 2007. 'In Search of South Africa's "Second Economy"'. Transcending Two Economies: Renewed Debates in South African Political Economy, Special Issue of the University of South Africa Development Studies. *Journal Africanus, November 2007* 37 (2): 145.

Ferguson, J. and A. Gupta. 2002. 'Spatializing States: Toward an Ethnography of Neoliberal Governmentality'. *American Ethnologist* 29 (4): 981–1002.

Gaule, S. 2005. 'Alternating Currents of Power: From Colonial to Post-apartheid Spatial Patterns in NewTown, Johannesburg'. *Urban Studies* 42 (13): 2335.

Gelb, S. 1987. 'Making Sense of the Crisis'. *Transformation* 5: 33–50.

Götz, G. and AbdouMaliq Simone. 2003. 'On Belonging and Becoming in African Cities'. In *Emerging Johannesburg: Perspectives on the Postapartheid City*, Richard Tomlinson, R. Beauregard, Lindsay J. Bremner and X. Mangcu, Routledge, 123–147.

Gupta, A. 1995. 'Blurred Boundaries: The Discourse of Corruption, the Culture of Politics, and the Imagined State'. *American Ethnologist* 22 (2): 375–402.

Hansen, T. B. 2001. 'Governance and State Mythologies in Mumbai'. *States of Imagination: Ethnographic Explorations of the Postcolonial State*: 221–254.

Hart, K. 1973. 'Informal Income Opportunities and Urban Employment in Ghana'. *Journal of Modern African Studies* 11 (01): 61–89.

Hunt, Stacey. 2009. 'Citizenship's Place: The State's Creation of Public Space and Street Vendors' Culture of Informality in Bogotá, Colombia'. *Environment and Planning D: Society and Space* 27 (2): 331–351. doi:10.1068/d1806.

Johannesburg Metro Council. 2002. *Informal Trading Development Programme*.

Johannesburg Metro Council. 2007. *Informal Trading Policy for the City of Johannesburg*.

Johannesburg Transitional Municipal Council. 1995. *Informal Trading Policy for the GJTMC Area*.

Legg, Stephen. 2007. *Spaces of Colonialism: Delhi's Urban Governmentalities*. Wiley-Blackwell.

Lipietz, B. 2004. *'Muddling-Through': Urban Regeneration in Johannesburg's Inner City*. Network Association of European Researchers on Urbanisation in the South.

Mabin, Alan. 1992. 'Dispossession, Exploitation and Struggle: An Historical Overview of South African Urbanization'. *The Apartheid City and Beyond: Urbanization and Social Change in South Africa*: 12–24.

Maylam, Paul. 1990. 'The Rise and Decline of Urban Apartheid in South Africa'. *African Affairs* 89 (354): 57.

Maylam, Paul. 1995. 'Explaining the Apartheid City: 20 Years of South African Urban Historiography'. *Journal of Southern African Studies* 21 (1): 19–38.

Meagher, Kate. 1990. 'The Hidden Economy: Informal and Parallel Trade in Northwestern Uganda'. *Review of African Political Economy* 17 (47): 64–83. doi:10.1080/03056249008703848.

Meagher, Kate. 2011. 'Informal Economies and Urban Governance in Nigeria: Popular Empowerment or Political Exclusion?' *African Studies Review* 54 (2): 47–72.

Mngoma, Sbusiso. 2010. 'Public Participation in the Informal Trading By-laws Amendment: The Case of Johannesburg Inner City'. Available at: http://wiredspace.wits.ac.za/handle/10539/8467.

Morris, Alan. 1999. *Bleakness and Light: Inner City Transition in Hillbrow, Johannesburg*. Witwatersrand University Press.

Moser, C. O. N. 1978. 'Informal Sector or Petty Commodity Production: Dualism or Dependence in Urban Development?' *World Development* 6 (9–10): 1041–1064.

Motala, S. 2002. *Organizing in the Informal Economy: A Case Study of Street Trading in South Africa*. SEED Working Paper No. 36. Available at: www.ilo.org/empent/Publications/WCMS_117700/lang--en/index.htm

Murray, Martin J. 2011. *City of Extremes: The Spatial Politics of Johannesburg*. Duke University Press.

Ngwane, T. 2003. 'Sparks in the Township'. *New Left Review* (22): 37–56.

O'Malley, P., L. Weir and C. Shearing. 1997. 'Governmentality, Criticism, Politics'. *Economy and Society* 26: 501–517.

Peberdy, Sally and Christian M. Rogerson. 2003. 'South Africa: Creating New Spaces?' *Immigrant Entrepreneurs: Venturing Abroad in the Age of Globalization*: 79–100.

Peyroux, E. 2007. 'City Improvement Districts (CIDs) and the Production of Urban Space in Johannesburg: Urban Regeneration, Changing Forms of Governance and New Meaning of Places'. Paper for *4th International Conference on Private Urban Governance and Gated Communities*, Paris.

Posel, Deborah. 1991. *The Making of Apartheid, 1948–1961: Conflict and Compromise*. Clarendon Press.

Reid, G. 2005. 'Reframing Johannesburg'. In *City Edge: Case Studies in Contemporary Urbanism*, edited by E. R. Charlesworth: 154.

Robinson, Jennifer. 1992. 'Power, Space and the City: Historical Reflections on Apartheid and Postapartheid Urban Orders'. *The Apartheid City and Beyond: Urbanization and Social Change in South Africa*, Routledge: 292–302.

Rogerson, C. M. 1999. 'Local Economic Development and Urban Poverty Alleviation: The Experience of Post-apartheid South Africa'. *Habitat International* 23 (4): 511–534.

Secor, Anna J. 2007. 'Between Longing and Despair: State, Space, and Subjectivity in Turkey'. *Environment and Planning D: Society and Space* 25 (1): 33–52. doi:10.1068/d0605.

Simone, AbdouMaliq. 2004. 'People as Infrastructure: Intersecting Fragments in Johannesburg'. *Public Culture* 16 (3): 407.

Skinner, Caroline. 2008. 'The Struggle for the Streets: Processes of Exclusion and Inclusion of Street Traders in Durban, South Africa'. *Development Southern Africa* 25 (2): 227–242.

Smith, David Marshall. 1992. *The Apartheid City and Beyond: Urbanization and Social Change in South Africa*. Routledge.

Sparks, Stephen. 2001. 'New Turks and Old Turks: The Historiographical Legacies of South African Social History'. *Studies* 27: 613–625.

Tissington, Kate. 2009. 'The Business of Survival: Informal Trading in Inner City Johannesburg'. Johannesburg: Centre for Applied Legal Studies.

Tomlinson, Richard. 1999. 'Ten Years in the Making'. *Urban Forum* 10: 1–39.

Wafer, Alex. 2010. 'Urban Governance, Informal Traders and the World Cup in Johannesburg'. In *Megaevent und Stadtentwicklung im Globalen Süden. Die Fußballweltmeisterschaft 2010 und ihre Impulse für Südafrika*: 230–243.

Williams, P. and I. Taylor. 2000. 'Neoliberalism and the Political Economy of the "new" South Africa'. *New Political Economy* 5 (1): 21–40.

8 Citizenship, contested belonging and 'civil society' as vernacular architecture

Morten Bøås

Introduction

Increasingly, the twentieth-century understanding of liberal citizenship is in crisis as people all over the world debate who belongs and who does not (see Weber 2008; Geschiere 2009; Bøås and Dunn 2013).[1] At every corner of the globe there is currently a sense of urgency, even nervousness and anxiety, connected to such conversations, but its most violent ramifications are first and foremost felt in fragile states and circumstances where the process of state-building and nation-building is incomplete or dysfunctional; there is little if any consensus on the composition of the polity, and social contracts between the governing body and those being governed are if not completely absent at the very least rapidly losing legitimacy. In such places, the outcome of such debates at times leads to social dramas pitting different groups against each other in 'wars on who is who' (see Marshall-Fratani 2006). Some violent, others latent, but nonetheless all with the capacity to transform social relations between different groups of people from cordial and collaborative to tense, suspicious and conflictual.

The question is therefore what this implies for our approach and understanding of civil society. Is it still a viable vehicle for peace and reconciliation in conflict-torn countries or has it been transformed into a 'vernacular architecture' that only embodies and facilitates perceptions of others as strangers, as *allogenes* without full rights to citizenship, be it in the state or in local communities?

Civil society as 'vernacular architecture' is therefore an organisational form of collective action that reflects an environment of ontological uncertainty and nervousness, bordering on pure social angst (see Bøås and Dunn 2013), born out of what Thomas Blom Hansen (2001: 2) depicts as the *paradox of identity*, that 'no identity and no imputed property of a place can ever be self-evident or stable. There are always multiple meanings and many narratives.' This is the case for all types of social organisation, but as Geschiere (2009) rightly points out, this uncertainty is currently linked to the inherent tension between the nation-state and global flows of capital and finance and how vulnerable they leave the already most fragile. The question is, therefore, if civil society under such circumstances can fulfil its assumed historical mission as an organisational

148   *M. Bøås*

form that combines autonomy from the state with its ability to create the bonds of trust and friendship that the concept's origin in European Enlightenment assumes?

This is undoubtedly a huge research agenda and thus not a question a chapter can aim to answer in full. Rather, my objective is much more modest, as it is to start raising some questions that must be discussed as several African countries with seemingly ever increasing passion discuss issues concerning belonging and identity, and thereby also the question of what it takes and means to be a citizen. This is of crucial importance as in its bare essence a citizen is just a member of a state. The ideas that we currently draw upon concerning civility and civic duties emerged as particular products of not only the European Enlightenment at large, but more specifically the historical transformations that created bourgeois European society.

It was this *Bürgerliche Gesellschaft* that created a space which made horizontal linkages in society not only possible, but also useful (see Turner 2008), and which in the words of Alexander (2006) enables a distinction between non-civil institutions (e.g. state, religion, family and community) that are particularistic and a civil society that is universalistic and societal. Without the latter, says Alexander (2008: 8), 'competition between rational actors in the state may well destroy political life through endless interpersonal conflict', thus bringing about an enclavisation of society that if it becomes too dominant will render the whole concept of national citizenship completely meaningless. This is partly, but only partly, what has happened in African countries as diverse as Côte d'Ivoire, Democratic Republic of the Congo (DRC) and Liberia.

By utilising three case studies that concern countries and conflicts generally seen as not having much in common, the chapter also aims to underscore that the commonalities that emerge when we approach them through this set of analytical lenses reveals that the basis of conflict revolves around issues concerning the enormous challenge of creating a national citizenship when its very essence and meaning remains undefined. This is very much the case for the conflicts in Liberia, Eastern DRC and Côte d'Ivoire. Their contemporary history is a 'modern history of violence', as even though they started at different times and had different triggers they were all concerned with the composition of their respective polities: who is a citizen and who is not (see Ellis 1998; Mamdani 2001; McGovern 2011). Integral to this history is the issue of access to the state and thereby state resources. The main point being that citizenship, even if it in itself does not secure this type of access, it at the very least allows those with this status a legitimate entry to the competition for state resources broadly defined (Mamdani 2002). There is therefore a direct link between contested citizenship and access rights issues. This chapter will therefore show how localised identity narratives under certain circumstances destroy as well as reformulate national identities and that insight from ethnographic work on autochthony issues can help us understand the contested space of 'civil society' in a broad range of African countries. This will be achieved through an emphasis on the formal and informal institutions that seek to regulate access to land. Here, they come in the form of the Liberian *stranger-father* institution, the Ivorian *tutorat* institution and Congolese law and nongovernmental organisations (NGOs). Each and every one is a manifestation of a vernacular architecture of civil society.

However, even if civil society of a more vernacular nature may be growing in importance, horizontal linkages and bonds of trust, friendship and solidarity beyond the immediate in-group is still not only possible, but also completely necessary for the preservation of the 'self'. It is therefore not the argument of this chapter that this development automatically leads to the destruction of political life. However, if a 'civil society' is emerging that is something other than what European history tells us, then that must be acknowledged. As such, this chapter will therefore also talk to important themes in this edited volume as: 'How do African politics challenge our understanding of the concept of civil society?'; 'How does civil society as a vernacular architecture interact with the state?'; and thereby also: 'Does "civil society" remain a meaningful concept in our attempts to understand social, political and economic interaction and practices in these countries?'

Autochthony, citizenship and soil

'Autochthony' literally means 'emerging from the soil', thus implying localist forms of belonging, referring to someone with a supposedly indisputable historical link to a particular territory (Ceuppens and Geschiere 2005); as Jackson (2007: 481) rightly observes, 'the laws regulating citizenship and nationality have become increasingly restrictive in a number of countries in the last couple of decades, particularly with regard to minority and/or immigrant identity groups.' The outcome is often violent 'vernacular' discourses.

Autochthony is a theoretical construct, but in real life it also exists as discourse and narrative. It is text, but also spoken words. Thus, for most practical purposes autochthony is just a word for a certain way of framing political debates. Once we acknowledge this we will also become aware of striking similarities between our different cases; commonalities that can best be described as 'tales of origin as political cleavages' (see Bøås and Dunn 2013). This is narratives arguing that certain groups have certain inalienable rights to land, to property, to employment, to social and economic organisation or to social benefits that other groups should not necessarily have. Where land (or employment and other rights for that matter) is perceived as scarce, one important asset may be the ability to stake your claim from the position of being autochthonous, e.g. as the 'son of the soil', whereas your counterpart is presented as a 'newcomer', as an 'immigrant' and *allogène*. This may be of primary importance as being recognised as a true citizen of the political unit in question (country, region, city or village) entitles you to legitimately enter the struggle for resources.

The protection of rights is therefore argued through tales of origin, and this will inform the 'civic' space in which 'civil society' emerges, forcing it to take a vernacular form because no other path is really available. Through various means of 'story-telling' a collective 'we' is constructed, and this unit can be anything from the nuclear family to the lineage, the community, the ethnic group

150　*M. Bøås*

or several ethnic groups faced with a perceived stranger, an intruder, an enemy: somebody threatening certain rights seen as the heritage of the 'sons of the soil'. The power as well as the contradiction of these discourses is that they underwrite as well as over-rule other identities, and thereby also informs the very social space of 'civil society'.

Land, belonging and the 'vernacular architecture' of civil society

The conflicts in Liberia, Eastern Congo and Côte d'Ivoire can be read as 'wars of modernity' (see Banégas and Marshall-Fratani 2007). As these conflicts therefore are concerned with the composition of their respective national polities: who belongs and who does not belong – who is a citizen and who is not a citizen – two different conceptions of citizenship are opposed against each other. One is rooted in a republican approach whereas the other is locked in the exclusionist language of autochthony. This is an important dimension of contemporary African politics, and the ability of African countries to find answers to the questions that this dimension raises will have huge ramifications for how future political debates are framed on the continent. However, as the case studies also reveal, these very contemporary debates are also deeply rooted in a long history of violence, and integral to this history is the issue of land.

Despite recent demographic trends that shows that Africa is becoming a much more urban continent, most African countries are still agricultural economies and land rights issues have increasingly become vulnerable to the politics of identity and belonging (see Hagberg 2004; Kuba and Lentz 2006). Land is not only a scarce commodity in certain areas; it is also the most essential element of rural life. Land is everything, as it is belonging to the land that guarantees the rights of present as well as future generations, and whereas it does not in itself secure the right to land, at the very least it allows those who are citizens to enter the political economy of land and land rights questions. Thus, there is a direct link between contested citizenship, the formation of civil society and land rights issues. 'Land is a special substance; it is not increasable, non-renewable, and central to both material livelihood and the politics of belonging' (Lentz 2006: 30). It must therefore also be protected at all costs. Many different attempts have been made to explain African wars. They range from ethnicity, to greed and resource wars, to the role of colonialism, and each and every one of them has made contributions to the debate. However, one advantage of an approach that places emphasis on autochthony-based explanations is that it combines ideational and material elements through the direct linkage made between discourse and narrative on one side and access to resources on the other side. This may not only help us to explain and give meaning to violence and make us better suited to understand the local dimension of most conflict on the African continent, it also helps us understand the contradictions of the post-conflict environment where most often institutions, be they formal or informal, civic or public, fail to play the role that the 'liberal peace' paradigm predicted that they would.

Finally, it must be stated that the conflicting claims concerning citizenship and land rights are not a novelty created by the so-called 'new wars' (see Kaldor 2001), but an enduring part of the history of these areas that is better seen along the lines of *la longue durée* than as a direct outcome of a crisis of modernity (see Braudel 1994). The conflicts in these areas have a long and complicated history that became ever more manifest with the establishment of the African state system and the post-colonial crisis taking place amidst an externally imposed

> recent drive towards political and economic liberalisation [that] has engendered a rapid intensification of struggles over belonging, an obsession with *autochtonie* and ever more violent forms of exclusion of so-called strangers, even when they are citizens of the same country.
>
> (Geschiere 2004: 237)

In some places, this has undermined the whole notion of national citizenship or radically changed its definition (see Geschiere and Nyamnjoh 2000).

The 'stranger-father' in Lofa County, Liberia

During the period from 1980 to 2003 Liberia became synonymous with war, chaos and destruction. The Liberian conflict was, however, not just one war. It was a series of local conflicts tangled up in each other, as Charles Taylor's rebellion against Samuel Doe's dictatorship pushed the Liberian state over the edge and into the abyss. This 'nationalisation' of local conflict created a 'logic of war' that dramatically affected the course of the war, the decision-making of the individuals involved and the subsequent militia formation (see Bøås and Hatløy 2008; Bøås 2010).

The Liberian war was therefore a national conflict constituted by a series of local conflicts. This is vividly illustrated by the conflict between the Loma and the Mandingo in Lofa County. Taylor's ability to tap into pre-existing conflicts, in Lofa and elsewhere in Liberia, triggered the war. However, the very same conflicts were also the combined outcome of conflict patterns preceding the Americo-Liberians and the administrative practices of their state. In fact, revisiting the Liberian civil war through the lenses of autochthony, the argument can be made that, viewed in this manner, the warlords, the grand plans, the elites and the international connections become less important and what we are left with is the intertwining of a series of local conflicts into a larger pattern. A violent zone of conflict that evolves and develops as local communities – dazzled and confused by the events unfolding in their midst – try to protect what they believe belongs to them. The question is what becomes of civil society under such circumstances? Can it reach across other societal divisions and ethno-political cleavages? Or will it by the very necessity of circumstances be constructed on a 'vernacular architecture'?

The answer to these questions can be illustrated by the ethnogenesis between the Loma and the Mandingo that formally assigns first-comer status and control of land rights to the Loma. The outcome has been an unstable system of political

152   *M. Bøås*

subordination that the Mandingo could often escape as they represented economic power through their trade networks. Thus, the Liberian civil war was the latest manifestation of a long history of co-operation but also prolonged spells of conflict between these two communities (see also Konneh 1996). The conflicting claims concerning citizenship and land rights is therefore an enduring part of the history of this area that is better seen along the lines of *la longue durée* than as a direct outcome of a crisis of modernity (see Braudel 1994).

Consequently, in Lofa, the relationship between the Loma and the Mandingo has been tense and hostile, particularly since the beginning of the civil war in 1990. The Mandingo accuse the Loma of supporting Taylor's forces when they reached this part of Liberia in the autumn of 1990, whereas the Loma believe that the attacks in 1992 on their towns by the Mandingo militia, United Liberian Movement for Democracy (ULIMO), were unjustified and mainly carried out to take their land and steal their belongings. Similarly, when the militia Liberians United for Democracy and Reconciliation (LURD) crossed over the border from Guinea in 1998–1999, the Loma claimed that LURD forces – also a Mandingo-dominated movement – attacked their villages indiscriminately.[2]

The war and Taylor's ability to tap into these sentiments increased the conflict, but did not create it. The historical relationship between the Loma and the Mandingo and their co-operation as well as conflict rests on a hierarchical stratification of rights based on the 'stranger-father' institution – an informal institution that can be seen as the very prototype of an institution emerging from a 'vernacular architecture' of civil society. When the Mandingo first arrived in Lofa in the seventeenth century it was most often as individual traders conducting long-distance commerce between the forest areas of Liberia and the savannah regions further inland, bringing with them much-needed goods as well as important skills such as blacksmithing. In many ways, the first Mandingo settlers must have had access to larger economic resources than the original Loma inhabitants. However, in order to settle permanently and gain access to land, the Mandingo had to enter into subordinate relationships through the 'stranger-father' institution. In basic terms, this means that a 'stranger' who seeks settlement in a village or community needs to be adopted by an autochthonous 'father': the 'stranger' must have a 'father' – a figure of authority who takes upon himself the responsibility to make certain that the 'stranger' behaves in accordance with the rules and regulations of the community. Thus, when a Mandingo first moved into a Loma village, he also entered into a subordinate position with a 'stranger-father', locking him and his lineage forever into a subordinate political position with regard to the decisions about land and land use. The product of this interaction was relatively fixed notions of political alignment in local everyday politics, creating a hierarchical political system that was supposed to regulate titles to land. Thus, even at the village level any 'civic' space would be at least partly determined by these cleavages and the narratives that constitute them.

However, even if the Mandingo were politically marginalised through the 'stranger-father' institution, they represented economic muscle by their access to Mandingo trade networks. The consequence in the immediate pre-war era in Lofa was therefore that the local Loma discourse centred on how the Mandingo had upset the balance and disturbed certain rights seen as inalienable. Thus, when the war came to Lofa in 1990, parts of the autochthonous population used it as a pretext to reclaim what they believed was their natural born rights.

Thus, the current conflict has a history that precedes the Liberian state and the making of the modern state system in West Africa. However, we must also recognise how the 'rules of engagement' changed with the imposition of modern statehood that tied citizenship to a specific territorially defined politics of place (Bøås 2009). The background for much of the crises in Eastern Congo and Côte d'Ivoire are remarkably similar. These wars are by and large agrarian conflicts preceding the modern state system, but sharpened by the crisis of modernity in post-colonial Africa (see Richards 2005).

North Kivu, Eastern Congo: the 'vernacularisation' of civil society

The province of North Kivu is located on the very boundary between the more centralised kingdoms of Rwanda and Uganda and the more fluid political systems of Central Africa's forest regions. It is a place of mighty mountains, active volcanoes, dense forests and fertile soil, but also of intense population pressure (see also Vlassenroot and Huggins 2005). It is a meeting place and a melting pot, but also an area that repeatedly has tasted the bitter fruit of conflict, most often between groups claiming the status of autochthony and those defined as 'strangers': migrants supposedly without the same level of attachment to a mythological native land.

Most of the migration has traditionally come from the east. Although many migrated from Rwanda during colonial times, e.g. after 1885, the presence of the Banyarwanda as they are called reaches back to pre-colonial times (Vansina 2004; Lemarchand 2006). The Banyarwanda are, in the simplest terms, the people who speak the language of Kinyarwanda. Once these people or their ancestors may have lived in what is currently known as Rwanda, but through a series of migratory waves they currently dwell in DRC as well as Uganda and Tanzania. This migration took place through the centuries, and the length of residence and its history have shaped these communities. It is therefore not possible to talk about the Banyarwanda as a homogenous group. It includes people of Hutu as well as Tutsi origin.

What these people have in common, however, is contested citizenship status and thereby also questions concerning their right to own land, to vote and to stand for election. According to the Congolese Constitution of 1964 there exists only one Congolese nationality:

> [I]t is granted, beginning from the date of 30 June 1960 to all persons having now, or at some point in the past, as one of their ancestors a member of a tribe or the part of the tribe established on the territory of Congo before the 18th of October 1908.

> (Jackson 2006: 104)

Thus, the Banyarwanda could claim Congolese citizenship on the basis of ancestors being native to the Congo as of 18 October 1908. Those falling into this category could claim ancestral land along with other autochthonous groups in North Kivu. However, as the immigration and settlement of this group had taken place at different times and for several reasons, only a few qualified as undisputable citizens. This changed in 1972 when the Director of the Office of the President, Barthélemy Bisengimana, a Congolese Tutsi and Mobutu crony, masterminded a new citizenship law. The new law bestowed Congolese citizenship to all migrants living in the Congo prior to 1960. This gave a number of Banyarwanda political and economic rights that they had previously not enjoyed – suddenly they could vote, stand for election and, not least, buy land (Vlassenroot and Huggins 2005). This also made it easier for them to organise, politically, but also in the civic sphere.

This entire framework was, however, changed again in 1981 when Anzuluni Bembe, another Mobutu strongman and an autochthonous Babembe from South Kivu convinced the Legislative Council to reopen the nationality question. With a pen stroke, the 1972 law was repealed and a new law formulated which set the qualifying date back to the Berlin Conference (i.e. 1 August 1885). This effectively disqualified almost all the Banyarwanda. Some undoubtedly had ancestors who had arrived in North Kivu as long ago as when this area constituted the western frontier of the powerful Nyiginya kingdom, founded sometime in the sixteenth century (see Vansina 2004), but it was almost impossible to prove that this was the case (Lemarchand 2006). The 1981 law was never fully implemented, but it still provided the institutional basis for increased discrimination against the Banyarwanda, and the issue resurfaced again in the National Conference in 1991 – a national conference also based on the participation of civil society organisations. The Banyarwanda had hoped that this conference would settle the citizenship issue, but instead had to witness the delegations that represented their interests refused admission to the entire conference as it became the very manifestation of a 'vernacular' organisation of society. In North Kivu this spilled over into interethnic skirmishes that exploded in anti-Banyarwanda violence in 1993 when armed youth groups of Nande, Hunde and Nyanga origin attacked Banyarwanda communities. The refugee flows that followed the Rwandan genocide further increased the tension because land became even scarcer, and the same was the case for the civil war that followed (Raeymaekers 2007). There is therefore a clear line of continuity between these historical events outlined here and the 2012 fighting in North Kivu.

There is therefore a line of continuity between the historical events outlined here and the fighting in North Kivu that erupted in 2012–2013 and led to the defeat of the Tutsi-dominated Movement of 23 March (M23). Most of the M23 leadership were previously part of Laurent Nkunda's National Congress for the Defence of the People (CNDP) that were integrated in the Congolese national army (FARDC) as part of an agreement in 2009. However, a group of these fighters mutinied from the FARDC in April 2012, accusing the Kabila government in Kinshasa of neglect and failing to fulfil the terms of the 2009 agreement.

Just as in the case of the CNDP rebellion, many of them also felt that they had no other choice than to fight as if not they would become permanent losers as a minority group in Eastern Congo (see Bøås 2012). This suggests that even if the joint forces of the Congolese army and the new special battalion of the UN in the Congo were able to defeat M23 this is not necessarily the end to the conflict as the underlying uncertainties concerning belonging and citizenship rights have not been addressed. Therefore there is still an open door to the social manipulation of these issues from below, as well as from certain leaders who find it in their interest to allow conflict and tension to continue.

The events outlined above also created a multitude of opportunities for clever, but cynical social engineering of the 'nationality issue' and the citizenship question. One example of this type of social engineering of a vernacular nature is former North Kivu Governor Eugène Serufuli. A Hutu member of the Banyarwanda ethnic minority, Serufuli was born in Rutshuru in North Kivu, attended Kinshasa University and worked as an anaesthetist at the Goma General Hospital when the war broke out, but he was also the head of the hospital trade union and a leading activist in MAGREVI, an organisation that campaigned for the rights of the Banyarwanda. When the Congolese civil war restarted in 1998, Serufuli used his various roles to propel himself into several important roles; one was as the main leader of the NGO *Tous pour le paix et le développement* (TPD). Formally an NGO that ran local development programmes, TPD was for all practical purposes an organisation for the interests of a small segment of the Banyarwanda elite, but it presented itself to the world with several faces. To potential funders in the international community it was a local NGO running much needed local development programmes; to the Banyarwanda community it was an organisation for their interests and as such a successor to MAGREVI, as TPD-members also alternated as a local militia it could flex its military muscles when the leadership felt that their interests were under threat; and it worked as an informal alternative political authority in North Kivu, at times, but not always, in collaboration with Rwandan interests. For a time, Serufuli and TPD had some success in pacifying North Kivu and bringing parts of the territory back under some form of administrative control. This was, however, short-lived, as the vernacular architecture of civil society that TPD was based on meant that it totally undermined reconciliation efforts by civil society organisations between the Banyarwanda and the other autochthonous communities of North Kivu. They felt marginalised within the province and blamed the Banyarwanda as a group, even if many Banyarwanda activists in fact openly spoke against the strategies of Serufuli and TPD (see also ICG 2003).

The consequence was therefore that the importance of confirming belonging to an area by ancestral connection to land increased even further. The 2005 Congolese Constitution may be a step in the right direction as it dates ancestral connections to Congolese soil to the time of independence and not 1885 or 1908. However, as nationality is still tied to membership in a community dwelling on Congolese soil at the eve of independence, and since so many of these also include people who arrived later, the door to uncertainty and manipulation of the

156 *M. Bøås*

citizenship question, and thereby to new conflict, is as the M23 rebellion of 2012 shows us not closed. The results of a field survey published in Bøås and Dunn (2013) illustrates this point as it showed that only people of Banyarwanda origin found it necessary to locate their right to land back more than one generation. This may sound strange, but the reason is obvious. For people of Hunde, Nande or Nyanga decent, this is not important, as their tales of origin are not questioned. Nobody claims that they are not proper Congolese citizens, whereas despite the 2005 Constitution, the people of Banyarwanda origin still constantly have to argue their claim to Congolese citizenship and thereby to land. With regard to civil society, as the TPD history proves all too well, the only possible outcome of this is several 'vernacular civil societies' that compete for access to the state and the loyalty of different segments of society at large.

Côte d'Ivoire – the *Tutorat*: inclusion, exclusion, war

Similar controversies concerning citizenship and land rights issues like the one in Liberia and Eastern Congo are also at the centre stage of the Ivorian conflict. In Côte d'Ivoire these issues had already surfaced in riots in the 1950s (see Crook 1997). However, from 1960 to 1993, the country was under the firm rule of Felix Houphouët-Boigny who used the spoils of the cocoa export crop economy to tie different elites (autochthon and *allogène*) to his regime.

The contemporary political economy and geographical stratification of cocoa production in Côte d'Ivoire is the outcome of a double movement of transformation: labour migration from the north to the cocoa-producing areas of the south, in combination with a relocation of production from south-east to south-west. The consequence is that land issues in Côte d'Ivoire are structured by an autochthon-*allogène* (migrant) dichotomy. Here, the smallholder cocoa economy initially expanded in areas of low population density. Thus, in order to expand production additional labour was needed. These workers came from the northern parts of Côte d'Ivoire, but also from neighbouring Burkina Faso and Mali. They came to work, but also in search for free land to establish their own farms.

These autochthon-migrant relations were institutionalised through what in Côte d'Ivoire is known as the *tutorat*, a 'civic' institution that functions according to the same vernacular logic as the Liberian 'stranger-father' institution. The *tutorat* establishes a bond of patronage between the autochthon and the migrant, to whom land rights are extended on the basis of the principle of a moral economy: any individual has a right to a piece of land necessary for his subsidence. Autochthons can therefore not deny land to a 'good stranger' – one who accepts the duties given to him by the local economy and respects the prevailing socio-economic order. As an institution, the *tutorat* therefore regulates both the transfer of land rights and the incorporation of the migrant into the local community. The migrant, however, also owes the *tuteur* gratitude (that is transferred to his heirs), expressed through gifts, labour and money. These gifts or payments do not conclude the agreement on land rights, but rather perpetuate it – it continues and is in principle never-ending (Colin *et al.* 2007). Thus, very much in

'Civil society' as vernacular architecture   157

the same way as the Liberian 'stranger-father' institution, the *tutorat* cements vertical linkages making the evolution of other horizontal social relationships than patron-client autochthon-migrant relations difficult. This implies that the 'significance of the stranger-host relationship often radiates into all areas of life' (McGovern 2011: 72).

In the first decades after the introduction of cocoa, the relationship between migrants and the autochthons in the cocoa-producing regions were cordial. Land was abundant and most were able to carve out a relatively good living from their involvement in cocoa production. However, as shown by Ruf (2001: 293–294), land rights issues evolve around the growth cycle of the cocoa plantation.

> Most booms can be interpreted as situations where local ethnic groups who control land, or at least have a moral claim to it, meet up with migrants, who initially bring or control labour. In this meeting, migrants are often the winners, at least initially, when labour is scarce. Some 20 to 25 years later when replanting becomes necessary, land can become scarce, and if relocation of production is not possible one may witness increased conflict between migrants and the autochthons.

In the central and western regions of Côte d'Ivoire, a combination of almost open land access and extreme labour mobility pushed the cocoa frontier westward, creating ethnically heterogeneous villages across most of the Ivorian south as hardwood forests were cleared to make room for small farms. Already in the 1920s, migrant farmers had received access to forest land from autochthon Bété, Dida and Gouro groups and began to invest in export crop production. The period from 1946 to 1960 was therefore marked by an even larger inflow of 'migrants' into this area. In the 1950s, this began to be perceived as a Baoulé invasion (see Chappel 1989). Boigny's rise to power and the maintenance of his rule is closely linked to the interest and hegemony of the Baoulé-dominated 'planter bourgeoisie'. For the first three decades of independence, the cocoa sector was vertically integrated in a system that represented Baoulé interests at three different levels. Baoulé planters as the biggest producers of cocoa dominated the co-operative structures supposed to represent the interests of all Ivorian cocoa farmers. Baoulé businessmen dominated the cocoa co-operatives, the marketing boards and the Ivorian side of the international cocoa business, and at the top, first president Houphouët-Boigny and later president Konan Bédié (both of Baoulé origin) presided over the inclusive, but still Baoulé-dominated one-party state (see McGovern 2011).

An integral part of this strategy was expressed in what became known as the policy of *mise en valeur*, where the government of Boigny granted land user rights to anybody who put idle land to use. This created a patron-client relationship between migrant planters and the state, effectively tying their political alignment to the Baoulé-dominated state. However, the same policy also constituted the basis for a whole range of unsolved questions concerning user rights vs. lineage-based claims to land that would later come back to haunt Côte

158　*M. Bøås*

d'Ivoire when land became scarce and the economy simultaneously went into recession due to a combination of falling international commodity prices (mainly cocoa) and economic mismanagement.

Thus, less than a decade after independence the Bété, Dida and Gouro found themselves in the process of becoming a minority in their original homeland, leading to a situation where the autochthonous Bété began rallying around Laurent Gbagbo and his party, Front Populaire Ivoirien (FPI) that had started calling for a 'second war of liberation (see also Banégas and Marshall-Fratani 2007). This was fuelled by the simple fact that the dynamic relocation of production had met its last frontier. The process could no longer recreate itself, as there was almost no free land left for the establishment of new farms. The integrative capacity of the forest belt is therefore rapidly diminishing and it can no longer sustain the traditional labour migration from the north to the south. In this situation, the autochthons are contesting past land rights transfers under the *tutorat* institution in order to establish a new land fee or even having their land back.

Land rights issues in combination with contested belonging are therefore an integral element also in the Ivorian crisis, and the post-Boigny era has been marked, as Colin *et al.* (2007: 5) note, by 'the return of autochthony in the guise of *ivorité*'. This is vividly illustrated in the 1998 land law that not only excluded foreigners from land ownership, but also contained the possibility of excluding the Ivorian Baoulé and Dioula and other northern groups from land and land registration in the southern cocoa-producing areas, as the law uses autochthony as the source of legitimate entitlement. Land, land rights questions and contested citizenship issues are therefore equally as burning issues in Côte d'Ivoire as they are in Liberia and in Eastern Congo.

Some final remarks: 'vernacular' civil societies

What these three case studies underscore is that with the making of the modern state, land tenure became a complex cocktail of socially and politically embedded rights that were negotiated in dynamic relationships between and among different groups of people and the respective states in which they lived. What was therefore established (and still exists) is a dual land tenure system, where the governments recognised both deed ownership and customary users' rights. In practice what this means is that the right to land is closely tied to membership in specific groups, be this the nuclear family or extended family, the larger descent group, the ethnic group, and their various relationships to modern property regimes.

Land rights are therefore often contested, always negotiable, and they change over time. The only thing that remains constant are that membership in a group of recognised 'citizenship' in the geographical area in question is essential in these processes. Land rights issues are therefore particularly vulnerable to the politics of identity and belonging, and one important asset in such situations is the ability to stake your claim to land from the position of being autochthonous, e.g. as the 'son of the soil', whereas your counterpart is presented as a 'newcomer', an 'immigrant' or a 'stranger'. The result is more often than not a combination of local and nationalist discourses framed along the line of exclusion as its opposite inclusion, belonging and 'membership' is tied to first-comer status. The end result is a localised type of 'ethnonationalism' that by its very nature is 'vernacular' and particularistic and subsequently creates a political climate ill-suited to the evolution of nationalist discourses of a more republican nature that are universalistic and societal (see Alexander 2008). This observation has important implications and ramifications for our approach to 'civil society' under such circumstances as 'civil society' does not exist in isolation from such contested terrains, but are in fact very much part of the 'terrains of war' in political spaces such as these.

The question is therefore whether current developments such as these entail the end of the grand national narratives and thereby also the end of the evolution of an African variant of the European enlightenment type of 'civil society', or if new modes of nationalism and civil society will emerge from the vernacular processes and struggles analysed in this chapter. The outcome of this will depend on the future trajectory of how 'civil society' as a vernacular architecture interacts with the state.

What is clear is that the twentieth-century formulation of citizenship and thereby also the related notions of 'civil society' are, if not a failing design, at least caught up in a number of crises as populations frenetically discuss who is who – 'who has citizenship but should not have it, and who should have it but does not have it' (Weber 2008: 125). In the three cases analysed in this chapter, different narratives arguing that certain groups have certain inalienable rights that other groups living in the same geographical territory should not possess have seriously undermined the whole notion of national citizenship and thereby also the evolution of a civil society that is horizontal and not vernacularly inclined. This undoubtedly has important implications for 'civil society' as an analytical concept to understand social, political and economic relationships and practices in these countries.

The situation in the Gagnoa region in Côte d'Ivoire illustrates this point. Originally, this was the homeland of the Bété, but due to the waves of labour migration described earlier in this chapter, Ivorian Baoulé and Burkinabe Mossi groups also inhabit this area today. For all practical purposes the Bété consider these two latter groups equally foreign. The very fact that the Baoulé carries Ivorian identification papers does not make them any more autochthonous than the Mossi. For the Bété they are both 'strangers' to Gagnoa, and therefore without the same kind of inalienable rights to land as the autochthonous population (see also Bøås and Dunn 2013). Such views make the whole notion of a civic national identity almost meaningless as formal citizenship is of little or no importance in local struggles over land and other assets. What one is therefore left with instead is a vernacular narrative of ethno-nationalism focusing on the expulsion of the 'strangers' from the homeland of the autochthon. It is hard to see what responses that focus on 'civil society' that fail to acknowledge this can achieve in such circumstances.

160 *M. Bøås*

Contemporary African politics is therefore challenging our traditional European enlightenment understanding of civil society, but this does not by necessity mean that the concept has lost all its analytical value in the circumstances of fragile states where the process of state-building is incomplete or dysfunctional, the composition of the polity is disputed and the social contracts between rulers and those being ruled over have lost legitimacy. Horizontal bonds of trust are still possible and also necessary. Both Liberian 'stranger-father' institution and the Ivorian *tutorat* show this. Thus, even if the tales of origin that underwrites them have a potential for social and economic exclusion, social conflict and war, they could also come to represent the very building blocks for a new nationalism that integrates national, regional and local identities into flexible modern African answers to the crisis of citizenship that has come to dominate large parts of African politics. In the case of Liberia, DRC and Côte d'Ivoire this must entail guarantees for minority protection and citizenship rights for those not considered proper citizens, but also the willingness of all concerned communities to renegotiate land rights issues based on a new flexible and inclusionary version of the Liberian *stranger-father* and the Ivorian *tutorat*. Transparent and legitimate treatment of land rights conflicts would in each case constitute a possible vantage point for reconciliation locally as well as nationally, and thereby also a possible new pathway from an exclusionist vernacular discourse to a more republican and societal approach to citizenship and civil society.

Notes

1 This chapter is a revised and expanded version of an article originally published as Morten Bøås, 'Autochthony and Citizenship: ' "Civil Society" as Vernacular Architecture?' *Journal of Intervention and Statebuilding*, 6, 1 (2012), pp. 91–105.
2 Former members of Samuel Doe's fragmented army and Liberian refugees established ULIMO in Sierra Leone. Most of the original ULIMO fighters were of Krahn and Mandingo origin. Under the leadership of Alhaji Kromah, a Mandingo and former Doe official, ULIMO first fought in southeastern Sierra Leone before it battled its way back to Liberia and Lofa County. LURD was established in Guinea as a successor to the Mandingo faction in ULIMO just after Taylor's victory in the 1997 elections (see Ellis 1998; Reno 2007; Bøås and Hatløy 2008).

References

Alexander, J.C. (2006) *The Civil Sphere*, Oxford: Oxford University Press.
Alexander, J.C. (2008) 'Civil sphere, state and citizenship: replying to Turner and the fear of enclavement', *Citizenship Studies*, vol. 10, no. 2, pp. 185–194.
Banégas, R. and R. Marshall-Fratani (2007) 'Côte d'Ivoire: negotiating identity and citizenship', in M. Bøås and K.C. Dunn (eds) *African Guerrillas: Raging against the Machine*, Boulder, CO: Lynne Rienner, pp. 81–111.
Braudel, F. (1994) *A History of Civilisations*, New York: Penguin Press.
Bøås, M. (2009) 'Funérailles pour un ami: des luttes de citoyenneté dans la guerre civile Libérienne', *Politique Africaine*, vol. 112, pp. 35–51.
Bøås, M. (2010) 'Militia formation and the nationalisation of local conflict in Liberia', in

'Civil society' as vernacular architecture   161

K. Mulja (ed.) *Violent Non-State Actors in World Politics*, London: Hurst & Company, pp. 257–276.

Bøås, M. (2012) *Prospects for Peacebuilding in Eastern Congo*, New York: Social Science Research Council, available at: www.forum.ssrc.org/kujenga-amani.

Bøås, M. and K.C. Dunn (eds) (2007) *African Guerrillas: Raging against the Machine*, Boulder, CO: Lynne Rienner.

Bøås, M. and K.C. Dunn (2013) *The Politics of Origin in Africa: Autochthony, Citizenship and Conflict*, London: Zed Books.

Bøås, M. and A. Hatløy (2008) 'Getting in, getting out: militia membership and the prospects for re-itnegration in post-war Liberia', *Journal of Modern African Studies*, vol. 46, no. 1, pp. 33–53.

Ceuppens, B. and P. Geschiere (2005) 'Autochthony: local or global? New modes in the struggle over citizenship in Africa and Europe', *Annual Review of Anthropology*, vol. 34, pp. 385–407.

Chappel, D. (1989) 'The nation as frontier: ethnicity and clientelism in Ivorian history', *International Journal of African Historical Studies*, vol. 22, no. 4, pp. 671–696.

Colin, J.P., G. Kouamé and D. Soro (2007) 'Outside the autochthon-migrant configuration: access to land, land conflicts and inter-ethnic relationships in a former pioneer area of lower Côte d'Ivoire', *Journal of Modern African Studies*, vol. 45, no. 1, pp. 33–59.

Crook, R.C. (1997) 'Winning coalitions and ethno-regional politics: the failure of the opposition in the 1990 and 1995 elections in Côte d'Ivoire', *African Affairs*, vol. 96, no. 383, pp. 215–242.

Ellis, S. (1998) *The Mask of Anarchy: The Destruction of Liberia and the Religious Dimension of an African Civil War*, London: Hurst & Company.

Geschiere, P. (2004) 'Ecology, belonging and xenophobia: the 1994 forest law in Cameroon and the issue of community', in Harri Englund and Francis B. Nyamnjoh (eds) *Rights and the Politics of Recognition in Africa*, London: Zed Books, pp. 237–259.

Geschiere, P. (2009) *The Perils of Belonging: Autochthony, Citizenship and Exclusion in Africa and Europe*, Chicago: University of Chicago Press.

Geschiere, P. and F.B. Nyamnjoh (2000) 'Capitalism and autochthony: the seesaw of mobility and belonging', *Public Culture*, vol. 12, no. 2, pp. 323–352.

Hagberg, S. (2004) 'Ethnic identification in voluntary associations: the politics of development and culture in Burkina Faso', in Harri Englund and Francis B. Nyamnjoh (eds) *Rights and the Politics of Recognition in Africa*, London: Zed Books, pp. 195–218.

Hansen, T.B. (2001) *Wages of Violence: Naming and Identtty in Postcolonial Bombay*, Princeton, NJ: Princeton University Press.

ICG (International Crisis Group) (2003) *The Kivus: The Forgotten Crucible of the Congo Conflict*, Nairobi/Brussels.

Jackson, S. (2006) 'Sons of which soil? The language and politics of autochthony in Eastern D.R. Congo', *African Studies Review*, vol. 49, no. 2, pp. 95–123.

Jackson, S. (2007) 'On "doubtful nationality": political manipulation of citizenship in the D.R. Congo', *Citizenship Studies*, vol. 11, no. 5, pp. 481–500.

Kaldor, M. (2001) *New and Old Wars: Organised Violence in a Global Era*, Oxford: Polity Press.

Konneh, A. (1996) 'Citizenship at the margins: status, ambiguity and the Mandingo of Liberia', *African Studies Review*, vol. 39, no. 2, pp. 141–154.

Kuba, R. and C. Lentz (eds) (2006) *Land and the Politics of Belonging in West Africa*, Leiden: Brill.

162 *M. Bøås*

Lemarchand, R. (2006) 'The geopolitics of the Great Lakes Crisis', in F. Reyntjens and S. Matsse (eds) *L'Afrique des Grand Lacs – Dis Ans de Transitions Conflictuelles: Annuarie 2005–2006*, Paris: L'Harmattan, pp. 25–64.

Lentz, C. (2006) 'Land and the politics of belonging in Africa: an introduction', in R. Kuba and C. Lentz (eds) *Land and the Politics of Belonging in West Africa*, Leiden: Brill, pp. 1–34.

Mamdani, M. (2001) *When Victims Becomes Killers: Colonialism, Nativism and the Genocide in Rwanda*, Princeton, NJ: Princeton University Press.

Mamdani, M. (2002) 'African states, citizenship and war: a case-study', *International Affairs*, vol. 78, no. 2, pp. 493–506.

Marshall-Fratani, R. (2006) 'The war of who is who: autochthony, nationalism and citizenship in the Ivorian crisis', *African Studies Review*, vol. 49, no. 2, pp. 9–43.

McGovern, M. (2011) *Making War in Côte d'Ivoire*, London: Hurst & Company.

Raeymaekers, T. (2007) 'Sharing the spoils: the reinvigoration of Congo's political system', *Politorbis – Zeitschrift für Aussenpolitik*, vol. 42, no. 1, pp. 27–33.

Reno, W. (2007) 'Liberia: the LURDs of the new church', in M. Bøås and K.C. Dunn (eds) *African Guerrillas: Raging against the Machine*, Boulder, CO: Lynne Rienner, pp. 69–80.

Richards, P. (2005) 'To fight or to farm? Agrarian dimensions of the Mano River conflicts (Liberia and Sierra Leone)', *African Affairs*, vol. 104, no. 417, pp. 571–590.

Ruf, F. (2001) 'Tree crops as deforestation and reforestation agents: the case of cocoa in Côte d'Ivoire and Sulawesi', in A. Angelsen and D. Maimowitz (eds) *Agricultural Technologies and Tropical Deforestation*, New York: CABI Publishing, pp. 291–315.

Turner, B.S. (2008) 'Civility, civil sphere and citizenship: solidarity versus the enclave society', *Citizenship Studies*, vol. 12, no. 2, pp. 177–184.

Vansina, J. (2004) *Antecedents to Modern Rwanda: the Nyiginya Kingdom*, Oxford: James Currey.

Vlassenroot, K. and C. Huggins (2005) 'Land, migration and conflict in Eastern DRC', in C. Huggins and J. Clover (eds) *From the Ground Up: Land Rights, Conflicts and Peace in Sub-Saharan Africa*, Pretoria: ISS, pp. 115–194.

Weber, C. (2008) 'Designing safe citizens', *Citizenship Studies*, vol. 12, no. 2, pp. 125–142.

9 Escaping state-building

Resistance and civil society in the Democratic Republic of Congo

Marta Iñiguez de Heredia

Introduction

State-building has become the policy panacea for post-Cold War conflicts where a link has been made between state-failure and war.[1] Thirty-two years of Mobutu's dictatorial regime and a subsequent war that partitioned the country, becoming one of the deadliest conflicts since World War II, have made the Democratic Republic of Congo (DRC) the paradigm of the failed state and thus a target of state-building strategies (Lemarchand 2003; Eriksen 2011). The priorities of these strategies have been to restore state authority over the whole of the territory, democratisation security sector reform and reform of the justice administration system (UN Security Council 2010). Many advances have been made since the war finished in 2002. They include the organisation of democratic elections twice since independence, the stabilisation of many areas in the country and improving macro-economic indicators, turning the DRC into one of the fastest growing economies in Africa (World Bank 2010). However, the DRC has also plummeted to the bottom of the International Development Index in the last ten years and the numbers of displaced are increasing (UNDP 2011; UNHCR 2012). The M23 rebellion in March 2012 added to an ongoing war in the eastern part of the country and to a mushrooming of militias in the last four years. Although state-building policies generally consider civil society a partner for reconstruction and democracy promotion, the context of the DRC makes civil society also a site for resistance.

Civil society building is a core foundation of post-conflict state-building. For the Organisation for Economic Cooperation and Development (OECD), for instance, state-building means 'to develop the capacity, institutions and legitimacy of the state in relation to an effective political process for negotiating the mutual demands between state and societal groups' (OECD-DAC 2008, p. 1). Thus defined, state-building needs to create a civil society that acts as a partner for carrying out the necessary reforms. In the DRC, civil society building is thought of as necessary in order to 'establish a credible and organized civil society that can participate in the national policy-making process on development' and turn it into 'a more reliable partner in terms of representing the population' (MONUSCO Civil Affairs 2012, para. 1 and 3). This is, however, not

164 *M. Iñiguez de Heredia*

straightforwardly the case in the DRC, where those outside the decision making process are most targeted by the continuation of conflict, while benefitting less from the improving macroeconomic indicators. Civil society in the DRC thus holds an ambiguous role.

The tendency in critical peacebuilding studies, as Paffenholz notes, is to call attention to civil society's role as a vehicle for '*gouvernmentalité* of the liberal peacebuilding grand narrative' (Paffenholz 2010, p. 60, italics in the original). However, scholarly and policy research on civil society's role in state-building has started to identify civil society's ambiguous role as a partner, as a *spoiler*, and as a site of resistance (DfID 2010, pp. 56–57; MacGinty 2011, pp. 15–17 and ch. 8; Richmond 2011, ch. 1; Kappler and Richmond 2011). This chapter wants to explore this aspect of civil society as a fruitful site for resistance. Following James Scott, it does so by focusing on civil society, not as an autonomous sphere that acts as a counter power and legitimates authority, but as a sphere of everyday self-help mitigating strategies of subordinate classes against domination. Achille Mbembe has argued that the nature of political authority in African post-colonial states provides no spaces for the exercise of 'autonomy, representation, and pluralism [to protect oneself] from the arbitrariness of both state and primary group (kin, tribe etc.)' (2001, pp. 38–39). It follows that civil society has to be theorised within its own historicity and not solely as the product of post-conflict state-building strategies. Civil society needs to be considered in its role as a site where strategies of mitigation provide the ground, not to foster and support state-building but also to reject it.

In a historical analysis of the African colonial state, Young already advanced that civil society presented 'an ambiguous challenge' (Young 1994, ch. 7). As a 'hodgepodge' of individual and collective solidarities, networks and associations, formed from different sectors and classes in society, civil society is better seen as a site, or as Fossaert puts it, a 'social space' (1981, 146). Civil society's ambiguity and not its univocality should be therefore taken seriously as a platform where resistance and state-building operate simultaneously. It is precisely its heterogeneity and ambiguous character that makes civil society a fruitful site to locate resistance in the context of state-building.

Based on fieldwork research undertaken between 2009 and 2011 in Kinshasa and North and South Kivu, the chapter analyses three concrete strategies of resistance that are undertaken or assisted by civil society organisations, networks based on proximity and kin.[2] The chapter starts with a discussion of the concept of resistance and civil society, followed by an analysis of resistance through discursive, violent and survival strategies. These are three prominent areas that interact with current state-building strategies and that provide an insightful standpoint from which to observe civil society's role as a site for resistance.

A framework of resistance vs. civil society

The connection between resistance and civil society is not new, but it can be somehow contradictory. Whereas political theory has often seen civil society as an arena of resistance (Boyd 2004), the notion of civil society used in contemporary state-building policies is one where 'civility' seems to be its most defining feature. This 'civilising' nature could be defined as the capacity to provide an autonomous political space for countering power but that falls within the limits power allows (Mbembe 2001, p. 37). Highlighting this aspect of civil society has been a trend in the critical literature on state-building, which has seen how civil society serves the purposes of state-building itself (Chandler 2010, ch. 8). Yet there is another angle to civil society that requires an analysis not just of the effects of the state-building policies but also of the 'enduring legacies' state-building meets, and thus the antagonising and resistance capacity of societies (Kurz 2012, p. 122). It thus require the exploration of the 'uncivil' or 'less-civil' nature of civil society (Keane 1998, pp. 114–156; MacGinty 2011, p. 205).

The problem of grasping the defining lines between 'civility' and 'resistance' is the relationship that these have with power and the complex nature of power in a postcolonial context. Achille Mbembe (2001) argues that the nature of power in the postcolony is seen partly in its capacity to exercise violence and wealth allocations using quotidian, even banal means. Thus for Mbembe, the spheres of power, the private and the public are muddled, rejecting the existence of arenas out of power as civil society or resistance, preferring to refer to relations of 'conviviality' (2001, pp. 128–129). Additionally, the nature of domination needs to be theorised not just as 'power over' but 'power through', noting the participation of those deemed dominated in their domination.

This horizontal power grid line has been raised in critical appraisals of civil society in Africa. For instance, Ferguson and Gupta argue that the recourse of Africanist scholars to notions of civil society as an arena outside or beyond the state is outdated (2002, p. 991). The exercise of power through nongovernmental channels establishes a horizontal dimension that challenges not just the vision of government and governed across a vertical line, but also shows that governmentality operates in a common framework through state and nonstate institutions (Ferguson and Gupta 2002). If Mbembe theorises from the point of view of relationships, Ferguson and Gupta do so from a notion of spatiality. They all conclude that state and civil society are not so much in opposition to one another but in connivance.

Behind this cautious differentiation between resistance and civil society lies Foucault's advice:

> Since the nineteenth century, civil society has always been referred to in philosophical discourse, and also in political discourse, as a reality which asserts itself, struggles, and rises up, which revolts against and is outside

166   *M. Iñiguez de Heredia*

government or the state, or the state apparatuses or institutions. I think we should be very prudent regarding the degree of reality we accord to this civil society.

(Foucault 2008, pp. 296–297)

Foucault argues that civil society has been created in the process of relations of power through history, turning into an element of governmental technology – 'technology of government whose objective is its own limitation as it is pegged to the specificity of economic processes' (Foucault 2008, p. 297). That is, civil society is part of a strategy to 'govern less' but to 'govern better'. But Foucault clarifies that civil society is 'not the sole product' of this governmental rationality (2008, p. 297). Civil society also responds to its own interests and intertwines societal solidarities and individual selfishness.

Civil society's character is better seen as what Young called 'an ambiguous challenge' (1994, p. 218). Its structure, composition and activities can be read as serving multiple purposes at once within and without a governmental rationality. An ambiguity also served by its heterogeneous composition as a 'social space' and as a receptacle and platform for multiple strategies. This space is not one necessarily of autonomy but as a site of resistance within and against the everyday experience of domination. This ambiguity is a historical feature of civil society in Africa. Ngonzola-Ntalaja asserts that anti-colonial resistance 'took place within the new structures colonialism itself had created' (2002, p. 41). Similarly Mahmood Mamdani notes that while customary chiefs and ethnic identities played a role as mediators and vehicles for the colonial enterprise, rebellions against colonialism were based on ethnic and customary institutions (1996, p. 24).

The problem with following Foucault's reading of civil society is that it corresponds to an analysis of the elements and techniques amenable to a modern rationality of government in which there is no similar analysis of the elements and techniques amenable to an account of resistance. As such, bearing in mind the dynamics of horizontality and conviviality, the argument this chapter proposes is that it is in the ambiguities and even through the same channels power operates, that resistance is found. This account of resistance needs to embrace the complexity of everyday life and not to reduce it to a simple binary of domination and resistance (Mbembe 2001, p. 103). Resistance needs to start, not from the public, organised, ideological undertaking but from the subtle quotidian forms of non-compliances and challenges to power, sexual exploitation, poverty and beliefs as well as in forms of creation, empowerment and discovery (Browdy de Hernandez *et al.* 2010, pp. 4–7). This chapter follows James Scott's framework of everyday resistance being rooted in such daily experiences of domination, for being able to account for those subtle quotidian ways in which power relations take place, while providing a strong and clear conceptual framework on which to base an empirical exploration of resistance.

James Scott and everyday forms of resistance

For Scott (1985, p. 290), resistance is:

> *any* act(s) by member(s) of a subordinate class that is or are intended either to mitigate or deny claims (for example, rents, taxes, prestige) made on that class by superordinate classes (for example, landlords, large farmers, the state) or to advance its own claims (for example, work, land, charity, respect) vis-à-vis those superordinate classes.

This definition identifies resistance as a practice of those outside the decision-making process. It identifies that resistance takes place as part of a relation of domination that has both symbolic and material bases, that can take place as a collective and individual undertaking and that it does not need to be organised or ideologically driven. It is rooted in the daily experience of claims and antagonist agendas. This definition does not rule out that individuals, members of a 'super-ordinate class', and those in a 'subordinate class', may act in connivance or may have similar agendas. It identifies historical patterns in relations of domination.

Scott's framework has been criticised for creating a binary understanding of the social world as well as a simplified understanding of power relations in which a category of dominated acts vis-à-vis the dominants (Mbembe 2001, pp. 103–110; Hibou 2011, Ch. 1). It does not take into consideration those horizontal forms of power and the nuanced ways in which domination might be consolidated by the actions of those deemed dominated, especially in an African context. These critiques are important for an analysis of civil society's ambiguity as resistance and as a vehicle for state-building.

Scott's definition of resistance does not capture enough how the framework is well-suited to account for the ambiguities that take place in power relations. Scott's framework, developed initially in the everyday relations of a small village in Malaysia captures a context of conviviality, double meanings, fake compliances and ambivalent gestures. Scott does not think of resistance so much as something that takes place outside power relations but through them, as a consistent pattern within them.

It is precisely its patternedness that differentiates resistance from any other random acts. Similarly, the definition does not clarify enough, besides the intention of mitigating or denying the claims made by the elites, what makes 'any acts' resistance and what not. It still needs to state clearly what makes these individual non-political acts into politico-social acts called resistance. Scott (1985, pp. 295–296, emphasis added) noted that:

> When a peasant hides part of his crop to avoid paying taxes, he is *both* filling his stomach and depriving the state of grain.... When such acts are rare and isolated, they are of little interest; but when they become a consistent pattern (even though uncoordinated, let alone organized) we are dealing with resistance.

168 *M. Iñiguez de Heredia*

Henceforth, the defining element of resistance in this framework is not *the act* but that this act is a pattern and a constant element in relations of domination, where claims made are denied or mitigated to pursue other agendas. This last element, acknowledging that subordinate classes pursue their own agendas, further asserts an extra dimension of ambiguity. As mentioned above, unearthing quotidian strategies of resistance does not rule out the existing connivance of agendas at certain times, or that these strategies may advance agendas that have nothing to do with a dynamic of power and resistance. The question is how to identify the actual practices that embody those practices of resistance. Civil society as resistance, and not just its role as a vehicle for governmentality, does not only illustrate an important dynamic of the everyday experience of state-building, it also illustrates an important aspect of the historicity of such societies. The following sections focus on three arenas that simultaneously speak to key aspects of state-building strategies and to how resistance to them takes place. Exploring civil society as a site of ambiguity and heterogeneity provides a view of civil society where alliances and solidarities can be found in order to resist the practices and effects of domination.

The discursive level

A first and important arena of resistance takes place at the discursive level. This discursive ground is significant because it shows the ideological foundations on which both power and resistance operate. On the one hand, these ideological tools of power serve to assert authority. On the other hand, they provide a platform on which to negate such authority and advance a different agenda. This discursive level is more clearly elaborated in Scott's theorisation of the 'hidden transcript'. Hidden transcripts respond to the patterns of everyday ideological insubordination, generally originated out of the reach of power, which ultimately create 'a critique of power' (1990, p. xii). They are the side effect of a 'public transcript' or 'pose', which illustrates the ways in which authority and subordinate roles are enacted, generally when in front of each other (1990, p. 5). However, Scott not only saw the 'hidden transcript' as an effect of the public transcript. Scott also saw the generation of a 'third realm', of a more ambiguous and fluid nature, between resistance and consent (1990, ch. 5).

Moreover, Scott pointed out that it would be misleading to see all that 'is said in power-laden contexts false and what is said offstage true', or to construct 'simplistically [...] the former as a realm of necessity and the latter as a realm of freedom' (1990, p. 5). Scott noted that to identify the existence of these transcripts was to identify the 'pose' that is enacted depending on which audiences, in which power relations determined to a large extent what is said and how one behaves. The criticisms of authority in the kitchen or the burst of talking when a teacher leaves the room were, for Scott, signals that there were different transcripts on which to read power relations (1990, p. 5). This does not mean, and Scott did not mean, that all that happens in the kitchen or after a class is a critique of the boss, the government or the teacher. They are analogies to illustrate

Escaping state-building 169

that there are individual actions and discourses that, if done in front of a figure of authority, would entail repression.

Civil society in the form of networks of proximity and kin, but also in its most organised form serve as a space for those transcripts to emerge. Counter-discourses in the form of denigration and slandering are deployed, giving foundation to other strategies of resistance and the construction of political alternatives. These hidden transcripts challenge state-building by exposing the contradictions between the material conditions of living experienced and the rhetoric of the mission.

In a workshop about participatory governance with high school children in Bukavu undertaken by NGO Group Jeremie in 2009, it became clear that even if 'participatory governance' sounded as if it had just been taken from any policy report from the UN Department of Political Affairs, its use had been changed to voice concerns about repression, to criticise the actions of the government and the international community regarding democracy and development, and to voice political alternatives, including redefining participatory governance as actual participation in decision-making processes (Participant Observation III 2009). Similarly, representatives from the local branch of the national platform of civil society organisations (SOCICO) stated that whenever they did workshops with residents and other smaller civil society representatives about the need to respect state authority and pay taxes it usually turned into a space to criticise corruption and voice rumours about hidden agendas of MONUC/MONUSCO (Interview with President of Civil Society – Masisi 2011).

Rumours are a feature of everyday conversation. What is striking is that in the stretch of almost 500 kilometres between Fizi and Butembo and around 1600 kilometres between these and Kinshasa, popular discourses share a common denominator: 'MONUC's soldiers traffic with coltan'; 'MONUC is there to serve Rwandan interests'. In Bunyakiri, Fizi and Masisi for example, a similar rumour was running around: MONUC provided the Forces Démocratiques de Libération du Rwanda (FDLR)[3] elements uniforms, weapons and food to sustain a war in Congo in order to keep Congo weak and easily exploitable. For MONUC/MONUSCO officers these rumours are evidence of the manipulation of politicians (Interview with MONUSCO Civil Affairs Officer (no. 145) 2010; Interview with MONUC Civil Affairs Representative (no. 1) 2009). Nevertheless, these rumours show, not that MONUSCO is not doing enough 'propaganda', but that people are not willing to look at MONUSCO in a positive light. Rumour resonates with a deeper political agenda. Whether these stories are true or not, whether they originate from a specific politician's agenda or even FARDC, they are used to discredit MONUSCO. As such they are also a symbol of social conflict.

Elites however also use denigration and slandering techniques to justify their indispensability. In line with Mbembe's vision of power as having the capacity to reach the banal level, it is not uncommon to hear UN officials and diplomats tagging Congolese as 'corrupt', 'lazy', 'opportunistic', 'selfish' or 'backward'. A MONUC officer for instance affirmed: 'We are dealing with people who are

170 *M. Iñiguez de Heredia*

helpless' (Interview with MONUC Political Affairs Officer (no. 7) 2009). These insults suggest that it is ultimately the fault of the Congolese, both elites and non-elites, for being in the situation they are. If we were to accept these complaints and critiques, we would immediately exonerate their interlocutors of their responsibility, acknowledging that they are doing their best against all odds.

The image of the selfless 'international community' is challenged by the denigration and slandering of subordinate classes where elites, national or international, are 'corrupt', 'only interested in material gains for themselves' and 'not committed to the real needs of the people'. By pointing to the hypocrisy of power, to other possible agendas and to the lack of commitment to power's own discourse, denigration is a way of de-legitimising the claims to power and political authority.

Mockery is also a common way to launch a critique and a form of resistance. Any visitor to the DRC can identify how the UN mission is caricatured. For instance, during the peak of violence from renegade soldier Nkunda, the popular saying 'no Nkunda, no job' referred to the common critiques that whether MONUC, as an actual accomplice of the continuation of the conflict, or as a hopeless conflict resolution agent, ultimately guaranteed the mission's continuation. In Kinshasa, the same day that MONUC changed to MONUSCO, with its change of mandate, people renamed the mission 'MONUSKOL' (as in the beer Skol, portraying a vision of UN workers as more interested in alcohol and night life than in peace). Soon after the government committed to the 'five pledges' (*cinq chantiers*) people renamed them the 'five songs' (*cinq chansons*), criticising the government for not realising them.

The problem is that this mockery expresses in humour what is otherwise a harsh experience. Programme Amani Leo is a Congolese military peace strategy supported by MONUC and many international representatives (2010). While this programme has been very effective in demobilising thousands of combatants from different armed groups, it has pushed negative consequences of its strategies onto subordinate classes. Subordinate classes in local villages not only have to host and feed soldiers but also to take care of the daily needs of demobilised soldiers dumped in the villages without resources for their reintegration in civil life. Those combatants that join the army or the national police are also likely to keep settling ethnic rivalries while living off the population because of lack of salary payment (Global Witness 2009, pp. 16–17). Further, issues of land, housing and ethnic rivalries brought by the return of refugees and IDPs are left for the populations to deal with. As such, when people on the ground mock the programme 'Amani Leo' (Peace today) calling it 'Amani Kesho' (Peace tomorrow) it actually vocalises a reality of poverty, increased sexual violence, repression and local conflict.

The discursive level allows us to observe the ideological patterns on which both power and resistance are justified. Portraying national and international elites as incapable, greedy, hypocritical and anti-democratic when not ridiculous are acts of resistance with important implications. First, they reject the authority and morality of the state-building mission and they conform to one of the only

Escaping state-building 171

ways to hold state-builders to account. Second, it is a way of voicing political alternatives. They are a form of resistance in so far as they articulate a critique of domination and not just demand better treatment from such domination. Chandler argues that civil society in state-building is a discourse that acts as a vehicle and as a justification of Western agendas to reproduce moral and civilisational divides for intervention (Chandler 2010, p. 171). Yet, as seen, civil society can channel a deeper critique to resist and even escape such agendas.

The not so weak weapons of the weak

That the everyday nature of everyday resistance is based on the lack of direct confrontation and on the deployment of discourses does not necessarily mean it is unarmed or without physical violence. As Scott argued, the struggle between resistance and domination is not just an argument, but a fight (1985, p. 241), which included extended guerrilla-style tactics (1985, pp. xvi–xvii). The relationship between civil society and violence has been explored within peacebuilding contexts as one that responds to the everydayness of violence, particularly in violent contexts (Mitchell 2011). It also deserves much more scrutiny. The use of violence is one of the arenas where, as Mbembe asserts, power sifts through all strata of society. 'The postcolony is a specific regime of violence' that 'privatizes means of coercion' while socialising violence across the population (Mbembe 2001, pp. 102, 51, 32 and ch. 2).

However, violence, as any other strategy, can be a tool of resistance and not only an instrument of power. In the greater picture of the discourses that have been analysed above and in the context of insecurity and poverty, it is possible to assert that violence is also used to escape state-building policies, attempt avenues towards one's own agenda and legitimate political authority outside the channels of state and state-building processes.

In these strategies, kin, family and personal networks are fundamental for the access of weapons and the support or creation of armed groups. This is then filtered through civil society organisations whose members might have a dual membership in these and local armed groups (either simultaneously or alternate) (Interview with Simba Mai Mai/MRS Combatant 2010; Interview with Demobilised Mai Mai Padiri Combatant 2009; Informal Conversation with Demobilised Mai Mai Padiri Combatant 2010). However, for the UN mission and the government, civil society organisations play a fundamental role in transmitting their message and acting on their behalf in the absence of an official authority.

This is best illustrated by analysing the solidarity with armed groups, and subsequent strategies of desolidarisation used by state-building. A first case is narrated by a UN officer:

> In Shabunda, there are not enough policemen or army. So Kinshasa sent in what they call 'Police d'Intervention Rapide' [Fast Intervention Police]. What happened is that this Police were setting up illegal detention centres, we heard cases of child abuse, sexual abuse … so they are causing more

trouble than their own local Mai Mai or armed groups. The situation became so ridiculous. We sent in a mission to do a bit of research and speak to the local population who were begging for this police to be redeployed, so that they could be left alone with Raia Mutombuki [local Mai Mai militia]. So when one of our officers went in and started talking to the local population about the idea of bringing in some regular tax officers, ministry of interior officers ... the response we had was that ... well you know we are quite used to Raia Mutombuki, they're not very nice, they tax us and they steal our crops, but we rather stay with what we know ... they haven't seen a regular civil servant for years, communities are living side by side with Mai Mai and a lot of the time these armed groups are the locals, they are the same people, so of course they accept them!

(Interview with MONUSCO Civil Affairs Officer (no. 145) 2010)

This passage reveals the reticence of the local populations towards Congolese authorities and even to the UN mission, and their preference for self-reliance. First, personal interrelationships become a more trusted authority than those 'foreign' ones, even if they come with the democratic, official, legitimate stamp on it. Second, rejecting state authorities reflects a lack of commitment towards them and an attempt to escape from them.

Another case is illustrated by the 'sensitisation workshop' organised by MONUSCO Civil Affairs in Fizi and Baraka (South Kivu) to ease the relations between the military and the populations, which had become very sour and were a source of insecurity. This area has long been a Mai Mai stronghold. It was the sparking centre of the Muleliste rebellion in the 1960s; it has granted refuge and logistical bases for many rebellions, including Laurent Kabila's, and it is now thought of as being the support and engine of many other Mai Mai groups throughout Eastern Congo (Informal Conversation with Demobilised Mai Mai Padiri Combatant 2010; Interview with Simba Mai Mai/MRS Combatant 2010). Additionally, the 23 March 2009 agreement, by which National Congress for the Defence of the People (CNDP) elements have integrated the army and been spread throughout the Eastern provinces, include many who only speak Kinyarwanda, feeding the conspiracy theories by which Rwanda would be attempting to annex part of the Kivus. Further, the military strategy of scattering an utterly under-resourced army throughout the territory, forcing it to live together with the population, where the populations have to provide them with accommodation, food, housing, sex and information, and the exactions committed by the military have created a *low* intensity war between the population and the military.

This workshop demonstrated two interesting factors, aside from the hostile relations just mentioned. First, the workshop illustrated that the civil society component, made out of local NGOs, religious representatives, local producers' cooperatives, had, by default, personal links to the Mai Mai militias. Two days after the workshop, members of this civil society, in an attempt to show good will, passed information on to the commander of the area to notify of an incoming attack to one of their battalions. This showed the channels of

Escaping state-building 173

communications between armed groups and civil society. A second factor was that despite the imbalance of power, people retained a substantial amount of control of what goes on the ground. As one UN officer in Kinshasa stated: 'the restoration of state authority depends in grand part on the local population' (Interview with Political Affairs Representative 2010). While there was a power imbalance between the military and the civil society representatives, the frustration of militaries and administrators is that without the help of the populations they could not get rid of the armed groups or fully deploy official authorities.

The jump to use violent methods to secure one's self and pursue certain political agendas poses a challenge to the monopoly of violence and authority the state-building mission attempts to grant to the state. The thin division between local militias and populations and the personal and collective decisions to accept or confront armed groups allow at the same time people to survive and violence to continue. This section has not attempted to suggest that these armed groups are a form of ethical resistance or that they are the symbol of the realisation of justice and peace in Congo. Indeed, they arguably generate their own dose of domination too. Rather this is to show that the multiple political avenues and the exercise of political agency through civil society take also the shape of violent and direct confrontation, and forms part of the spectrum of everyday resistance to state-building.

Providing social services, producing the social fabric

If there is one place where the actions of civil society become more present in providing a space for mitigating violence and dispossession it is in the delivery of social services. This provision is not new but war has accentuated it. Congo's history as one of relative state absenteeism in its social and arguably administrative role (Renton *et al.* 2007, p. 44; Jewsiewicki 1986) peaked with the famous claim made by Mobutu in the 1970s of 'fend for yourselves' (*debrouillez-vous*). Mobutu literally meant that the state was withdrawing from providing basic services to the population. This absenteeism, or 'delinquency', as Kankwenda puts it, 'has had as a response the emergence of an active and dynamic civil society, organised to take control of everyday survival, education, health, neighbourhood security, etc' (Kankwenda 2005, p. 176). MacGaffey saw that with the Zairian state withdrawal, a second economy flourished that allowed for people to survive. She was conscious that the state still played a role, at times intervening itself through informal channels. However, she asserted, 'through the second economy, the citizenry may not only evade civil obligations but also express resistance to the state and to the class which controls it' (MacGaffey 1991, p. 10). More so, arguably through the provision of social services, where civil society is especially visible, a particular social fabric is produced where subordinate classes retain substantial control. It is actually this control that makes these strategies not only a form of survival but a form of resistance.

Seeing the actions of civil society in this way is not straightforward. Chabal, for example, argues not only that the state has an actual control and operates

174   *M. Iñiguez de Heredia*

though informal channels but also that making subordinate classes provide all sorts of social services is a sort of extortion by the state (2009, pp. 132, 151). Chabal points to Foucault's conception of governmentality where the logic of self-provision and more so using the channels of civil society could fit a logic of neoliberalism of the state's withdrawal or self-limitation. However, seeing only the effects of domination occludes what is the response to these regimes. This is not to say that people opt to be exploited but that to observe just this feature is to ignore the daily strategies of escapism to this form of exploitation (Scott 2009).

MacGaffey argued that 'participat[ing] in the second economy could be seen as a political option' (1987, p. 157). Not only that, she saw this option not as a result of the successful political economy of the state, but as a contestation to the legitimacy of the state. She asserted that 'by contesting what is defined as legitimate, people confront a predatory state which fails to provide them with the opportunity to earn a living wage, with a functioning economic infrastructure or with basic social services' (MacGaffey 1987, p. 157). What this points to, once again, is to configure the space of civil society as an ambiguous one where resistance in different forms seeks alternatives to the daily effects of domination. Let us go through a few examples.

In Mabuku (North Kivu), for instance, there is an established payment for teachers, nurses and doctors; the women of the village have built the maternal wing of the small hospital/health centre by collecting materials around the area and making their own bricks (Participant Observation II 2010). In other places, whilst the hospital may have been built by the state with the contribution of international NGOs, still the management relied on local Catholic or Protestant churches, which, at the same time, relied on the contributions made by the patients (Participant Observation XII South Kivu General Hospital, Bukavu 2010). In Butembo every 60 or so houses buy a generator together and set up its own electricity system. One house hosts the generator and everyone makes a contribution to the petrol, providing electricity in the evenings.

But the same goes for peace strategies and refugee flow management, which seem to fall even more directly under the government's responsibility, especially in times of conflict. In Bunyakiri, the organisation Action pour la Paix et la Concorde (APC) organises and manages the flow of refugees around the territory where the town of Bunyakiri is found. Refugees present a problem in particular to the issue of land. When a family returns, the land may have been taken or given away by the customary chief. This is very important since land is at the heart of the conflict. When people are displaced and they flee the area or the country, upon their return they may find that there are new occupants on their land (Interview with APC Representative 2010). This may be families, politicians, military or police members. As such, this generates multiple conflicts. This is added to the fact that land is a resource for agriculture, cattle farming and mining and therefore a source of conflict. However, when asked about the policy in regards to all these issues and land to an MP for one of the Eastern territories he stated 'we do not have a policy' (Interview with Deputy for Masisi 2010). The fact that people have organise themselves to address these problems, even seeking international NGO support over and above the government, points to an attempt to keep a degree of independence and control from state authority. As Moore (1978, p. 27) observed: 'By and large, it appears that the efforts of subordinate groups to work out their own rules for settling internal disputes represent attempts to maintain some degree of independence in respect to superior authority.'

The use of civil society space through the hodgepodge of organisations, networks based on kin and personal links as well as associative life, provides subordinate classes their own means of survival in ways that substitute, escape and subvert the authority of state-building. Although this could be seen as successful extortion on the part of the state, and although part of the success of the peace strategies relies on the capacity of people to precisely deal with the problems on the ground, this space left to subordinate classes generates a substantial amount of control on their part. It is in the capacity to retain the state at a distance and seek alternative channels to provide for one's survival that these strategies are in themselves a form of resistance. They establish the ground to enact creative ways of social organisation and new forms of political authority.

Conclusion

This chapter has argued that civil society can play a role not only in facilitating state-building, but also as a site of resistance to it. Civil society's character as a heterogeneous and ambiguous arena does not make it straightforwardly a partner for state-building and reconstruction. As Richmond argues, the instrumental vision of civil society that liberal peacebuilding has is subverted by the fact that this civil society is 'empty' and composed of 'individuals and communities who do not accept this agenda' (2011, p. 67). 'Civil society' does demand democracy, development and peace, but what is rejected is the daily experience of domination, which state-building does not only not resolve, but makes this civil society the most affected by its failures. Civil society demonstrates society's own historicity and multiplicity creating a resistance barrier to projects that precisely marginalise such civil society (Mbembe 2010, p. 28). In this form, resistance is better explored not in its organised form, or as an ideologically driven and direct confrontation, but rather as the quotidian strategies of mitigation, avoidance and escapism. Following James Scott, the chapter examined three areas of resistance that highlighted the self-help mitigating strategies against domination as evidence of the patterns in relations of domination.

Three strategies were proposed, including counter-discourses, alliances and creation of armed groups and the control of the social fabric through social service provision. The discursive level gave an account of the ideological basis on which both the state-building mission and resistance rely. Civil society both in its formal and informal form creates the spaces for criticism, mockery, denigration and slandering, where subordinate classes reject the authority of state-building and voice alternatives to it. These alternative discourses point out the contradiction between the experience of violence and poverty in their everyday

176 *M. Iñiguez de Heredia*

lives and the rhetoric of the mission. This is not just a demand for services in the civilising role that state-building reserves for civil society, but rather a critique of processes and structures by which those outside the decision-making process continue to experience the worst consequences of war and poverty. These criticisms and alternative political visions slip through the ongoing and contradictory support to armed groups and the search of alternative ways of social organisation through the self-management of all sorts of social services.

The alliances and solidarity links that populations maintain with armed groups further show different loyalties and the establishment of political authorities outside of the state-building mission. Similarly, the provision of many social services showed a substantial amount of control of the social fabric, even the production of it, on the hands of subordinate classes. The idea that the state's strategy of self-limitation equates to its control over this social arena is therefore limited. These are not an exhaustive list of forms of resistance, but rather some important areas of state-building where civil society is seen ambiguously as a site for resistance.

For state-building, civil society is fundamental in legitimating the uses of violence and political economy by the state. For subordinate classes, civil society serves as a space of encounter for the formulation of political critique, of redistribution and even production of means of survival and even as a channel to sustain militias and establish political authority. Ambiguity and heterogeneity makes civil society a fruitful site where to locate quotidian strategies of state escapism. These actions do not account for random acts of defiance or for the future revolutionaries of Congo, but for the patterns of resistance to the conduct of state-building and the multiple political projects this entails. An important implication of these contending spheres of action is, first, that if civil society is to continue to be a useful concept it is by highlighting its ambivalent role. With that it follows that civil society has a history and cannot be solely conceived of as the product of state-building or other intervening strategies. Exploring the role of civil society as a facet within a heterogenous space with an 'enduring legacy' means to take account of the different forms civil society plays as an actual mechanism for activism and as a representation of historical societal organisation. In this regard, civil society may be the expression of historical aspirations and traditional ways of solidarity and struggle that illustrate both continuities and change towards the new and old forms of domination that are embedded within state-building processes.

Notes

1 This chapter is a revised and expanded version of an article originally published as Marta Iñiguez de Heredia, 'Escaping Statebuilding: Resistance and Civil Society in the Democratic Republic of Congo', *Journal of Intervention and Statebuilding*, 6, 1 (2012), pp. 75–89.
2 Field research was carried out in the summers of 2009, 2010 and 2011 in Kinshasa and most territories of North and South Kivu for a PhD thesis (Funded through an ESRC +3 studentship ref. number: EH/H17704/1). The research was based on semi-structured

interviews, participant observation and field observations. Three major groups were targeted: the Government, UN officials and the Population/Civil Society. Within this last category, participants were chosen: (a) for their direct relation with the UN Mission; (b) for their instrumentality in providing services to the populations; (c) for their links with armed groups; (d) for being representative of subordinate classes, including credit cooperatives, street sellers and peasants associations. A total of 158 formal interviews, three focus groups, and 19 participant observations have been carried out. This is added to field observations and informal conversations.

3 A Rwandan armed group remnant from the Rwandan genocide that attempts to oust Kagame.

References

Boyd, R., 2004. *Uncivil Society: The Perils of Pluralism and the Making of Modern Liberalism*, Lanham, MD: Lexington Books.

Browdy de Hernandez, J. *et al.*, 2010. Introduction. In J. Browdy de Hernandez, P. Dongala, O. Jolaosho and Anne Serafin, eds, *African Women Writing Resistance: Contemporary Voices*. Cape Town: Pambazuka Press, pp. 3–11.

Chabal, P., 2009. *Africa: The Politics of Suffering and Smiling*, London and New York: Zed Books.

Chandler, D., 2010. *International Statebuilding: The Rise of Post-Liberal Governance*, epub: Adobe Digital Editions 2.0.67, New York: Routledge.

DfID (Department for International Development), 2010. *The Politics of Poverty: Elites, Citizens and States – Findings from ten years of DFID-funded research on Governance and Fragile States 2001–2010 – A Synthesis Paper*, London.

Eriksen, S.S., 2011. 'State failure' in theory and practice: the idea of the state and the contradictions of state formation. *Review of International Studies*, 31(1), pp. 229–247.

Ferguson, J. and Gupta, A., 2002. Spatializing states: toward an ethnography of neoliberal governmentality. *American Ethnologist*, 29(4), pp. 981–1002.

Fossaert, R., 1981. *La société: les états*, Vol. 5, Paris: Editions du Seuil.

Foucault, M., 2008. *The Birth of Biopolitics: Lectures at the College de France 1978–79*, New York: Palgrave Macmillan.

Global Witness, 2009. *Faced with a Gun, What can you do? War and the Militarization of Mining in Eastern Congo*, London: Global Witness. Available at: www.globalwitness.org/library/faced-gun-what-can-you-do (accessed 6 December 2012).

Hibou, B., 2011. *Anatomie Politique de la Domination*, Paris: La Découverte.

Jewsiewicki, B., 1986. Belgian Africa. In *Cambridge History of Africa: From 1905–1940*, Cambridge: Cambridge University Press, pp. 460–493.

Kankwenda, M.J., 2005. *L'Économie Politique de la Prédation au Congo Kinshasa: Des Origines à nous Jours 1885–2003*, Kinshasa, Montréal and Washington: Icredes.

Kappler, S. and Richmond, O., 2011. Peacebuilding in Bosnia and Herzegovina: resistance or emancipation? *Security Dialogue*, 42(3), pp. 261–278.

Keane, J., 1998. *Civil Society: Old Images, New Visions*, Cambridge: Polity Press.

Kurz, C., 2012. The limitations of international analyses of the state and post-conflict statebuilding in Sierra Leone. In B. Bliesemann de Guevara, ed., *Statebuilding and State-Formation: The Political Sociology of Intervention*, Abingdon: Routledge, pp. 114–131.

Lemarchand, R., 2003. The Democratic Republic of Congo: from collapse to potential reconstruction. In R.I. Rotberg, ed. *State Failure and State Weakness in a Time of Terror*, Washington: Brookings Institution Press, pp. 29–70.

178 *M. Iñiguez de Heredia*

MacGaffey, J., 1987. *Entrepeneurs and Parasites: The Struggle for Indigenous Capitalism in Zaire*, Cambridge: Cambridge University Press.

MacGaffey, J., 1991. *The Real Economy of Zaire: The Contribution of Smuggling and Other Unofficial Activities to National Wealth*, London: James Currey.

MacGinty, R., 2011. *International Peacebuilding and Local Resistance: Hybrid Forms of Peace*, New York: Palgrave Macmillan.

Mamdani, M., 1996. *Citizen and Subject: Contemporary Africa and the Legacy of Late Colonialism*, Chichester: Princeton University Press.

Mbembe, A., 2001. *On the Postcolony*, Berkeley: University of California Press.

Mbembe, A., 2010. *Sortir de la Grande Nuit: Essai sur l'Afrique Décolonisée*, Paris: La Découverte.

Mitchell, A., 2011. *Lost in Transformation: Violent Peace and Peaceful Conflict in Northern Ireland*, London: Palgrave Macmillan.

MONUSCO Civil Affairs, 2012. Support to Civil Society Organisation (CSOs). Available at: http://monusco.unmissions.org/Default.aspx?tabid=10712&language=en-US (accessed 29 January 2013).

Moore, B., 1978. *Injustice: The Social Bases of Obedience and Revolt*, London: Macmillan.

Nzongola-Ntalaja, G., 2002. *The Congo: From Leopold to Kabila: A People's History*, London: Zed Books.

OECD-DAC (Organisation for Economic Co-operation and Development, Development Assistance Committee), 2008. *State-Building in Situations of Fragility: Initial Findings*, Paris. Available at: www.oecd.org/dac/fragilestates (accessed 26 April 2011).

Paffenholz, T., 2010. Civil Society and Peacebuilding. In T. Paffenholz, ed., *Civil Society and Peacebuilding: A Critical Assessment*, Boulder: Lynne Rienner Publishers, pp. 43–64.

Programme Amani, 2010. Site officiel du Programme STAREC. Available at: www.amanileo.net (accessed 18 April 2010).

Renton, D., Seddon, D. and Zeilig, L., 2007. *The Congo: Plunder and Resistance*, London: Zed Books.

Richmond, O., 2011. *A Post-Liberal Peace*, epub: Adobe Digital Editions 2.067275, London: Routledge.

Scott, J.C., 1985. *Weapons of the Weak: Everyday Forms of Peasant Resistance*, New Haven: Yale University Press.

Scott, J.C., 1990. *Domination and the Arts of Resistance: Hidden Transcripts*, New Haven: Yale University Press.

Scott, J.C., 2009. *The Art of Not Being Governed: An Anarchist History of Upland Southeast Asia*, New Haven: Yale University Press.

UN Security Council, 2010. *Resolution 1925*. Available at: http://documents.un.org (accessed 13 December 2010).

UNDP (United Nations Development Programme), 2011. Congo (Democratic Republic of the) – Country Profile: Human Development Indicators. *International Human Development Indicators*. Available at: http://hdrstats.undp.org/en/countries/profiles/COD. html (accessed 20 April 2012).

UNHCR – Democratic Republic of the Congo, 2012. 2012 UNHCR Country Operations Profile – Democratic Republic of the Congo. *UNHCR 2001–2012*. Available at: www. unhcr.org/pages/49e45c366.html (accessed 9 September 2012).

World Bank, 2010. Democratic Republic of Congo – Country Brief. *World Bank*. Available at: http://go.worldbank.org/VU4KGZ3JX0 (accessed 5 May 2010).

Young, C., 1994. *The African Colonial State in Comparative Perspective*, New Haven; London: Yale University Press.

List of interviews, informal conversations and participant observations

Interview with APC Representative, 2010.
Interview with Demobilised Mai Mai Padiri Combatant, Kinshasa, 2009.
Interview with Deputy for Masisi, Goma, 2010.
Interview with MONUC Civil Affairs Representative (no. 1), 2009.
Interview with MONUC Political Affairs Officer (no. 7), 2009.
Interview with MONUSCO Civil Affairs Officer (no. 145), Bukavu, 2010.
Interview with Political Affairs Representative, 2010.
Interview with President of Civil Society – Masisi Centre, Masisi, 2011.
Interview with Simba Mai Mai/MRS Combatant, 2010.
Informal Conversation with Demobilised Mai Mai Padiri Combatant, 2010.
Participant Observation II, 2010. Mabuku Environments and Village Life.
Participant Observation III, 2009. Peace workshop organised by Group Jeremie, College Alfajiri, Bukavu.
Participant Observation XII South Kivu General Hospital, Bukavu, 2010.

Index

Abrahamsen, Rita 7, 111
accountability 23, 25, 26, 27, 29, 32
acquiescence, puzzle of 8–9
Action pour la Paix et la Concorde (APC) 174
ActionAid Sierra Leone 30
African agency 14
Africare 52
agri-business 81, 117
agriculture: Tanzania 76–7, 81; Zambia 117, 118, 119; Zimbabwe 41–2
Alexander, J. C. 148
Amani Leo programme, DRC 170
anthropology of the state 130
anti-money laundering regimes 35
Anvil Mining 99, 101, 102
apartheid 131–3
APC see Action pour la Paix et la Concorde (APC)
Aretxaga, Begoña 142, 143
armed groups, DRC 171–3
autochthony issues 149–51, 158–60; Côte d'Ivoire 150, 156–8, 159, 160; Eastern Congo 150, 153–6, 160; Liberia 150, 151–3, 160

Banyarwanda 153–6
Beall, J. 134
Beavon, Keith 131, 132
Bembe, Anzuluni 154
Bernstein, Steven 69, 70
BIDs see Business Improvement Districts (BIDs)
big picture analysis 5
bio-power 46
biofuels 81, 83
Bisengimana, Barthélemy 154
Booth, David 34, 36, 70, 71, 83
Brassett, James 69, 70, 83

BRICS-Bank 13
BRICS countries 13–14
Brockington, Dan 80
business community, Johannesburg 133–5, 138
Business Improvement Districts (BIDs) 133, 134

capacity building 24
capillary conception of power 59
CARE International 52
CBOs see Community-Based Organisations (CBOs)
Central Johannesburg Partnership (CJP) 133, 134
Chabal, P. 173–4
Chandler, D. 165, 171
Chatterjee, Partha 130, 139
chieftaincy system 58–9; DRC 100–1; Sierra Leone 31–2; Zimbabwe 50, 51, 52–3
Child Supplementary Feeding Program, Zimbabwe 55
choiceless democracies 9
citizenship, contested 148, 149–51, 158–60; Côte d'Ivoire 150, 156–8, 159, 160; Eastern Congo 150, 153–6, 160; Liberia 150, 151–3, 160
City Improvement District, Johannesburg 134
CIVICUS survey, Sierra Leone 32, 33
civil society: community-based 28–9, 108–9, 111–13, 114–16, 118–24; counter-hegemonic potential 112–13, 117–18, 119, 121, 122–3, 124; and development agencies 24–5, 102, 108–9, 113, 120–1; engineering in Ghana 25–9, 34–5; engineering in Sierra Leone 29–34, 35; and environmental

Index   181

mainstreaming 66–7; and good governance agenda 110–11; liberal concept of 22–4; and national democratic participation 121–3; participatory community development 92, 93–5, 97–103; and resistance to state-building 163–6, 169–76; Tanzania 78, 82; Zambia 114–16, 118–20, 122–3; *see also* vernacular architecture of civil society

civil wars: DRC 154–5, 163; Liberia 151–3; Mozambique 44; Sierra Leone 29

CJP *see* Central Johannesburg Partnership (CJP)

Clark, Ian 69

cobalt 95, 102

cocoa 156–8

coercive paternalism 92, 95–7

colonial government: DRC 95–7; indirect rule 94; Johannesburg 130–1; and the liberal project 34; resistance to 166

Community-Based Organisations (CBOs) 28–9, 108–9, 111–13, 114–16, 118–24

community development, participatory 92, 93–5, 97–103

conduct of conduct 6, 9, 47, 68

conflicts 4–5; *see also* civil wars

Congo *see* Democratic Republic of Congo (DRC)

conservation, wildlife 80, 83

contradictions 4–5

Cooke, B. 94–5, 101

copper 95, 102

corporate risk management 93, 97–102

corporate social investment 99–100

corporate social responsibility (CSR) 92, 100, 101

corruption: Tanzania 79, 83; Zimbabwe 44

Côte d'Ivoire 150, 156–8, 159, 160

counter-hegemonic potential of civil society 112–13, 117–18, 119, 121, 122–3, 124

Cox, Robert W. 4, 112

critical theory 3–6, 13–15

Cross, John Christopher 138–9

CSR *see* corporate social responsibility (CSR)

DanChurchAid 114

data collection and analysis, Tanzania 76, 81

decentralisation policies: DRC 100; Sierra Leone 31; Tanzania 77; Zimbabwe 51

decentralised despotism model 94, 95

deliberative processes, Tanzania 77

democracy, perceptions of 9

democratic participation, and community groups 109, 121–3

democratic procedures 70, 71; Tanzania 77

Democratic Republic of Congo (DRC): autochthony issues 150, 153–6, 160; mining companies 91, 95–103; resistance to state-building 163–4, 169–70, 171–3, 174–5

democratisation 58–9, 110–11

Department for International Development (DfID), UK 24, 26, 30, 31, 73, 74, 102

Department of Wildlife, Tanzania 79

development, Zimbabwe 41–5, 49, 51–2, 54–8, 59–60

development agencies 13, 25–9, 30–4, 75, 82; and civil society 24–5, 102, 108–9, 113, 120–1

developmental patrimonialism 13

DfID *see* Department for International Development (DfID), UK

Dill, Brian 82, 108, 120

disciplinary paternalism 95–7

disciplinary power 46, 49, 93

discursive strategies of resistance 168–71

dissent 112–13, 122–3

Doe, Samuel 151

donor agencies *see* development agencies

DRC *see* Democratic Republic of Congo (DRC)

Duffield, Mark 98

Eastern Congo 150, 153–6, 160, 172

economic crisis, global 102–3

economic indigenisation 55–6

economic reform, Zimbabwe 42, 44, 49, 53–4, 60

Economic Structural Adjustment Programme (ESAP), Zimbabwe 44–5, 49, 53–4

education: Zambia 117; Zimbabwe 42, 44, 54, 55–6

effectiveness 70, 72

elections 8; DRC 100, 163; Zambia 116, 122

electricity generators 174

ENCISS (Enhancing the Interface between Civil Society and the State to Improve Poor People's Lives), Sierra Leone 30, 32

Engels, Friedrich 4

Englebert, P. 8–9

182 Index

entrepreneurship: Johannesburg 136, 138;
  Zimbabwe 55–7, 59–60
environmental mainstreaming 66–7, 70–2;
  Tanzania 73–8, 82–3
environmental NGOs 75
ESAP *see* Economic Structural
  Adjustment Programme (ESAP),
  Zimbabwe
ethical issues 5–6, 14
ethno-nationalism *see* autochthony issues
Europe: agricultural policy 117;
  disciplinary regimes 96
extraction industries *see* mining companies
Extractive Industries Transparency
  Initiative 35

FARDC (Congolese national army) 154–5
Ferguson, James 9, 14, 67, 110, 113, 165
Fertilizer Support Program, Zambia 118
food-for-work programmes, Zimbabwe 54
food security, Tanzania 82–3
foreign investment, Tanzania 76
Foucault, Michel 4, 6–9, 14, 45–9, 58,
  59–61, 68, 165–6
free trade 117
freedom, power through 9, 47, 48, 56, 61,
  68, 69, 93
Front Populaire Ivoirien (FPI) 158

Gbagbo, Laurent 158
gender equality 114–15
Geschiere, P. 147, 149, 151
Ghana 25–9, 34–5, 132
Ghana Anti-Corruption Coalition 26
global economic crisis 102–3
global market, and Zambia 116–18, 122–3
good governance agenda 24, 71, 110–11
Götz, G. 136, 137, 138, 143
Gould, Jeremy 79
governing at a distance 93
government: avoiding excessive 49;
  indirect private 94; *see also* colonial
  government; local government
governmental rationalities, Tanzania 75–8
governmentality 6–9, 14–15, 47, 48, 61,
  93, 174; and legitimacy 68–70
Gramsci, Antonio 112, 122
Green, M. 120–1
green revolution 117
Gupta, A. 165

Habermas, Jürgen 112
Hansen, Thomas Blom 142–3, 147
Harrison, Graham 27, 79, 81

Hart, K. 132
healthcare: DRC 174; Zambia 117;
  Zimbabwe 42, 44, 54
Hearn, J. 124
hegemony, and civil society 112–13,
  117–18, 119, 120, 121, 122–3, 124
hidden transcripts 168–9
HIV/AIDS projects 52
Houphouët-Boigny, Felix 156, 157
hybrid authority structures, Tanzania
  78–80

identity, paradox of 147
income generation, community 120, 123
India 111, 131, 142–3
indirect rule 94–5, 100–2
Indonesia 100
informal economy 132
informal street traders, Johannesburg 129,
  130–7, 138, 139–42
input legitimacy 70, 71
internal self-regulation 49
International Development Index 163
International Institute for Environment and
  Development (IIED) 73
International Relations 7

Jackson, S. 149, 153
Johannesburg 129, 130–42, 143
Johannesburg Summit 71
Johannesburg Well of Development and
  Training (JOWEDET) 141–2
Joseph, Jonathan 7, 8, 48
juridico-political model of power 45–6, 59

Kankwenda, M.J. 173
Katanga, DRC 95–103
Kilimo Kwanza policy, Tanzania 76–7, 81
Kolwezi Artisanal Mining Project 102
Kyoto Protocol 70

labour camps, DRC 96, 98
labour market deregulation, Zimbabwe
  54–5
land acquisition programme, Zimbabwe 42
Land Administration Projects, Ghana 28
land-grabbing, Tanzania 81, 83
land rights 149–51, 158–60; Côte d'Ivoire
  150, 156–8, 159, 160; Eastern Congo
  150, 153–6, 160; Ghana 28; Liberia 150,
  151–3, 160; of refugees 174–5;
  Zimbabwe 52, 56
Land Tenure Commission, Zimbabwe 52
Landell-Mills, Pierre 25

Index   183

Leadership Code, Zimbabwe 43–4
legal systems, traditional: Ghana 27–8;
   Zambia 116
Legg, Stephen 96, 130, 131
legitimacy: concept of 67; and
   governmentality 68–70
legitimating mechanisms 69–70;
   environmental mainstreaming as 66–7,
   70–2, 74–8
Lemke, T. 47, 49
Lewis, D. 113
liberal interventions 7–8
liberalism 21, 68; and civil society 22–4
Liberia 150, 151–3, 160
lighthouse politics 35
Lipietz, B 134
local government 58–9; DRC 100; Sierra
   Leone 31, 35; Zimbabwe 43, 50–3,
   57–8, 60
Lofa County, Liberia 151–3
logic of power 59
Loma 151–3

M23 (March 23 Movement), DRC 154–6,
   163
MacGaffey, J. 173, 174
MAGREVI, DRC 155
Mai Mai militias, DRC 171–3
Mamdani, Mahmood 50, 58, 94, 110, 148,
   166
Mandingo 151–3
Marcuse, Herbert 112
markets, Johannesburg 129, 130–2, 133,
   136–7, 140–1
Marx, Karl 4
mass movements 14
Mbembe, Achille 61, 94, 96, 164, 165,
   167, 171, 175
MDC see Movement for Democratic
   Change (MDC), Zimbabwe
Mercer, C. 110, 120–1, 124
Metro Mall, Johannesburg 129, 138, 140,
   143
militias, DRC 171–3
Millennium Development Goals 71, 82
mining companies: DRC 91, 95–103;
   Tanzania 79
missionaries 96
Mkandawire, Thandika 9
MKUKUTA strategies, Tanzania 73–8, 81,
   82–3
MNCs see multinational companies
Mobutu Sese Seko 163, 173
mockery 170

Mohan, G. 124
MONUC/MONUSCO see United Nations
   Mission in the Democratic Republic of
   Congo (MONUC/MONUSCO)
Moore, B. 175
Motala, S. 139
Movement for Democratic Change
   (MDC), Zimbabwe 52
Mugabe, Robert 44, 46, 47, 61
multinational companies (MNCs) 91,
   92–5; agri-business 117; DRC 95–103

National Congress for the Defence of the
   People (CNDP), DRC 154, 172
national democratic participation, and
   community groups 109, 121–3
National Strategies for Sustainable
   Development (NSSDs) 71–2; Tanzania
   72, 73–8, 82–3
National Strategy for Growth and the
   Reduction of Poverty see MKUKUTA
   strategies, Tanzania
natural resources: Zimbabwe 52–3; see
   also environmental mainstreaming;
   mining companies
neoliberalism 9, 58, 68, 113, 116–18, 174
new governance mechanisms 71, 79
NGOs: DRC 99, 102–3, 155; Ghana 25,
   26; local African 120–1; and
   multinational companies 100, 102;
   Sierra Leone 30; Tanzania 75, 79;
   Zambia 114–15, 117, 118–20;
   Zimbabwe 51–2, 55, 56, 60
normative issues 5–6, 14
North Kivu, DRC 153–6, 174
NSSDs see National Strategies for
   Sustainable Development (NSSDs)
Nyerere, Julius 75, 80
Nzongola-Ntalaja, G. 166

Obama, Barack 1
ODI see Overseas Development Institute
   (ODI)
Ojanen, Julia 79
one-party system, Zimbabwe 42–3, 46
Organisation for Economic Cooperation
   and Development (OECD) 163
output legitimacy 70, 72
Overseas Development Institute (ODI) 26,
   70, 78
Oxfam 75

Pact Congo 99, 102–3
Paffenholz, T 164

184 *Index*

participatory community development 92, 93–5, 97–103
paternalist discipline 95–7
PF ZAPU (Zimbabwe African People's Union) 42–3, 44
philanthropy, strategic 99–100
Plan International 52
pluralism 112, 122
policing 97–8, 101
popular mass movements 14
poverty: and informal economy 135; Zambia 120; Zimbabwe 41–5, 49, 51–2, 54–8, 59–60
poverty-reduction strategies: Tanzania 79, 82; Zimbabwe 41–5, 49, 51–2, 54–8, 59–60
Poverty Reduction Strategy Papers (PRSPs) 71; Ghana 26, 27; Sierra Leone 30; Tanzania 73, 75; Zambia 122
power 6, 45–8, 58–9; bio-power 46; disciplinary 46, 49, 93; and legitimacy 69; sovereign 9, 45–6, 58, 59, 60, 61, 93; state 112, 129–30; through freedom 9, 47, 48, 56, 61, 68, 69, 93
private government 94
private sector: Tanzania 76–7, 82; *see also* business community, Johannesburg
Programme Amani Leo, DRC 170
project approach, to urban development 137–8
protests: DRC 98, 101; Johannesburg 129
PRSPs *see* Poverty Reduction Strategy Papers (PRSPs)
public consultation, Tanzania 77
public works scheme, Zimbabwe 54

refugee flow management 174–5
rent-seeking, Tanzania 79, 83
resistance to state-building 163–76; and civil society 163–6; defined 167–8; discursive strategies 168–71; social service provision 173–5; violent strategies 171–3
Richmond, Oliver 175
risk governance 93, 97–102
Rose, Nikolas 15, 93
Rotberg, Robert 8
Ruf, F. 157
rural poverty: Zambia 120; Zimbabwe 41–5, 49, 51–2, 54–8, 59–60

SANTRA *see* South African National Traders Alliance (SANTRA)

SAPs *see* Structural Adjustment Programmes
savings club projects, Zimbabwe 55
Scott, James 164, 167–8, 171
SDA *see* Social Dimensions of Adjustment (SDA) programme, Zimbabwe
second economy 134, 136, 173, 174
Secor, Anna J. 142, 143
security governance 93, 97–102
seed banks 119, 123
seeds, agricultural 117, 119, 123
Selby, Jan 7, 8
Self-Help Development Foundation (SHDF) 56
self-help projects, Zimbabwe 55, 56–7, 60
self-regulation, internal 49
Serengeti National Park, Tanzania 75
Serufuli, Eugène 155
service delivery protests 129
Sheridan, Michael 80
Sierra Leone 29–34, 35
Simone, AbdouMaliq 136, 137, 138–9, 142, 143
slandering techniques 169–70
slum clearance 131
small and medium enterprises (SMEs), Zimbabwe 55, 56
Social Dimensions of Adjustment (SDA) programme, Zimbabwe 49, 54, 60
social engineering: DRC 155; Ghana 25–9, 34–5; Sierra Leone 29–34, 35
social investment 99–100
social reforms, Zimbabwe 42, 44, 49, 54–7, 59–60
social service provision 173–5
socialist ideology, Zimbabwe 42–3, 53
South Africa *see* Johannesburg
South African National Traders Alliance (SANTRA) 139–40, 142
sovereign power 9, 45–6, 58, 59, 60, 61, 93
sovereignty, classical theories of 45–6
Soweto Electricity Crisis Committee (SECC) 129
STAR-Ghana 26, 27
state-building, resistance to *see* resistance to state-building
state phobia 60–1
state power 112, 129–30; *see also* sovereign power
state-sponsored violence, Zimbabwe 43
stranger-father institution, Liberia 152–3, 160
strategic philanthropy 99–100

street traders, Johannesburg 129, 130–7, 138, 139–42
Structural Adjustment Programmes (SAPs): Tanzania 74; Zambia 117; Zimbabwe 44–5, 49, 53–4
subsistence agriculture, Zambia 117
survival strategies of resistance 173–5
sustainable development 71, 72

Tanzania 72, 73–83
Taylor, Charles 151, 152
terrorism 1–2
Tocqueville, Alexis de 112
town planning ordinances, Johannesburg 131
TPD (*Tous pour le paix et le développement*), DRC 155
Traditional Authorities 58–9; Ghana 27–8; Sierra Leone 31–2, 33; Zambia 116; Zimbabwe 50, 51, 52–3
Traditional Leaders Acts, Zimbabwe 52, 53
Tsingou, Eleni 69, 70, 83
tutorat, Côte d'Ivoire 156–7, 160

UNDP (United Nations Development Programme) 31, 73, 74
Union Minière du Haut Katanga (UMHK) 95–7
United Kingdom, attitudes to democracy 9
United Nations Mission in the Democratic Republic of Congo (MONUC/ MONUSCO) 169–70, 171–2

USAID 24, 102

vernacular architecture of civil society 147–51, 158–60; Côte d'Ivoire 156–8; Eastern Congo 153–6; Liberia 151–3
village development committee (VIDCOs), Zimbabwe 50, 51, 57
violence, state-sponsored, Zimbabwe 43
violent strategies of resistance 171–3

ward development committee (WADCOs), Zimbabwe 50, 51, 57
Welker, Marina 100
wildlife conservation 80, 83
Willowvale Scandal, Zimbabwe 44
women, entrepreneurship in Zimbabwe 56
Women for Change, Zambia 114–15
World Bank 24–6, 27–9, 31–2, 81
World Summit for Sustainable Development 71
World Vision 52

Young, Crawford 8, 164

Zambia 114–20, 122–3
Zambuko Trust 56
ZANU PF (Zimbabwe African National Union – Patriotic Front) 41, 42–5, 46, 47, 56, 57–8, 61
Zimbabwe 41–5, 46, 47, 48–62
Zimbabwe African People's Union (PF ZAPU) 42–3, 44

Taylor & Francis
eBooks
FOR LIBRARIES

ORDER YOUR FREE 30 DAY INSTITUTIONAL TRIAL TODAY!

Over 23,000 eBook titles in the Humanities, Social Sciences, STM and Law from some of the world's leading imprints.

Choose from a range of subject packages or create your own!

- ▶ Free MARC records
- ▶ COUNTER-compliant usage statistics
- ▶ Flexible purchase and pricing options

- ▶ Off-site, anytime access via Athens or referring URL
- ▶ Print or copy pages or chapters
- ▶ Full content search
- ▶ Bookmark, highlight and annotate text
- ▶ Access to thousands of pages of quality research at the click of a button

For more information, pricing enquiries or to order a free trial, contact your local online sales team.

UK and Rest of World: online.sales@tandf.co.uk
US, Canada and Latin America:
e-reference@taylorandfrancis.com

www.ebooksubscriptions.com

A flexible and dynamic resource for teaching, learning and research.

CPSIA information can be obtained
at www.ICGtesting.com
Printed in the USA
BVHW061359271218
536476BV00007B/40/P